SECRET GERMANY

THE ITALIAN LIST

SECRET GERMANY

MYTH IN TWENTIETH-CENTURY GERMAN CULTURE

FURIO JESI

Translated by Richard Braude

With an Introduction by Andrea Cavalletti

LONDON NEW YORK CALCUTTA

SERIES EDITOR
Alberto Toscano

Seagull Books, 2023

Originally published as Furio Jesi, *Germania segreta* by Silva
Editore in 1967; republished in February 1995 by Giangiacomo
Feltrinelli Editore, Milan, Italy

© Giangiacomo Feltrinelli Editore, 1995

Introduction and appendices © Nottetempo srl, 2018

First published in English by Seagull Books, 2021

English translation © Richard Braude, 2021

ISBN 978 1 8030 9 194 5

British Library Cataloguing-in-Publication Data
A catalogue record for this book is available
from the British Library

Typeset by Seagull Books, Calcutta, India
Printed and bound by WordsWorth India, New Delhi, India

CONTENTS

TRANSLATOR'S NOTE

This volume has been prepared for a reader with an interest in German literature but with no particular knowledge of the Italian language. Nevertheless, I note here that two central terms—'guilt' and 'darkness'—provide significant problems of translation due to the triangulation between Italian, German and English. The English noun 'guilt' corresponds easily enough to the German *Schuld*; the Italian term *colpa*, however, has a much broader meaning, encompassing 'blame', 'fault' and 'error', often with an implicit religiosity. The English adjective 'guilty' is, however, in turn broader than the Italian *colpevole*, the English containing a sense of shame not included in the Italian, which instead equates to the 'guilty' of a juridical trial. Sometimes the solution has been to use 'guilt-ridden' when the sense is merely adjectival, i.e. somehow 'pertaining to' guilt. This is significant as Jesi's discussion of Heidegger or Wagner being 'guilty' does not necessarily imply a discussion of shame or self-consciousness.

A second central and problematic term is the Italian adjective *oscura*, which comprises 'shadowy', 'dark', 'obscure' and 'hidden'. The ambiguity is important for Jesi's exploration of myth, death and the 'dark God'; it also implies a relation to the 'secrecy' of the 'secret Germany' of the title. The title itself is a translation of an enigmatic phrase, *geheimes Deutschland,* used by the circle of writers around Stefan George who, in Adorno's judgement, 'spoke from the soul of the quantitatively significant groups of the pre-Hitlerian reactionary German bourgeoisie'.[1]

References and citations in the original work have been completed where Jesi often left them enigmatic; they have also been updated, and references to available English translations have been provided for the most part. Where Jesi's translations (or those he drew upon) from German to Italian have departed from the original text significantly, this has been noted. German fictional prose has often been translated anew to maintain the salience to Jesi's argument rather than rely on other translators' alternative priorities. All translations are my original, unless otherwise stated. Notes using asterisks are original to the translation. My thanks to Alfonso Geraci, Judith Jochum and Giorgia Listì for suggestions and advice.

Richard Braude

---

1 Theodor W. Adorno, 'George (1967)' in *Noten zur Literatur*, Vol IV (Frankfurt: Suhrkamp, 1974), p. 49. [English translation: *Notes to Literature*, VOL 2 (Shierry Weber Nicholsen trans.) (New York: Columbia University Press, 1991), p. 181, modified.]

MYTHOLOGY AND JUSTICE

ANDREA CAVALLETTI

1. At the beginning of May 1965, Károly Kerényi added a unique dedication to his latest article, 'Nietzsche zwischen Literatur- und Religionsgeschichte' (Nietzsche between Literary and Religious History): 'To Furio Jesi, in order to distract him from an unrealizable Cyclopean project with *justice* [Gerechtigkeit].'[1]

The young scholar from Turin had been corresponding with Kerényi for a year by this point but considered him to have been his mentor 'since adolescence'.[2] Accompanied by a brief letter, Jesi had just sent him the first paragraph of a book he wanted 'to call *Secret Germany*' and which was 'going to focus on the survival of mythic images in nineteenth- and twentieth-century German culture'.[3] The four typewritten pages made up a 'kind of initial programmatic declaration', one that was

---

1 Cf. Károly Kerényi and Furio Jesi, *Demone e mito. Carteggio (1964–1968)* (Andrea Cavalletti and Monika Kerényi eds, with an essay by Andrea Cavalletti) (Macerata: Quodlibet, 1999), pp. 52–3n1. Kerényi's article had appeared in *Neue Zürcher Zeitung*, 2 May 1965, p. 4 onwards, under the title 'Der Sprung: Nietzsche zwischen seinem Roman und seinem Evangelium'. It was republished in Karol Kerényi, *Wege und Wegenossen 2, Wekausgabe 2* (Monika Kerényi ed.) (Munich: Langen-Müller, 1988), pp. 133–58.

2 Furio Jesi to Károly Kerényi, 16 May 1968, in *Demone e mito*, p. 117.

3 Jesi to Kerényi, 2 May 1965, in *Demone e mito*, p. 44.

then removed from the final draft but which nevertheless contains concepts that would reappear in the (much altered) work, either rethought or completely revised. As Jesi wrote:

> Developments over the last fifty years have made the need to take very a precise position with regards to that which is defined as Germanism dramatically clear. This choice, which must now be posed to all men of conscience, is above all a moral choice [. . .]. Yet the Second World War, in all the excess of its horrors [. . .] taught us so painfully to be all the more cautious. When the errors can be so serious and the world so fully and fundamentally overturned, it becomes difficult to apply moral criteria with any strictness.[4]

Jesi continued, recalling that 'one of Stefan George's last great lyric poems is called *Geheimes Deutschland*, "Secret Germany"' and that the same phrase 'can be found in Norbert von Hellingrath's essay on "Hölderlin and the Germans"' in order to express 'that distorted, concealed German soul which Hölderlin intended to task with reinvigorating the greatness of classical civilization' and indeed, finally, that the last words of Claus von Stauffenberg, the man who made an attempt on Hitler's life, were 'secret Germany lives' (*Es lebe das geheime Deustchland*). Jesi then claimed that if these recurrences were to construct

> the conclusion and not the beginning of our discussion, we might be accused of sympathizing with—or at least being fooled by—a Germanic substrate that can be all too easily confused with the Germanism of Hitler's own disciples. For us,

---

4 Jesi to Kerényi, 2 May 1965, in *Demone e mito*, p. 45.

however, *Secret Germany* is a symbol of that which remains human in Faust even after his pact with Mephistopheles. It is a symbol of those abysses of the human psyche in which the god of love and the demon of evil are simply names without meaning, no more than empty, arbitrary terms within an inappropriate language.

The mystery of our 'model' of the human psyche lies outside of symbolic consciousness, an eternal reservoir of realities and images that can overwhelm humankind. This overwhelming is not susceptible to the limitations of conscious will and thus finds itself beyond the morality of responsibility. The only real responsibility is that which falls upon the behaviour of whoever stands witness to the unfolding of such images of the unconscious and treats them lightly—i.e. without suffering and uncertainty—and as determinants of his or her activity or even as an object for devotion.

But responsibility is not the only conceivable basis for a morality.

If that which emerges from consciousness and its domination leads to the idolatry of death, it would be correct for a human community to condemn those who unwillingly submit themselves to its possession. Whoever does so commits evil: not a metaphysical evil but damage to those similar to themselves, an attempt on their very survival.

Once morality is reduced as such to a practical morality, what reaction can one have in relation to those who welcome such images of death within themselves without, nevertheless, seeking death? So long as their activities do not become murderous, do they remain morally innocent?[5]

At the time, Kerényi could only respond by sending his article, along with the 'perhaps Oracular dedication'. But he wrote again, on 17 May, to explain his own reservations better:

First of all, I wanted to call attention to some unsolved psychological problems, the solution to which would be necessary in order to reach an objective judgement of German influence on the nineteenth and twentieth centuries. Nietzsche was one the most influential Germans in intellectual history. Yet he was also, at the end of an epoch, the most influential and undisciplined figure, a madman—and where madness begins, there the quality of 'the German' regresses to that of 'sickness'. Hitler himself belongs to the first order of those completely distorted through mental alienation. That said, one cannot put him together with Nietzsche at the same time—or perhaps one can, if we were to think in terms of pathology?[6]

Kerényi referenced various figures mentioned by Jesi as well as Thomas Mann's position, who he problematically defined as 'a complete devotee to the images of death that emerged fascinatingly from his psyche, while at the same time—aware of the dangers that lay within them— forthrightly opposed those who wanted to derive rules of behaviour from those images.' He continued:

---

5 Jesi to Kerényi, 2 May 1965, in *Demone e mito*, pp. 47–8.

6 Kerényi to Jesi, 17 May 1965, in in *Demone e mito*, p. 54.

The problems presented by these comparisons and juxtapositions are enormous. Lukács—who represented Thomas Mann as a communist Jesuit through Naphta [in *The Magic Mountain*]; as a character in a novel, Mann attributes him with greater dignity than that which he is due— is not German. Gottfried Benn is not so far from Goebbels as Frobenius is from Rosenberg. There is some injustice [*Ungerechtigkeit*] done to the great ethnologist in mentioning the two of them in one breath [. . .]. Thomas Mann as 'a complete devotee to the images of death'? This was the criticism made of him for the most part by nationalist critics on the publication of *The Magic Mountain*, and one need only note that everything is treated with irony in the book, including death, something that garnered the resentment of many. One has to read both volumes of his letters (all that has been published of his daily correspondence) to be reminded of the misconceptions that have been built up around him. And what of Rilke and his own relation with death? I do not think I really have to remind you of this![7]

2. On 18 February of the same year, Jesi had put together an outline of *Secret Germany: Myths in Twentieth-Century German Culture* for the publishing house Silva, a plan for a book of 'around 200 pages' to be completed within 'one year of work' and subdivided into three sections—or, one

---

7 *Demone e mito*, pp. 54 onwards. Kerényi had recently read and greatly appreciated Jesi's essay 'Rilke e l'Eggito', *Aegyptus* 44(1–2) (January–June 1964), later published in Furio Jesi, *Letteratura e mito* (Turin: Einaudi, 1968), pp. 85–94. See *Demone e mito*, p. 41.

might say, the whole conceptual development articulated in three moments. The first (one which recalls the title closely, combining studies not only by Kerényi but also Frobenius, Propp and Warburg) was to be dedicated to a *Morphology of the survival of three fundamental mythic motifs*: 'woman', 'city' and 'shadow'. This dealt above all with examining the afterlife (that is, the reverberations and distortions) of the ancient image of *kore*, the adolescent female divinity, the mythic virgin reborn in German literature and figurative arts as a hybrid creature, human and animal or plant, ambiguously infernal (as with Frank Wedekind's Lulu) or 'monstrously deformed'. The 'motif' of the city, on the other hand, was understood—mythologically speaking—as the resolution of collective and social problems: the Expressionist city, the dark bourgeois metropolis to which the veterans of the First World War return. This is a space experienced as isolation from the genuineness of myth or (and for Jesi the two experiences coincide) as the impossibility of an authentic collective life. It is, therefore, the location of a closed and autonomous community, organized according to individual interests, the defence of which—as Jesi observes, in terms that could not seem more contemporary—leads to 'the desperation of closing oneself within a surrounding wall, confronted by the threatening advance of those forces that had always been excluded from the "serene" microcosm, in correspondence with an intrinsic weakening of that microcosm's internal defences'.[8] The section deals with the heavenly and infernal city and its metamorphoses, corresponding ('in revolutions and particularly in the Spartacist revolution') to changes in the relation to myth: the city changes from being 'the entrenched site of the bourgeoisie . . . to the site of the

---

8 See below, p. 120.

battle against them'.[9] The individual's relation to myth, on the other hand, corresponds with the social level, reflected for Jesi in the 'shadow' of the self or in the symbol of the double, the other—which in turn brings the schema full circle to the 'external projection [. . .], i.e. to the image of "the woman" '.[10]

In the second moment, Jesi planned to deal with the theme of *Relations between literary survivals and scientific research into motifs of myths*. This was meant to investigate the different ways of knowing myth, whether esoteric or philological, as well as their relation to artistic categories. The analysis was to focus on broadly right-wing authors (Stefan George, Ludwig Klages, Oswald Spengler) but, as Jesi eventually did in the penultimate chapter, would focus in particular on the works of Nazi theory and finally Leo Frobenius in opposition to Kerényi and Kerényi in opposition to Martin Heidegger. This reflection on mythological knowledge was then, in a third and final moment, meant to lead to the recognition and description of *the two basic solutions of the relation to myth*: 'De-mythification or *mystic union*'. At the heart of the former solution lay 'Parody (which does not exclude "private ecstasy") as Thomas Mann's provisional solution. Parody and "alienation effect" in Brecht.'[11]

The schema (which we have included in the Appendix to the current volume) clearly represents an extremely important document, not only for understanding *Secret Germany*: the attentive reader will easily recognize many of the protagonists (with the notable exception of Carl Sternheim), works and some of the principles or, better

9 See Appendix, below, p. 273 and p. 135.

10 See Appendix, below, p. 274.

11 See Appendix, below, pp. 274–5.

still, conceptual pairings that not only structured the final draft of the book but which Jesi would continue to develop from this point on in other compositions and essays. *Secret Germany* is, in effect, his second or even third book, following *Tales and Legends from Ancient Rome* written in 1956 with his mother, Vanna Chirone, and *Egyptian Ceramics* two years later. Thought it is perhaps the fourth book he planned,[12] it is nevertheless the work that provides us with the first, unified version—the original image—of the Jesi laboratory. The essays immediately preceding it, collected in 1968 as *Literature and Myth* and those that came to follow from *Spartakus* up to *Right-Wing Culture*, as well as the last essays, partly collected in *Mythological Materials* or, more recently, the posthumous anthology *Time and Festivity* are already contained in its potential. It represents a complex initial gesture that truly reveals the author's intellectual physiognomy, an act both of anticipation and recapitulation.[13]

After reading the Appendix, the reader will thus be able to return to the book or, ideally, go over it once more, bringing together its subtle turns, isolated elements, conceptual juxtapositions and fulcra that at first sight seem to be brief fragments dispersed in the flow of the argument.

---

12 The papers Jesi left behind include the draft of a book from his youth, dedicated to Sigfried Giedion and entitled *La ceramica musulmana* (Mulsim Ceramics). It is likely to have been conceived between 1958 and 1960.

13 Furio Jesi, *Spartakus: The Symbology of a Revolt* (Alberto Toscano ed., Andrea Cavalletti introd.) (London: Seagull Books, 2014); Furio Jesi, *Materiali mitologici. Mito e antropologia nella cultura mitteleuropea* (Andrea Cavalletti ed.) (Turin: Einaudi, 2001[1979]); Furio Jesi, *Cultura di destra. Con tre inediti e un'intervista* (Andrea Cavalletti ed.) (Rome: Nottetempo, 2011 [1979]).

The reader can thus easily place, for example, the third chapter and its concept of mythological morphology in the city, and rethink these pages or even those of *Spartakus* in terms of their relation to the theme of the double or the metamorphosis of the mythical female figure, the modern *kore*—distorted, violated, the Queen of Hades—here an object of exorcisms capable of leading 'her lovers to death itself'. And if Rilke's name can be found in the schema, curiously omitted from the 'programmatic declaration', the reader will also note that the wonderful interpretation of the *Duino Elegies* provided in the current volume does not appear either (an anticipation of the issue of Rilkian esotericism and, through the reduction of images to 'rubble', the theory of semantemes that no longer say anything).[14] And the reader will now understand that the opening words, which seem to be written for our own eyes are in reality only so by reflection, seen through the privileged gaze of another reader—for in truth they resound with a response to Kerényi's poignant question as well, perhaps with some irony, following his own drastic conclusion on György Lukács–Leo Naphta ('he is not German'): 'And what of Rilke and his own relation with death?'

> Our research into the demonic aspects of the relations between myth and artist in twentieth-century German culture cannot disregard the works of Rainer Maria Rilke, even if we are here

---

14 See Furios Jesi, 'Esoterismo di Rilke' in *Esoterismo e linguaggio mitologico. Studi su Rainer Maria Rilke* (Macerata: Quodlibet, 2002[1976]), pp. 45–52; and Furio Jesi, 'R. M. Rilke, Elegie di Duino' in *Il tempo della festa* (Rome: Nottetempo, 2013), pp. 147–64.

dealing with a poet who [. . .] never belonged
to the German nation.[15]

3. As with Jesi's 1965 essay 'Myth and the Language of
Collectivity',[16] *Secret Germany* begins with a homage to
the conference 'From Genuine Myth to Technified Myth'[17]
that Kerényi held in Rome in 1964. As has been noted,
after decades of having attempted 'to not say the word
myth inasmuch as he was a mythologist', Kerényi finally
distinguished 'genuine myth'—the original phenomenon
(*Urphänomen*, using Goethe's expression) that arises
spontaneously from the depths of the soul—by isolating
it from myths used instead with 'calculating intention' for
political ends, a myth that is false, deformed and—as the
grotesque evocations of totalitarianisms had demonstrated—tragically dangerous. 'Genuine myth' is both the
event of truth and, each time it appears, is also the new
event that precedes the word by which a language can, at
least partially, embrace it: the 'solemn, elevated, original
word of the poet, clear in itself. Word as *agalma*, an image-
word!'[18] The kind of transparency of the *agalma* is

---

15 See below, p. 49.

16 Furio Jesi, 'Mito e linguaggio della collettività', *Sigma* 7 (1965):
76–84, republished in *Letteratura e mito*, pp. 33–44.

17 In *Archivio di Filosofia: Tecnica e casistica, Atti del congeno
internazionale di Rome, January 1964* (Rome: Istituto di studi
filosofici, 1964), pp. 153–68. Now in Károly Kerényi, *Scritti italiani
(1955–1971)* (Giampiero Moretti ed.) (Naples: Guida Editori,
1993), pp. 113–26.

18 Károly Kerényi, 'Dal mito genuino al mito tecnicizzato' (1964)
in *Scritti italiani*, p. 120. Kerényi already includes a comparison to
Goethe's 'primal plant' (*Urpflanze*) in his introduction to C. G. Jung
and Karl Kerényi, *Science of Mythology: Essays on the Myth of the
Divine Child and the Mysteries of Eleusis* (R. F. C. Hull trans.). New
York and London: Routledge, 2002[1942], p. 28.

achieved through an art capable of helping man reach the joy of being, an art that, Kerényi continues,

> does not have the quality of philosophy but of poetry. The language of mythology is, *de facto*, always poetic, to the extent that sometimes it is impossible to distinguish mythology from pure poetry. If such a thing is possible, the poetic word is able to embrace even the image within it.[19]

'Whether man can be healed from his demons', i.e. whether 'the terrifying or bewitched [. . .] are to be ascribed to Being or to man, is a philosophical question'.[20] This was the problem that Jesi wanted to confront in his plan for *Secret Germany*, yet he could only solve the problem and begin to truly write the book after he had met Kerényi in the flesh. Again, we can trace this process through their correspondence.

Having received 'the article on Nietzsche, with the admonishing dedication', Jesi immediately responded to his 'mentor' in very clear terms:

> I am not certain that *giustizia* is a perfect translation for *Gerechtigkeit*, but I believe that the concepts are more or less the same. I think I am aware of the dangers inherent in becoming so close to a horrific, fatal event—as I have proposed that I do. That kind of evil finds fertile territory for contagion within us. But, living as I do through work, and personally feeling the need to find some clarity in that part of me closest to and least defended against the dark forces working

---

19 Károly Kerényi, 'Discussione' [following the conference 'Dal mito genuino al mito tecnicizzato'] in *Archivio di Filosofia*, p. 168. On 'agalma' see Károly Kerényi, 'Agalma, Eikon, Eidolon' (1962) in *Scritti italiani*, pp. 83–97, esp. p. 95.

20 Kerényi, 'Discussione', p. 168.

within German tragedy, I hope that mine will be a labour of catharsis.

And yet my consciousness forbids me from making such excuses under your watch. If I might be allowed to appeal to a literary comparison instead, my current situation is similar to that of the characters in Hesse's *Demian*: an approach, when faced with the divine or extra-human, that does not exclude its most terrifying part, that of horror and destruction. This is the reason why I wrote to you in the past with some doubts about the possibility and efficacy of man 'healing'.[21]

Ten days later, between 27 and 28 May 1965, Jesi and Kerényi met each other in Turin and went to the Egyptian Museum and the Sabauda Gallery together. On the 30th, Jesi wrote once more to Kerényi:

In the moment in which I felt at my weakest in reacting against 'non-genuine' myth, that which is deformed through the lens of demonism, I had in reality been the closest to the beginning of 'healing': in the moment in which the demon no longer appeared to me as an integral part of god. But I also had the feeling of 'healing' when, looking at Albani's paintings, you said to me 'This is genuine mythology. *And there aren't any demons.*' Even the abductor of Kore, as you noted to me, was a god.

As much as this might seem rhetorical—although I do not believe it will to you—the words you uttered in front of those paintings,

---

21 Letter from Jesi to Süden, 16 May 1965, in *Demone e mito*, pp. 50–1.

together with your comments to me on Thomas Mann and 'Fiore', revealed to me that which was already in preparation within myself, i.e. that myth—*genuine* myth—is not the essence of good and evil, examined and conjoined together, but 'a place higher up', where the demon does not exist, as the demon can only be inside us, as a tragic 'error of vision' or a force to be conquered, lying there within our gaze, not on the horizon of reality itself.[22]

From this moment on, Jesi's position could no longer be assimilated to that of *Demian* nor to a form of Junghianism.[23] Indeed, we read in *Secret Germany* that Hesse's novel, completed at the peak of a widespread spiritual attitude within German culture of the time, carries out an exorcistic deification of the demon: here 'god and demon are conjoined in an image which draws on aspects of Gnostic thought and directly inspired the teachings of Carl Gustav Jung, whose "Manicheism" would be noted by Martin Buber'.[24] There is an explicit reference here to the 1964 conference ('Buber defined Jung's mentality as

---

22 Letter from Jesi to Kerényi, 30 May 1965, in *Demone e mito,* pp. 60–1. [Jesi wrote 'Appiani' here instead of 'Albani']. During the days spent in Turin, Kerényi was working on his speech to mark Thomas Mann's 90th anniversay, dedicated to the 1905 work *Fiorenza* and the characters (far from their historical selves) of Lorenzo de' Medici and Savonarola in the play, and thus to the 'divine Fiore', Lorenzo's courtesan and loves. See Károly Kerényi, 'Thomas Mann zwischen Nordern und Süden' in *Wege und Weggenossen 1* (Monika Kerényi ed.) (Munich: Langen-Müller, 1985), pp. 340–50. On *Florence*, also see Furio Jesi, *Thomas Mann* (Florence: La Nuova Italia, 1972), pp. 30–2.

23 In relation to this, also see 'Quando Kerényi mi distrasse da Jung' in *Il tempo della festa*, pp. 223–31.

24 See below, p. 14.

Manichean,' Kerényi recalled). But these pages by Jesi are also full of references to the letter of 30 May, entirely hidden from the standard reader ('god and the devil', or rather 'good' and 'evil', 'examined and conjoined'), included here instead for the mentor's sake as a sign of respect and homage:

> In reality, the genuine myth never includes the 'monsters of the night': even Kore's hellish abductor was neither monster nor demon but a god. In its original sources, Greek mythology did not include the deification of monsters but is characterized by their absence. In both the overworld and the underworld, there are only divine figures: originally divine, not subsequent to a human process of deification. It is men who have seen deified monsters in the gods of the underworld, reflecting their own evil in the guise of myth.[25]

Here, on the horizon of healing, there where *there are no demons*, silence also falls on the ambiguous disguise of that 'contemplating devotee of those deathly images that emerge fascinatingly from their psyche, who at the same time is the declared enemy of those who would derive rules of behaviour from such images'. Mann appears here as the creator of a 'genuinely mythic' figure, Fiore:

> Superior to the conflict between Lorenzo and Savonarola, distant from both the competitors and their desires, Fiore lives out a reality which could be accused of corrupting men only by those who, like the Savonarola of the play, passionately distort and debase that reality,

---

25 See below, p. 14.

constricted as he is from accessing it. [. . .]. [W]hoever wants to possess Florence, and therefore deform the myth to this end, cannot possess Fiore—that is, genuine myth.[26]

If Fiore is the authentic, clear apparition of the mythic virgin, whose monstrous metamorphoses are 'born from the observer's broken gaze',[27] Mann is the artist who 'despite all these torments [is capable of approaching] the purity of myth',[28] or, rather, capable of experiencing in a limited manner the events and thoughts of those on whom guilt and error weigh. As with Goethe, he is the writer born in a bourgeois house, in which the genuineness of myth remains prohibited, but at the same time 'right from the first he was marked by a faculty of serene and human connection with the mysterious forces of myth, a destructive element within bourgeois society'.[29]

In *Spartakus*, Jesi outlines this paradigm once more, here reprising the theoretical nucleus of *Secret Germany* and describing the process of 'self-destruction' that might allow contact with myth in its collective dimension, eliding the bourgeois components that work within us. In these pages, he mentions genuine inspiration as the spiritual ability to finally be a man among men—no longer alone, but one among others—i.e. as 'devotion to man, to his soul, twisted and tormented by myth and history.[30]

---

26 See below, pp. 68–9.

27 See below, p. 84.

28 See below, p. 75.

29 See below, p. 75.

30 See below, p. 210. For these themes in *Spartakus*, see below pp. *xxvi–xxvii*, nn42–3.

4. Myth and History. Introducing Jesi's *The True Earth*, Georges Dumézil wrote that 'in any case, the last thing to do would be to juxtapose these two terms as fiction and happening, imagination and recorded facts'. In relation to this, he recalls a personal memory:

> After the First World War, while I was preparing for my final exams at the Ecole Normale [. . .] a 'talas' friend of mine—that is, a Catholic activist —came home one evening fairly shocked. He had asked a child: 'Who do you think Jesus Christ was?'—'He was a good person, who was shot by the Germans.' Historicised myth? Mythologized history? It matters little: the two processes combine.[31]

Secret Germany revolves around this combination— indeed, one might say, so does the entire Jesian mode of speculation. The process of 'healing' in this book corresponds to understanding the relation between historical time and mythical time, an understanding that is philosophical in the narrow sense of philosophy as the *ancilla humanitatis*.[32] This does not only overcome a Jungian horizon (or Manicheanism) but also Ludwig Klages' concept of the struggle between soul (the reign of eros without possession, of elusive image and their eternal life) and spirit (the rule of the concept, the possession of things, death). In this regard, one must also recall the shock with which Walter Benjamin, writing to Gershom Scholem in 1930, noted how a commonplace, unseemly metaphysical dualism lived alongside ideas that were otherwise truly

---

31 Georges Dumézil, 'Mito e storia. Appunti di un comparatista' in Furio Jesi, *La vera terra. Antologia di storici e di altri prosatori greci sul mito e la storia* (Turin: Paravia, 1974), pp. *x–xi*.

32 See below, p. 57.

new and important.[33] Yet Jesi—who may very well have known this letter (published as it was in 1966)—does not make reference to Benjamin here.

Instead, writing against the very author whose 'profundity and singular genius, on the other hand, we would never dare to deny', Jesi attempted to 'utilize Klages' thought'[34] by resolving it through a mutual identification of the conscious (or spirit) and the unconscious (soul). This strategy, which is in truth characteristic also of Benjamin, in all likelihood relies on Max Scheler and the section entitled 'contra Klages' in his 1928 essay 'Die Stellung des Menschen im Kosmos' (The Human Place in the Cosmos): spirit and life, one reads here, are each necessary for each other; to view them as involved in a struggle against each other, or part of an original enmity is a grave error. Jesi picks out the following maxim from Scheler's masterpiece: 'That which only can make man "man" [. . .] is *a principle in opposition to life in general and to life within man.*' Jesi substitutes Scheler's dualistic opposition for Klages', demonstrating the eccentricity of a principle that marks life itself, its momentary manifestation.

From the beginning of the 1950s, Jesi defines the meeting between man and the mysterious forces of myth through an idiosyncratic development of the concept of 'emotion' (*Ergriffenheit*) as coined by Frobenius. The extremely dense final chapter of *Secret Germany* forms the reprisal of this concern of the young Jesi and descends into the context of the modern re-emergence of myths. This deals initially with rethinking 'emotion' at the point

---

33 Walter Benjamin, 'An Gerhard Scholem' (15 August 1930) in *Briefe* (Gerhard Scholem and Theodor W. Adorno eds) (Frankfurt: Suhrkamp, 1978), p. 515.

34 See below, p. 58.

in which man leaves the original level that had consigned him to history through placing him in a paradoxical relation to the mythical dimension—that is, 'outside of time and space'. The game of images, previously 'bound to one another through elective affinities extraneous to logical relations', now becomes 'ruled by the illusion' of time and space.[35] As one can read in an unpublished text from 1960, on a primitive level these images stemmed from the flow of *Ergriffenheit*, understood as 'the capacity to allow oneself to be subjugated by a sensation or thought while attempting to know it',[36] and thus

> they crystallize into perennial forms. Man perceives them as the grip of emotion; here, his 'grasped' being did not represent a limitation but rather the very faculty for expansion. To use extremely approximate terminology, man lived in 'the Other World'.[37]

With the loss of this condition and the entrance into historical time, space—which corresponds to this—determines the structures of the mythic epiphany. Jesi thus investigates the transformations undergone by the idea of space-time through divine intervention or the influence of the Other World on the world and therefore the resolving attribution of otherworldly values to spatial and temporal elements. He refers back to Kerényi's reflections on the magical figure of the *mandala*, previously

---

35 Furio Jesi, *La ceramica egizia* (Turin: editrice S.A.I.E, 1958), pp. 17–20.

36 Furio Jesi, *Nuove ricerche sulle connessioni architipiche, I, La nascita dello spazio-tempo*, unpublished [1960–61]. Three handwritten manuscripts (in pen and pencil) signed: 'Archivio 1–3', Notebook 1, p 23.

37 Jesi, *Nuove ricerche sulle connessioni architipiche, I*, Notebook 2, pp. 5–6.

studied by Jung, and on the union of the square and the circular *mundus* in the foundation of Rome.[38]

On the no-longer-magical-religious horizon of *Secret Germany*, in which the mythic epiphany no longer coincides 'with the legitimate revelations of the divine',[39] Jesi's attention turns instead towards those works (initially Max Klinger's *Beethoven* and the young Wassily Kandinsky's mirrors, but also stories by Mann and Broch . . .) in which transient, sensory appearance and a form of existence that, in comparison to myth, shows itself to be ephemeral and fleeting—that is, death, the stigma of historicity—are interwoven with the eternity of myth and reflected in or drowns within it. Here it is as if myth embraces death within it. In its historical appearance, its being of the past *par excellence*, myth absorbs the appearance of death into itself, while death, in mythic forms, acquires a 'enduring reality, without nevertheless losing its destructive characteristics'.[40]

Durable does not mean crystallized, however: the form is no longer perennial. The artist's activity operates within historical time and death provides the image with a dynamic character; as such, a new production becomes necessary as soon as the epiphany is reached: another

---

38 Jesi refers above all to the fifth section of Kerényi's introduction to *Science of Mythology*, pp. 11–16. Jesi returned to Franz Altheim and Carl Jung's studies of the square city, reprised and developed by Kerényi, not only in the youthful notebooks ('Archivio 3', p. 6 onwards) but also at the beginning of the third chapter of *Secret Germany*, that focussing on the bourgeois city: 'Their research has shown the existence of an image behind the appearance of the bourgeois city, one that is inherently resistant to classist qualifications: a genuinely mythical image, and therefore profoundly and uniquely human.' See below, p. 120. See also the Appendix, p. 273.

39 Appendix, see below, p. 288.

40 See below, p. 256.

work—everything has to be remade, even though this does not necessary include any expansion of consciousness.[41] In this new version of emotion, it is essential that the space in which it takes place and that structures the mythic epiphany (the *mandala* or the ancient magical union of the square city and the circular foundation of the *mundus*) is interiorized, i.e. that it transforms into an 'interior space' of death, an 'an underground cavity dug within the life of each human being, and populated with figures more real than those included within historical space.'[42] Those mythic images that do not exist in quotidian time are thus protected within the flow of days: through them, death lasts within us, remaining internal to life itself.

On one hand, myth can thus be exploited, technified or deformed as an outside power. In this way—and herein lies the crime and guilt—it is capable of subjugating and destroying life. But those who would possess Florence cannot possess Fiore: imagining a genuine myth in the modern context of Germanism means, on the other hand, developing a fitting idea of emotion, i.e. of a life that is not subjugated to the enemy, of a destruction that coincides with duration and only effects that which impedes the spontaneous flow of images within us.

---

41 See below, p. 263.

42 See below, p. 263–4. Here one can also recognize an echo of Kerényi's 'unterweltlich' *mundus*: 'the *mundus* is the *arché* into which the older world of the ancestors, the subterranean seedhouse [*unterweltlich Kornkammer*] of everything that will ever grow and come to birth, flows' (*Science of Mythology*, p. 13, modified). Kerényi's text includes a series of para-synonyms: *Korn* ('seed'), *Keim* ('germ'), *arché*. In *Spartakus*, Jesi reprises the idea of myth and notably also 'the time of myth' which 'can be said to be the hour of death inasmuch as it represents the eternity with which human being is commingled. It is the deep shelter, the secret room in which the spirit draws on its reality . . .' (p. 153).

Genuineness here acquires a character that is both existential and political. If, as Kerényi claimed, Mann knew how to treat even death with irony, then by the same token Jesi was able to write that 'interior space'

is the fundamental image of my book. Meaning that space and time are partial truths, no one dies and no one is born, no history passes by, death and life are experienced simultaneously by the human creature, death as the end or as the beginning of another life is an optical illusion, the soul is faculty of dying life and living death.[43]

In the lasting, continual, philosophical process that heals the error of sight within us, it is justice that guides the investigation and discovery of such space.

5. 'One can speak with God, but not of God.' Martin Buber's claim has a special role in the pages of *Secret Germany*: Jesi writes that it could be an epigraph to the fourth chapter, which focuses on Nietzsche and Benn's dark God, and on Kafka's *The Castle* and *The Trial*. Buber's role can be seen within Jesi's interpretation of *The Castle*, or rather through the document that guides it: Max Brod's letter from 21 December 1964, cited in the

---

43 Furio Jesi, Letter to Giulio Schiavoni, 26 January 1970, in *Cultura tedesca* 12 (1999) (monographic issue on Furio Jesi, edited by Giorgio Agamben and Andrea Cavalletti): 173–4. For the development of this theme see, again, *Spartakus*, pp. 153–9. 'What man draws from his inner space of death is objective and collective, even if the act through which he does this is intimately subjective' (p. 156). This move recalls that in *Secret Germany*: 'this solitary devotion is also transformed into a common emotion thanks to the collective value of the genuine epiphany of myth' (see below, p. 264).

text.[44] Replying to Jesi's observation that the Castle is inaccessible, Brod wrote: 'In my opinion, it is not "impossible à atteindre"—but, rather, *extremely difficult to reach* or "*perhaps* impossible to reach". That Kafka may have believed in the possibility of reaching Being=Duty can be seen from his aphorisms, diaries etc.'[45]

Nevertheless, one needs to place these words next to those which Jesi sent to Scholem on 26 November 1966:

> I have studied Jewish mysticism in scholarly works (though still not through the original texts) and in this I have been your student. I received moments of enlightenment that healed my spirit but I have also been disturbed by the claims of these mystics regarding the nature of God. Is it possible to speak of God? I would merely observe that God lies in the shadows, and I then would keep quiet.[46]

This keeping quiet, which goes beyond theology, involves mysticism or indeed can become so radical as to lead to Buber's 'speaking with God'. But here going 'beyond' theology and mysticism means beyond mythology and poetry, outside of every form of knowledge and creation, of every image and word:

---

44 See below, p. 201. Brod's letter is conserved among Jesi's papers, along with the copy of the response, published in Andrea Cavalletti and Enrico Lucca (eds), 'Dossier Furio Jesi: Lettere e Materiali', *Scienza & Politica* 25(48) (2013): 103–09.

45 On 15 February 1965, Jesi responded to Brod: 'this possibility that you suggest to me not to rule out is very important to me.' See Cavalletti and Lucca, 'Dossier Furio Jesi', p. 103.

46 The letter was tracked down by Enrico Lucca in the Scholem Archive in Jerusalem and published by him (with commentary) in *Scienza & Politica* 25(48) (2013): 111–16.

I speak of 'healing' beginning with myth not because genuine myth alludes to a correct relationship with the divine (Buber is very dear to me, but I would not join him in saying that 'one can speak with God') but rather because in genuine myth I see merely a serene 'station' in the process of consciousness. And this is not a 'final station' nor does it allude to the End, but is simply a station of humanity richer than that of horror. I say nothing of the 'End' and I do not think I could speak of it.[47]

The absolutely ineffable—Jesi writes in relation to Benn, making reference to Kerényi—does not coincide with the non-being that the Greeks attributed to Hades' form. It is not nothingness as an 'eternal matrix of forms' but, rather, 'a nothingness beyond the nothing: [...] beyond that image of nothing of which men can conceive'.[48] By contrast, this 'beyond'—corrupted neither by speech nor image, but the pure absence of relation—makes healing possible through freeing the genuineness of myth that 'which corresponds to the realm of humanity' alone,[49] a mythology or music that is finally Mozartian and joyous, in which 'justice' and 'playfulness' reign in the artistic creation. If it is not impossible to reach the Castle but only extremely hard, if genuine myth can coincide with history in the continuous and patient destruction of the apparatus of technification—an apparatus that impedes emotion and consciousness—then this is because the source of justice remains radically eccentric, just like

---

47 Jesi, Letter to Schiavoni, 26 January 1970, p. 173.

48 See below, p. 191.

49 See below, p. 212.

Rilke's 'pure stars' [*reines Gestirn*],[50] from which the serene, purified and healed gaze derives.

'You will surely say'—Jesi continued in his letter to Scholem—'that the problem ought be resolved in my own conscience . . . '. If this problem does not coincide in a simple way with the personal relation of Jesi to *Demian*, to Mann's approach, or to the difficult legacy of German culture, it nevertheless remains inseparable from it—or, rather, it includes it. On 7 February 1967, Kerényi wrote to Jesi after reading *Secret Germany*:

> I followed your work with great engagement in relation to the problem of genuine myth, because even if you chose 'German myths' as your example, this effort—as you write with great insight in your letter—touches on your own problem. Connecting in this manner one's own problem with a general one is perfectly legitimate, and finds a basis in the object itself [. . .]. I deeply regret that Thomas Mann was not able to read your analyses . . . [51]

---

50 See below, p. 264.

51 Kerényi to Jesi, *Demone e mito*, p. 111.

SECRET GERMANY

CHAPTER 1

Over the last hundred years of German culture, myth has appeared sometimes as medicine and sometimes poison, both as a source for renewed humanism and as an instrument for barbarism and criminality. The above distinction between a *source* and an *instrument* mirrors Károly Kerényi's own distinction between *genuine* and *technified* myths, the former flowing spontaneously from out of the depths of human being, the latter artificially called forth from within, directed towards a pre-determined goal.[1] The distinction is based on the recognition of a genuine mythological quality, but it would not be right to conclude, therefore, that there is medicine within the history of every genuine myth and poison in every technified one. Genuine myth seems to be a positive and beneficent element in human civilization on its own but, in the moment in which it is embraced by an artist's life experience, it can suffer dark, terrifying transformations and metamorphoses. And conversely, technified myth, while omitting the genuine side of mythological activity, can in fact be used for ends which, at the very least, are not morally reprehensible.

---

1 Karl Kerényi, 'Dal mito genuino al mito tecnicizzato' in E. Castelli (ed.), *Atti del colloquio internazionale su 'Tecnica e casistica'* (Rome: Istituto di Studi Filologici, 1964), pp. 153–68. [Kerényi was visiting professor in Rome at the time, hence the text is in Italian; the letters between him and Jesi are now published in Károly Kerényi and Furio Jesi, *Demone e mito. Carteggio (1964–1968)* (Andrea Cavalletti ed.) (Rome: Quodlibet, 1999).]

From a moral point of view, when genuine myth takes on a horrific and dangerous appearance under the activity of an artist, it assumes the iniquitous purpose of the tech-nified myth. This appearance has been noted many times and for this reason there are even those who have con-demned all artists, in one fell swoop, who have inter-preted the genuine outpouring of myth in a horrific form, equating them with the truly guilty and criminal techni-fiers of myths. But unless one can demonstrate the artist's intention to impose such horrific meaning on genuine myth—i.e. to illuminate the deliberate technification of the myth—then instead one ought to speak of the *sickness* within those artists who give myth a semblance of horror as opposed to the *guilt* of real criminal technicians.

As soon as one considers this sickness of artists how-ever, one must also ask if there might be a component of horror that lurks in the depths of genuine myth or whether that horror exists only through the manner in which some absorb myth into their being. This was a cen-tral concern in twentieth-century German culture, and forms the opening of Thomas Mann's *Doktor Faustus*. It is exactly this nucleus of doubts and fears that assails Serenius Zeitblom, the humanist biographer of Faustian artist Adrian Leverkühn, as he begins to narrate the life of 'this dear and so terrifyingly haunted man, lifted up so high only to be so frightfully cast down.'[2]

---

2 Thomas Mann, *Doktor Faustus* (Stockholm: Bermann-Fischer Verlag, 1947), p. 9: 'des teuren, vom Schicksal so furchtbar heimgesuchten, erhobenen und gestürzten Mannes'. [English translation: *Doctor Faustus: The Life of the German Composer Adrian Leverkuhn As Told by a Friend* (John E. Woods trans.) (New York: Vintage, 1999); henceforth, 'Woods translation'. The quote is from p. 7, modified].

Of course, Zeitblom does not speak explicitly about the horrific component of myth, but refers instead to the demonic component of genius. Nevertheless, the relationship between myth and artistic genius is so intimate that any conclusion regarding the apparent demonism of genius makes an implicit claim about the horror intrinsic either to myth or to the genius who has accessed it. In both its genesis and epiphany, the work of art is always made real through myth: indeed, the question arises as to whether the work of art is always demonic, or whether in truth such demonism applies only to some artists, those who possess (or suffer from) an 'impure heightening of [their] natural gifts'.[3] Similarly, we might ask whether genuine myth possesses an intrinsic and fundamental horror, or if it takes on its horrific semblance only through certain artists' development of terror and darkness.

This intimate bond between art and mythology always emerges in biographies of Faustian musicians. Mythic images—such as the butterflies that appear in Leverkühn's childhood and recur periodically throughout his life—undergo metamorphoses which depend on an ever-deeper relation between myth and artist. The *Haetera esmeralda*—the butterfly that Adrian discovers as a child in his father's illustrated books and through which he maintains an ironic detachment from the marvels of nature—later finds another form in the prostitutes in the brothel in Leipzig, a transformation which seems to reflect an aspect of the classical figure of Psyche, herself both butterfly and girl.[4] The circuit is closed in the

---

3 Mann, *Doktor Faustus*, p. 12: 'eine "unlautere" Steigerung meiner natürlichen Gaben'. Woods translation, p. 10.

4 The image of the butterfly-adolescent, which Erwin Rohde studied in *Psyche* within the limits of the context of antiquity and soul-butterfly symbolism, is a recurrent hybrid in early-twentieth-

brothel: Adrian no longer laughs when faced with the *Haetera esmerelda*, but enters into contact with it; the ironic distance from mythic imagination is abandoned, and replaced with a bond imbued with fate. Although he runs away from the brothel, Adrian meets a prostitute and finally sleeps with her, in an embrace which arouses a 'religious shudder'[5] in the biographer. The *Hetaera esmerelda*, first butterfly, then woman, makes another, final metamorphosis, becoming a musical cipher: *B-E-A-E-E♭*. The circle has closed—the mythic image has become an intimate part of artist's creation.

Myth also forms the landscape of Adrian's infancy and adolescence, both on the Buchel estate that bears witness to his birth—and which, later in life, will provide

---

century European culture. Rilke had already referred to it in his lyric on the bone-shaped butterfly in the air-cemetery, also to be found in some of the drawings of Koloman Moser (especially the sketches for the book covers: the body of the butterfly-adolescent is found on the back of the book, and the wings extend across the plates). The butterfly-adolescent, the snake-adolescent, the flower-adolescent are all hybrids born from the renewal of mythic epiphanies of the divine virgin (on this point, see Chapter 2, especially pp. 105–06). [Rohde's *Psyche* was published in two volumes in 1890–94. Rilke's poem referenced here is 'Am Kirchhof zu Königsaal'. See Rainer Maria Rilke, *Sämtliche Werke. Band 1* (Frankfurt: Insel, 1955), pp. 47–8. The design by Moser is that intended for Ewart Felicie's *Jugendschatz*, 1897.]

5 Mann, *Doktor Faustus*, p. 206: 'ein religiöses Erschauern'; Woods translation, p. 224. Adrian and the *Hetaera*'s embrace effectively possessed a religious charge, for in its survival through into a transformed form, the reason for this hierogamy becomes 'witchcraft'. The embrace with the *Hetaera* establishes a profound relationship between Adrian and the *Deus inversus*, the demon. We have already seen that the butterfly, imagined as Psyche, is a symbol of Kore, from whom derives the mythical 'bewitching woman' in the novel. See below, pp. 173–4 and 260.

the model for his house in Pfeiffering—and through the village of Kaisersaschern that symbolizes the dark substrate of Germany. Just as with the image of Buchel, Adrian never abandons the image of the village; in the dialogue at Palestrina, the devil claims: 'If you only had the courage to tell yourself: "Where I am, there is Kaisersaschern," then everything would be fine.'[6]

Buchel provides the environment of Adrian's infancy, Kaisersaschern that of Germany. We will speak first about the latter, in order to then move onto the former with greater clarity; moreover, Adrian is more a symbol of German man than that of the autonomous figure of the musician. No moment in his life can be understood without Kaisersaschern.

Kaisersaschern, with its 'latent psychic epidemic'[7] and bizarre, deformed people, represents the German past—or, better still, the altered image of the past as it survives in modern German society. Kaisersaschern is not a genuine ancient Germany—just as Professor Kumpf is not Luther—but rather its altered and deformed residual image. Similar survivals recur throughout the novel and at certain moments directly engage Adrian: albeit in parodic form, he begins to use a wilfully arcane language in the language of his letters and in his final tragic confession. We will return to the relation between these

---

6 Mann, *Doktor Faustus*, pp. 301–2: 'Wenn du den Mut hättest, dir du sagen: "Wo ich bin, da ist Kaisersaschern", gelt, so stimmte die Sache auf einmal.' Woods translation, p. 328.

7 Mann, *Doktor Faustus*, p. 52: 'von latenter seelischer Epidemie'. Woods translation, p. 53. *Seelische* here refers more explicitly to the soul [*anima*] rather than the psyche, leaving the moral and physical nature of the epidemic somewhat ambiguous. Analogously bizarre forms had already been included in Lübeck in *Buddenbrook*.

deformed survivals of an ancient Germany and the modern Doktor Faustus; what interests us here is to point towards that vitiated relationship with the past typical of modern bourgeois German culture. It is a culture characterized by a desire to return to the past as a primordial source of strength and renewal (think of Deutschlin's speeches on the youths of Germany in Chapter 19 of *Doktor Faustus*: 'To be young means to be original, to have remained closer to the sources of life [. . .] to plunge again into the elemental'[8]), yet it contains the past only as a deformed, damaged, unfaithful image, like modern furniture modelled in the style of the German Renaissance.

This phenomenon has been given the term 'reversion of the myth' by scholars. The original myth is no longer understood in its genuine sense but survives in an altered form, turning positive into negative: the image of the mythical protagonist is replaced by a wizard or the witch of the forest, the image of the underworld by that of an ogre.

Why do myths change from their pure and genuine forms through the upheavals of centuries and forms of life? This can happen when a myth decays to the level of a fairy tale, which can occur along with an alteration in those social institutions which render images of the past comprehensible, thus forcing such myths to be reinterpreted according to new forms of life. However, in the case of Kaisersaschern, the myth has decayed not only to the level of a fairy tale but also to that of a horrific and demonic image on which humanity can construct its guilt-ridden behaviour. That the myth assumes this

---

8 Mann, *Doktor Faustus*, p. 159: 'Jung sein heisst ursprünglich sein, heisst den Quellen des Lebens nahe geblieben sein [. . .] wieder unterzutauchen im Elementaren.' Woods translation, p. 170.

horrific appearance is not the fault of the myth itself, but of those who have altered it, making it reflect their own sickness. They have discovered in the past (the mythical 'precedent' to present actions) the 'precedent' of their own sickness, and thus their own criminal soul. Instead of referring to a genuine myth and an authentic past, the criminal refers instead to a crime or some other action for which they are to blame, and hides this 'precedent' with an altered version of the past. Whether intentionally or otherwise, his objective guilt comes to appear as a collective 'precedent' and therefore his personal responsibility is replaced by the notion of an inevitable culpability, a guilty legacy.

The concept of such a past, the survivals of which have become sterile and deformed, emerges in the image of the archive that dominates the city of the victims of a monstrous enchantment in Alfred Kubin's novel *The Other Side*, in Kafka's *The Trial* and in Herman Hesse's *The Journey to the East*.[9] In *The Other Side*, the inhabitants of the city of Pearl are put under the spell of their 'Führer' Patera, wearing antiquated clothes and making use of

---

9 Beyond this we could also recall the weight of the broken relationship with the past in the novel *The Golem* by Gustav Meyrink. In this novel (as in Kubin's which belongs to the same literary world) the horror of the past with which there is an unhealthy bond is manifested through the supernatural animation of ruins and old houses. Every 33 years the Golem, a magical automaton, reappears and spreads terror through the ghetto, showing that the relation with the past is worked out through a perennial nightmare. In *The Golem*, it seems, on the other hand, that in the important image of the 'lost chamber' (that is, of the chamber where the Golem might live: the room exists in a house but is inaccessible and never found) one can recognize the darker side of the past that survives on the margins of the present: the space of death within life, of which we will speak in Chapter 6.

tools and objects from another era. In founding the city of Pearl, Patera collects and relocates ancient buildings from across Europe. Other than their antiquity, each of these buildings shares the quality of having been a crime scene. It would be hard to imagine a more explicit allegory for the criminal evocation of the past within recent German bourgeois culture.

The description of Kaisersaschern in Chapter 6 of *Doktor Faustus* also contains a brief but profound hint regarding the meaning of another typically German experience of the vitiated relationship with the past. Mann mentions, along with other monuments of the city, the sepulchre of the Emperor Otto III

> who was titled *Imperator Romanorum* and *Saxonicus*, not so much because he wanted to be Saxon, but after the fashion in which Scipio took the appellative *Africanus*: because he had conquered the Saxons. In 1002, when Otto died following his expulsion from his beloved Rome, the spoils were carried back to Germany and buried in Kaisersaschern Cathedral—much against his wishes, as he was the master of anti-German sentiment and throughout his long life had suffered from being German.[10]

---

10 Mann, *Doktor Faustus*, p. 51: 'der sich Imperator Romanorum und Saxonicus nannte, aber nicht, weil er ein Sachse sein wollte, sondern in dem Sinne wie Scipio den Beinamen Africanus führte, also weil er die Sachsen besiegt hatte. Als er im Jahre 1002 nach seiner Verteibung aus dem geliebten Rom in Kummer gestorben wr, wurden seine Reste nach Deutschland gebracht und in Dom von Kaisersaschern beigesetzt—sehr gegen seinen Geschmack, denn er war das Musterbeispiel deutscher Selbst-Antipathie und hatte sein Leben lang unter seinem Deutschtum gelitten.' [The Italian translation used by Jesi omits that Otto III is said to have died from the sorrow of his expulsion from Rome.] Woods translation, p. 52, modified.

Mann says no more than this. We can nevertheless interpret the significance of the imperial sepulchre in Kaisersaschern, recalling that, around the year 1000, Otto III attempted to instigate a rebirth of the preceding era in Rome, in order to resurrect the spirit of the Roman emperors within his own life, inspired by the Byzantine customs inherited from the classical world. Indeed, it is known that he compiled a Latin formulary (drawn partly from the *Origines* of Isidore, partly from the *Book of Ceremonies* of Constantine Porphyrogennetos), that he gave Roman and Byzantine ranks to his officials and that he wanted to restore the use of Greek language to the speech and official documents of court.

The pseudo-rebirth of antiquity which Otto III wanted to establish lasted only a short while, too brief a period to have any real effect. It was replaced by the act of consolidating German imperial power, rather than escaping into a past which was long dead and whose interpretation left the truth untouched. That would be enough to explain the presence of the imperial sepulchre in Kaisersaschern, which bears witness to the spiritual adventure of a German who refused to be German but who could find no cure in the classical past, unable to establish any genuine relations with it. There is, however, another element which in all likelihood did not escape Mann (even though he makes no reference to it) and which casts the events of Otto III's life in a Faustian light, quite appropriate for the city of Adrian Leverkühn. Otto III's teacher (who introduced him to the world of antiquity) and spiritual adviser in his attempted Renaissance, was Gerbert d'Aurillac, later Pope Sylvester II. In medieval tradition, Gerbert d'Aurillac holds the figure of magician, a scholar gifted with extra-human powers obtained from the devil in exchange for his soul. It was thus a Faust of antiquity in papal robes who inspired, therefore, the broken relation with the past which provided the basis for the attempted classical Renaissance carried out by Otto III, the German who did not want to be German. There is a tradition which claims that Gerbert, on becoming Pope Sylvester II, had a bronze bust installed in his palace in Rome, a bust which possessed the magical power of being able to answer 'Yes' or 'No' to any question demanded of it, cast by Gerbert himself with the devil's assistamce. The medieval writers who recorded this tradition could not have but noticed, nevertheless, that the image of the magical and prophetic bust (a frequent appearance in Mediterranean myths and folklore, as much as in Northern and Eastern Europe) has a singular connection with another man who held great influence over Otto III: St Adalbert, bishop of Prague, who was also so great an admirer of Italy that he twice abandoned his Northern diocese to find refuge in Rome. Adalbert died as a martyr in Prussia and Otto showed the greatest of devotion to his memory, dedicating a convent to him in Ravenna, a church in Aachen and a basilica in Rome, on the Tiber Island, at the location of the ancient sanctuary of Asclepius. Here the salient point is that in the legend of St Adalbert's martyrdom there is consistent reference to his severed head, evoked powerfully by a bronze relief on the portal of Gniezno Cathedral, depicting the saint's burial.[11] On the headboard of the funerary bed on which the mummified body of the saint lies, one can make out a head on a pole, the severed head of the martyr. At the same time, it also represents the miraculous survival of

---

11 In relation to this, see: Furio Jesi and Philippe Derchain, 'Enqête: Sur les influences osiriaques', *Chronique d'Egypte: Bulletin périodique de la Fondation Egyptologique Reine Elisabeth* 35(69–70) (1960): 184–9.

prophetic heads. As such, the bronze bust which magically advises the Faustian pope, Sylvester II, Otto III's teacher, is reconnected to the legend of this other figure who inspired the emperor's fractured Renaissance dream. The image of 'the head which speaks', once as genuinely mythical as was the myth of Orpheus, is here emblematic of the Faustian pact in the exact moment in which it casts its shadow over the non-genuine relation with the past that this German attempted to construct, embarrassed by his Germanness.

In Kubin's *The Other Side*, the crumbling of the city of Pearl and Patera's reign is determined above all by the coming of 'the American', a figure who symbolizes society's turn towards the future, deprived of roots, just as with the American millionaire in Mann's *Royal Highness*. But the protagonist of *The Other Side* bears a unique revelation: when he finally gains a *tête-à-tête* with Patera, one notices that the latter constantly changes face, even resembling the American himself. Such a vision, in which good and evil are revealed to be two faces of one supernatural reality, is symptomatic of the attitude assumed by one morally 'good' part of German culture faced with the crisis that showed itself in the broken relationship between myth and the past. This attitude also emerges in the words of Serenus Zeitblom, when he claims that civilization ('Kultur') endures 'exactly through the pious, regulating and, I would say, propitiatory entrance of the monsters of the night into the cult of the gods.'[12] These are the words of a humanist of the old tradition, an honest and noble soul mired in a crisis destined to leave

---

12 Mann, *Doktor Faustus*, p. 17: 'dass Kultur recht eigentlich die fromme und ordnende, ich möchte sagen begütigende Einbeziehung des Nächtig-Ungeheueren in den Kultus der Götter ist.' Woods translation, p. 16, modified.

behind the very fundamentals of the old humanism. In reality, the genuine myth never includes the 'monsters of the night': even Kore's hellish abductor was neither monster nor demon but a god. In its original sources, Greek mythology did not include the deification of monsters but is characterized by their absence. In both the overworld and the underworld, there are only divine figures: originally divine, not subsequent to a human process of deification. It is men who have seen deified monsters in the gods of the underworld, reflecting their own evil in the guise of myth.

Zeitblom's thought, advocating the deification of the demon via exorcism is, as we have seen, the expression of a spiritual attitude which was widespread among a section of German culture, fully formulated in Herman Hesse's novel *Demian*, one of the books most treasured by the young generation prior to the First World War. In *Demian*, god and demon are conjoined in an image which draws on aspects of Gnostic thought and directly inspired the teachings of Carl Gustav Jung, whose 'Manicheism' would be noted by Martin Buber. Mann's suspicion of psychoanalysis was founded exactly on a consideration of the risks of possible moral implications demonstrated here. In *Doktor Faustus*, the conjoining of god, demon and the cosmological necessity of the existence of the demon are all present as typically philo-demonic symptoms in Professor Schleppfuss' demonic instruction. Here, under a moral sterilization deriving from a supposedly scientific basis, other residual contortions of the German past (the kind typical of 'Kaisersaschern') are made apparent.

The 'gnostic' solution to the relation with myth—according to which a terrifying demonism surfacing in the reversion to genuine myths would mean the shadowy return of God—thus becomes classical humanism's final attempt to confront the tragic situation of the present. Even a humanist of the old mould would maintain that myth is indispensable: because myths contain images that include a genuine element granted a terrifying appearance, the humanist claims that such terror is 'another face' of God.[13] Participating in the fate of bourgeois culture from which they have not freed themselves, the humanist observes that myth has undergone a profound reversal: god has become demon; and as such, in order to maintain a precarious equilibrium, the theory of the god-demon is created, both wondrous and horrifying.

We can now return to the modern Doktor Faustus: Adrian Levekuhn. His own relation with those mythic images is destined to decay into horror along with all that which is polemical and ironic in Kaisersaschern. Adrian demonstrates his mirth even before facing his father's naturalist curiosities, including the *Hetaera esmeralda*. His laughter resounds painfully and tragically from the first chapters of *Doktor Faustus*:[14] he has no passion for

13 In Zeitblom's thought, set within the framework of twentieth-century Germany, the evocation of classical religious intuitions goes along with other esoteric doctrines which were developed in the same years (Randolph, Crowley, Maria de Naglowska) and which built upon esoteric thought of the nineteenth century (that of Eliphas Levi, for example) around the 'black Jehovah'. [The reference is to the frontispiece of E. Levi, *Dogme et rituel de la haute magie*, 2 VOLS (Paris: Germier Baillière, 1861), which depicts a 'white' and 'black' Jehovah.]

14 Similarly, in *The Magic Mountain*, Hans Castorp is seized with fits of irrepressible laughter when faced with the first images of death which the world of the sanatorium presents to him: tragic images, like those of bodies carried down the valley with sleds. Castorp's laughter could be a symptom of defence against the mountain's atmosphere of illness and death, but in reality it is merely the manifestation of a conviction of 'superiority' over nature, destined soon to transform itself into the weakness

anything. Nothing—and he adds with fear, not even music—can win out over his ironic 'coldness'. In the student debates of his university days in Halle, he always opposes his irony to an apology for Germanism, which is an apology for 'Kaisersaschern'; and he is accused of being 'cold'. Because the object of his mirth is a horrific, deformed survival of the German past, one might suppose that this attitude is an ironic rejection of horror and the demonic: an apparently healthy moral attitude; but this optimistic hypothesis is destined to receive the strongest disapproval later on in the novel. Adrian's 'coldness' is that of the demon; the demonic horror which emerges from Kaisersaschern—the roots of the deformed Germanism—will find both its greatest exponent and victim in Adrian. Not merely a victim however, because the *Hetaera esmeralda* and its demonic contagion are deliberately chosen by him, and it is exactly this choice that forms the Faustian pact. Adrian wants to be infected, not cured. The importance of this standpoint on moral responsibility has often been played down by various scholars, Hans Mayer for example, who claimed that Adrian 'is already marked *before* the specific "infection". He is devoted to magic—that is, to the devil, as the book says—from birth. His artistic vocation assumes the form

---

inherent to the demonic pact. From this one could deduce—above all through reference to *Doktor Faustus*—that Mann allowed the transformed image of the laughter of the classical deities survive in the laughter of man's 'superiority' over nature (see Kerényi, *The Religion of the Greeks and the Romans* [Christopher Holme trans., London: Thames and Hudson, 1962], p. 199), which in its original form symbolized the abyss between men and gods, and now becomes symptomatic of the human illness. [The Italian translation of the German manuscript was published in 1940; the original German not until 1941.]

of original sin.'[15] Due to his artistic nature, Adrian is no doubt predisposed to the Faustian pact from birth, and this is not a specifically Germanic but a universal element. Mythic images pregnant with demonism surround him even from childhood: the symbolic migraine of the father and his naturalist curiosities allow one to speak of a kind of hereditary predisposition. The obscure events of the parents' lives have slowly prepared their progeny, according to the mysterious paths which Mann traced back to Goethe:[16]

> . . . for an ancient house does not replicate
> the demigod, nor the monster . . .

Yet to go further and claim, as Mayer does,[17] that 'the story of Adrian Leverkühn is also the suicide of Christian theology' as it demonstrates a case of absolute, extra-human, predetermined behaviour, seems to miss the most profound lesson of *Doktor Faustus*. There is no suicide of Christian theology in the novel, because Adrian Leverkühn is not a man but rather a pedagogical symbol of a society destined for the abyss: bourgeois society. Even the most severe condemnation of a society, its institutions and its convictions cannot exclude the salvation of those who comprise it. The structures of an exhausted society can even fall apart, but they cannot take with them all of those who take part in it. The possibility of redemption and salvation always exists within man, provided that he wants to choose the road of confession, humility and

---

15 Hans Mayer, *Thomas Mann: Werk und Entwicklung* (Berlin: Volk und Welt, 1950), p. 346.

16 Goethe's *Iphigenie*, Act 1, Scene 3, cited by Thomas Mann in *Neue Studien* (Frankfurt: Suhrkamp, 1948), p. 15: ' . . . denn es erzeugt nicht gleich / Ein Haus den Halbgott, noch das Ungeheur . . .'

17 Mayer, *Thomas Mann*, p. 346.

renovation; provided, in other words, that he wants to reject the demonic. *Doktor Faustus* is not only a novel of desperation: 'that resounding note hanging in the silence, which is no more, which only the soul can hear, that which was once the final knell of sorrow but is that no more, has changed its meaning, and now appears like a light in the dark.'[18]

But what is the meaning of Adrian's irony towards these survivals of Germanism? It is an irony which separates the Faustian artist from Nazi criminals, but not in terms of moral discrimination. In the novel, Adrian's music is prohibited by the Nazi regime: but not because it was healthier than the ideology of the 'gangsters', but rather because it was, in its tragic demonism, too explicitly symbolic of destruction, and its highest intellectual qualities contrasted too sharply with a regime founded on the death of the intellect. Adrian's irony is the icy, aristocratic detachment from the baseness of criminals indulging in their crimes; it is the symbol of the life of a great spirit who chooses demonic terror as the road to its own completion; it is the emblem of the spiritual life of Nietzsche—a man who, like Adrian, disdained Germanism.

Adrian's irony also forms a parodic relation between the artist and the past, and between the artist and myth, a parody indicative of both a return and an overcoming. Adrian's parody of 'The Marvels of the Universe'[19]—the title of his symphonic opera—becomes that of music

---

18 Mann, *Doktor Faustus*, p. 651 (end of Chapter 46): 'der nachswingend im Schweigend hängende Ton, der nicht mehr ist, dem nur die Seele noch nachlauscht, und der Ausklang der Trauer war, ist es nicht mehr, wändelt den Sinn, steht als ein Licht in der Nacht.'

19 Mann, *Doktor Faustus*, p. 365: '*Die Wunder des Alles*'. Woods translation, p. 397.

itself. Adrian does not even love music in itself—and with some foresight, before embarking on his musical 'career', had written to Wendell Kretzschmar of the fear that music would have the capacity to bore him.[20] Just as with theology, he had searched above all for the supreme confirmation of the self and of contact with the demonic, in music too he searches to fully realize his own self and to access 'shadowy forces': two desires which for him are inseparable. An overcoming even of music, therefore; but also of that which, in reality, will be engulfed in the images of the past, a return to childhood—Germany's childhood—and of those images which, though surviving, are nevertheless artificial and non-genuine, just as the home of Adrian's adulthood in Pfeiffering only mirrors artificially that of his childhood in Buchel.

It is an irony which does include moments of emotion —but a 'demonic' emotion which presides over Adrian's choices and the development of mythical subjects in his compositions. With the advance of the musician's creative activity and his ever-closer relation with the demon, this irony becomes ever-more explicit. Latent in the choice of Brentano's songs—in which the ancient mythic images survive, but decayed to the level of a fairy tale—it manifests itself openly in the desire to set the *Gesta romanorum* to music, which Adrian reads with that same icy laughter that met his father's naturalistic wonders as an adolescent. At this point Adrian's irony becomes ferociously destructive of anything human; now entirely subjected as a demonic 'servant', he destroys the man, leaving behind only God and the marionette. The compositions of the *Gesta romanorum* are formed through the representation of marionettes, which Adrian studies via the celebrated essay by Kleist, and the name of the poet

---

20 Mann, *Doktor Faustus*, pp. 173–4. Woods translation, p. 188.

Juncker tragically echoes on the threshold of the First World War—the era of the *Gesta's* development—when, in the meeting which Zeitblom holds with Adrian before leaving for the war, 'the final chapter of the history of the world'—as Kleist defines the story of the marionettes—seems to foretell the imminent events. The 'advance' of Germanism is identified with the 'advance' of the man who strives for self-realization. Adrian, albeit with some ironic inflection, asks: 'and who denies that a real break-through is worth what the tame world calls a crime!'[21] According to this morality—one that imitates the devil's own morality, the destruction of every kind of human-ism—'unconditional grace' is 'reserved for puppets and for God, that is, for the unconscious and for infinite con-sciousness.'[22] To speak of grace as reserved for the uncon-scious means to have already anticipated the years in

---

21 Mann, *Doktor Faustus*, p. 419: 'Und wer leugnet denn, dass so ein rechter Durchbruch das schon wert ist, was die zahme Welt ein Verbrechen nennt!' Woods translation, p. 445.

22 Mann, *Doktor Faustus*, p. 410. 'der freien Grazie, die eigentlich dem Gliedermann und dem Gotte, das heisst dem Ubewusstsein oder einem unendlichen Bewusstsein vorbehalten ist'. Woods translation, p. 440. One can presume that Mann, in attributing a work for puppets to Adrian, was thinking both of the educational puppet theatre of Wilhelm Meister (in a parodic key) and above all of the marionettes which, in the second of Rilke's *Duino Elegies*, is counterposed to the Angel; see below, p. 260. Furthermore, Karl Kraus had already evoked Kleist's words in the face of the tragedy of the war, with a tragic parody. Kraus' 'apocalyptic' drama is in fact titled *The Last Days of Mankind*, just as Kleist had spoken of 'the last chapter in the history of the world', in the drama itself 'masks of tragic carnival' play out the roles: 'the masks parade through Ash Wednesday, but do not wish to recognize one another.' [The quotation is from the foreword of Karl Kraus, *Die letzten Tage der Menschheit: Tragödie in fünf Akten mit Vorspiel und Epilog* (Salzburg: Jung und Jung, 2014[1919]).]

which a monstrous capacity for discipline will be proffered to men in order to render them marionettes in a
blood-soaked drama, and destined for a grace to be symbolized through the Iron Cross, awarded by the Führer
personally.

This ironic comportment cannot draw on genuine
myth and its restorative faculties: first, because this cannot be accomplished by an irony that comes so close to
vanity and the acceptance of the demonic, destroying the
human basis of myth. An inhuman myth, a myth of gods
or marionettes, is not a genuine myth but the horrific
development of the survival of myth. We could even talk
of the technification of myth, which for Adrian would
mean the realization of the self and the explication of his
own guilt, while for the champions of Germanism it
would mean the criminal consequences of their own
potential.

Hesse chose a line from Nietzsche as the epigraph to
his novella *Zarathustra's Return*: 'Sickness is always the
answer, whenever we are inclined to doubt our duty to
follow our mission, whenever we begin to make matters
easier, one way or another.'[23] The personal events of
Nietzsche's life and those of *Doktor Faustus* both demonstrate the tragic error of this claim. The sickness which
struck both Nietzsche and Adrian was a direct consequence of their desire to realize their own potential at any
cost. Artistic *guilt* overlaps with that of artistic *sickness*.
Nietzsche fell sick, in the medical sense of the term, and

23 The line is taken from *Nietzsche contra Wagner*. ['Krankheit ist
jedes Mal die Antwort, wenn wir an unsrem Recht auf unsre
Aufgabe zweifeln wollen, wenn wir anfangen, es uns irgendworin
leichter zu machen.'] In Friedrich Nietzsche, *The Anti-Christ, Ecce
Homo, Twilight of the Idols and Other Writings* (Judith Norman
trans.) (Cambridge: Cambridge University Press, 2005).

it would be all too difficult to separate off the horror within his thought from sickness and madness. Indeed, one ought recall that Mann would have this image of Nietzsche before him throughout the entire process of writing *Doktor Faustus*.[24] He analysed the last morsel of Nietzsche's thought, framing its creative experience within the historic events of bourgeois culture and traditional humanism. At the point at which the image of the butterfly appears in *Doktor Faustus*, Mann refers back to Nietzsche's own words. It has been established that the episode in the Leipzig brothel is a citation from Nietzsche's own life, evoking the image of the butterfly through the 'daughters of the desert'.* These butterflies, which his friend Erwin Rohde had studied as symbols of the soul in his *Psyche*—a celebrated philological work!— in Nietzsche's words become images of demonism, the counterpart to which we find in the *Haetera esmeralda*.

Mann provided an interpretation of Nietzsche's illness which corresponds textually to the narrative of *Doktor Faustus*: Nietzsche's illness, according to Mann, was the result of a deliberate choice, a desire for extensive destruction even within the biological sphere, a religion of death whose acts even had a mortal effect on the

---

24 Mayer, *Thomas Mann*, p. 321 onwards. See in particular the letter by Mann to Kerényi on 23 September 1945, and Kerényi's relevant considerations in the preface to Karl Kerényi (ed.), *Gespräche in Briefen* (Zurich: Rhein, 1960). English translation: Thomas Mann and Karl Kerényi, *Mythology and Humanism: The Correspondence of Thomas Mann and Karl Kerényi* (Alexander Gelley trans.) (Ithaca, NY: Cornell University Press, 1975).

* [The episode to Nietzsche's own life is related in P. Deussen, *Erinnerungen am F. N.* (Leipzig, 1901), p. 24; see *Selected Letters of Friedrich Nietzsche* (Christopher Middleton ed. and trans.) (Chicago: University of Chicago Press, 1969), p. 8n5.]

human body.[25] In *Doktor Faustus*, these concepts are the basis for Adrian's sickness and the psyche's effect on the organism is part of the demonic Schleppfuss' instruction. These selfsame concepts are found throughout Mann's works, from *Buddenbrooks*—in which the adolescent Hanno 'wants' to die of typhus—to his essay on August von Platen, where Mann recalled that 'Platen died in Syracuse from some typhus-like disease, the only reason given for his death, to which he knowingly consigned himself from the start.'[26] And again, in his novella *Tristan*, Frau Klöterjahn dies due to having been weakened by the overwhelming seduction of music and an artist. *Death in Venice* is more explicit still, however: here the artist Gustav von Aschenbach is killed by a cholera that only seems to be the pretext for his death. In reality, death comes to Aschenbach along with his passion for the adolescent boy, a truly 'divine youth', a mythic image. A genuine myth? Perhaps. But pregnant with horror, destruction and death all the same. A form of horror for which the myth is 'to blame'? Certainly not; instead it is Aschenbach's fault that, through his passion for the Polish adolescent, he accepts the religion of death, a love which is sterile and bound for death. Death is announced to Aschenbach within a dream of a Dionysian orgy that recalls the most terrifying aspects of Euripide's *Bacchae*. It is not Dionysus, therefore, who announces the artist's death to him, but an altered image of Dionysus, in which

---

25 These concepts are clearly outlined by Mann in his essay on Nietzsche. [Mann, *Neue Studien*.]

26 Thomas Mann, *Adel des Geistes. Sechzehn Versuche zum Problem der Humanität* (Berman-Fischer: Stockholm, 1945), p. 447: 'stirbt er zu Syrakus an einer undeutlich typhösen Krankheit, die nichts war als der Vorwand des Todes, dem er vor Anbeginn wissentlich anheimgegeben war.'

men have intermingled horror, fanaticism and the unchecked and inhuman expression of guilty desires. The orgy without healing; murder.[27]

---

27 This explicitly mythological evocation—but of a myth deformed in its survival—in Aschenbach's dream corresponds to the mythological 'dream' of Hans Castorp following his frostbite in *The Magic Mountain*. In this dream too the mythic imagery of the ancient Eleusian religion (that celebrated rebirth through the experience of death, overshadowed with symbols of horror), Castorp, during his vision, finds himself on a threshold of the appearance of 'a group of statues, two stone female figures on a pedestal, mother and daughter' ('einer Statuengruppe, zwei steineren Frauenfiguren auf einam Sockel, Mutter und Tochter'). But in this sanctuary represented by the figures of Demetra and Kore, two witches perform terrifying activities:

> Contemplating the group of statues, Hans Castorp's heart, for shadowy reasons, was filled with still greater fear and foreboding. He hardly dared to, and yet was forced to turn away from the statues and hide behind the next double row of columns . . . Two grey women, half nude, with ragged hair, with sagging witch-breasts and nipples long like fingers, were busying themselves with a horrific brazier among the flames. They were tearing up a baby over a cauldron. [Original translation; equi-valent to pp. 493–4 in Thomas Mann, *The Magic Mountain* (H. T. Lowe-Porter trans.) (New York: Alfred A. Knoff, 1927); henceforth 'Lowe-Porter translation'.]

> ('In der Betrachtung des Standbildes wurde Hans Castorps Herz aus dunklen Gründen noch schwerer, angst- und ahnungsvoller. Er getraute sich kaum und war doch genötigt, die Gestalten zu umgehen und hinter ihnen die nächste doppelte Säulenreihe zurückzulegen . . . Zwei graue Weiber, halbnackt zottelhaarig, mit hängenden Hexenbrüsten und fingerlangen Zizten, hantieren dort drinnen zwischen flackernden Feuer-pfannen aufs grässlichste. Uber einem Becken zerrissen sie ein kleines Kind.' Thomas Mann, *Die Zauberberg* [Frankfurt: Fischer, 1950], p. 451.)

The Platonic references in *Death in Venice* seem to introduce a belief that Aschenbach's guilt was inevitable, implicit in his condition as an artist: an artistic 'original sin.' The same can be said for Adrian. The reality seems different however: Aschenbach receives death with the myth not because genuine myth intrinsically carries horror within it, but because Aschenbach is the symbol of bourgeois art, projecting its own guilt onto myth and thus condemning itself to find horror within myth.

The notion of the influence of psyche on the organism is already present in *Death in Venice*, in that the demonic guilt of the artist transforms itself into a force of bodily destruction. The image of St Sebastian, stoically tolerating his pain, is Aschenbach's emblem, just as the terrible sufferings of Andersen's mermaid are Adrian's.[28] The little mermaid suffers terrible pain through the transformation of her fish tail into human legs: the infiltration of the demonic into the human.

The theory of a psychic influence on the human organism is evoked again by Mann in *The Magic Mountain*; but the great pedagogic novel also offers a warning against these demonic influences. Settembrini, the demon's antagonist, is again a sick man, and an incurable one; but—as Maurice Boucher so acutely noted—'he

---

The two 'ladies' of Eleusis have become the witches of fairy-tale tradition, decaying mythical figures, deformed, bringing horror with them rather than healing. The immersion of the adolescent Trittolemo in flames has become the murder of the child, a figure which recurs frequently in the Inquisition's accusations against heretics.

28 The Christian martyr is revealed, furthermore, in the traditional imagery in which Mann saw a feminine element which corresponded to Aschenbach's homosexual love, and which also flows into the figure of the mermaid for Adrian.

hides his sickness and finds it humiliating.'[29] Furthermore, in the paragraph titled 'Schnee' ('Snow'), Castorp
recognizes all the seductions of death, but manages to
reject them.[30] That is perhaps not assurance enough for
when, descending from the mountain, he will find himself in the horrors of war, but these horrors do not go
beyond those risks in which, without any devotion to
death, one must confront when the history of the world
is influenced by the will of those who worship death,
those for whom 'progression' is no more than the justification of crime.

The theory of the influence of the psyche on the
human organism reflects, on one hand, the doctrines of
an advanced (and esoteric) strain of psychoanalysis,
while on the other this is also a doctrine that reaches
back to Hellenic esoterica, the theme of the lesson given
by Professor Nonnenmacher, that which Leverkühn
and Zeitblom follow with enthusiasm in Halle. But this
is also the esoterica of Neoclassicism and German
Romanticism. The religion of death which cuts across all
Romantic culture had already manifested itself fully in
the Neoclassical age: the references to Winckelmann in
Goethe's monologue in *Lotte in Weimar* are very explicit,
documenting—as Mann would have been well aware—

---

29 Maurice Boucher, *Le roman allemand (1914–1933) et la crise de
l'esprit* (Paris: Presses universitaires, 1961), p. 24.

30 In the events of Castorp's life there is a juxtaposition (perhaps
intended) with the fate of Knulp in the eponymous novel by Hesse.
Knulp, in fact, dies under the snow, and in the instant of
abandonment to death, finds God. Castorp's story, rather, presents
activity, the opposite of abandonment, as the only possibility of
salvation'. In this juxtaposition one can already see in embryonic
form the basis for Mann's 'response' (*The Transposed Heads*) to
Hesse's *Siddharta*. See below, p. 102 and p. 110.

the ambiguous and mysterious attitude of European culture in its confrontation with classicism and its myths.

'Ah yes, Winckelmann . . . "Precisely speaking, one
may say that there is but one single moment in which a
beautiful man is beautiful".' Goethe reflects on this in
Lotte in Weimar;[31] a little further on in the same marvel-
lous monologue, there is a unique reference to Winckelmann's moral 'guilt'—which was also that of Plato, of the
'giving oneself over to death'—that is to homosexuality:

> My darling, aching, acutely sensitive swooner
> and lover, so absorbed in the intellectually sen-
> sual! I do know your secret, don't I? The inspir-
> ing genius behind all your knowledge, that
> modern commitment-free enthusiasm which
> binds you to Hellas? For your *aperçu* only really
> applies to the manly pre-manly, to that beautiful
> moment of male youth captured in marble
> alone. You're lucky that 'Man' is masculine, for
> in that way you can mould the masculinity of
> beauty according to your heart's desire.[32]

31 Thomas Mann, *Lotte in Weimar*. (Frankfurt: Fischer, 1939),
p. 355. 'Winckelmann ... "Genau genommen kann man sagen, es
sei nur ein Augenblick, in welchem der schöne Mensch schön sei"'
[English translation: *The Beloved Returns* (H. T. Lowe-Porter
trans.) (Berkley and Los Angeles: University of California Press,
1968), p. 357, modified].

32 Mann, *Lotte in Weimar*, pp. 355–6. 'Teurer, schmerzlich
schardsinninger Schwärmer und Liebender, ins Sinnliche
geistreich vertieft! Kenn ich dein Geheimnis? Den inspirierenden
Genius all deiner Wissenschaft, den heute bekenntnislosen
Enthusiasmus, der dich mit Hellas verband? Denn dein Aperçu
passt ja eidentlich so recht nur aufs Männlich-Vormännliche, auf
den im Marmor nur haltbaren Schönheitsmoment des Jünglings.
Was gilts, du hattest das gute Glück, dass 'der Mensch' ein
masculinum ist, und dass du also die Schönheit masculinisieren

This is beauty as life that cannot generate life, beauty as death. This ideal of Neoclassicism, grasping the mortality of beauty in the dynamic process of human life, is fundamentally also its reversion to myth: the recalling of the transformed survival of the past, and an act of mourning. But every act of mourning of the past, if it manages to totally imprint itself upon life, is an act of guilt against the present, against action, against moral behaviour. When myth is qualified by 'the past', not in the sense of a primordial foundation of human experience deriving from the depth of man, but as emblematic of the experience of man long-gone, it always maintains the risk of a mutation and mythological deformation. Winckelmann's myth was the symbol of society and culture's mourning a bygone form of life: as such, it was an emblem which carried within it the symbolic reality of the desire for death, the *cupio dissolvi* of Romanticism. The student Deutschlin, in Chapter 14 of *Doktor Faustus*, claims that 'Youthful courage is the spirit of dying and becoming, the knowledge of death and rebirth.'[33] Thus Deutschlin, who in his Germanism is an apologist for Kaisersaschern, reconnects himself to the teachings of Romanticism: the doctrine that developed the Neo-classical thought of beauty marked by death, so that the reversion of the classical myth, transformed into an emblem of death, might give rise to resurrection. Furthermore, *Doktor Faustus* indicates that it is not possible to base resurrection and salvation on an experience of death borne from the return to genuine myth, that is,

---

mochtest nach Herzenlust'. [*The Beloved Returns*, p. 357, modified.]

33 Mann, *Doktor Faustus*, p. 159: 'Jugendmut, das ist der Geist des Stirb und Werde, das Wissen um Tod und Wiedergeburt.' Woods translation, p. 170, modified.

from the projection of the sickness—the desire for death—onto genuine myth. But if Winckelmann had been right, and if the romantic devotees of death had been right, the human organism would have been nothing more than a wondrous receptacle for a moment of death—and of beauty. Its own bodily reality would be, at least for an instant, a hypostasis of death.

When Mann claims that Nietzsche—and Adrian Leverkühn—wanted and determined an illness. i.e. their own bodily destruction, he transferred the guilty experience of the religion of death onto a level of universal, divine justice. The punishment of the devotees of death is the execution of their own proposal: death. The reduction of myth to images of the past, thus deformed as much as depositories of death, was the guilty act of a society and of a culture that projected its own evil deeds into the mirror of genuine myth, helping itself to strength and life through the justification of its own guilt.

In Halle, Zeitblom and Leverkühn attend the lessons of Kolonat Nonnenmacher (a name which derives from a parody on that of Schleiermacher). Mayer notes quite rightly that Nonnenmacher 'does not follow Schleiermacher's Platonism, but moves from Pythagoras and the pre-Socratics to Aristotle, and those Aristotelian principles of philosophy which were ideas at one remove from scientific empiricism, transferring to late medieval thought a mysterious metaphysics of the relation between form and matter.'[34] It is therefore in Kaisersaschern that the partial interpretation of classical thought is formed, from which emerges Adrian's notion of esoteric musical horror as the demonic version of Pythagorism, and of the 'Führer' as that of the *autos epha*.

---

34 Mayer, *Thomas Mann*, p. 350.

Zeitblom himself—it is important to note—follows Nonnenmacher's lessons with enthusiasm.[35] His traditional humanism allows him to flirt dangerously with deformed myths, an action that he will carry to an apparently sacred level through an apologia for the deification of demons. In the environment of bourgeois German culture, the tutors of classical instruction embrace the surviving deformations of myths, foreshadowing the 'gangsters' pseudo-myths. Humanists and artists—even if these two categories ought be considered in opposition—are all mutually involved in the crisis of the society in which they take part.

The problem of the artist's sickness is nevertheless still not entirely resolved. That which we have understood from Mann's work allows us to hear the great pedagogue's admonishment: the influence of the psyche on the organism is, fundamentally, a punishment for being devoted to death; it is a punishment that comes 'from within', and therefore from a radical coherence to the presuppositions of the religion of death. But if the story of Adrian Leverkühn represents an admonishment, it is not the narration of a historical event; the events of Nietzsche's life are historically real. Nietzsche's tragedy was carried out historically, not borne out of thought of an artist or moralist, and his sickness and madness, beyond being a symbol, were of course also clinically verifiable. Madness really was a part of the metamorphosis of German culture at the end of the nineteenth century, just as, perhaps, it has been in the events of more recent German history.

In confronting the presence of madness, the problem of guilt is intertwined primarily with those who choose madness as their own guide. Nietzsche was not to blame

---

35 Mann, *Doktor Faustus*, p. 127. Woods translation, p. 134.

for his madness, but for his interpretation, in a horrific mode, of the genuine myths which arose within him. Nietzsche's spiritual experience was of universal depth, but carried within it the projection of his myths of guilt and elements of horror which were his own, inasmuch as they were also supreme representations of German society and culture. Madness thus impressed the seal of demonism and the destruction of the human onto a horrifying mutation of the genuine sources of myth.[36]

One might object that Nietzsche's authentic guilt, that is, his deformation of myth, may have depended on his latent madness. This objection—a certain validity of which one cannot entirely refute, at least hypothetically—only diminishes Nietzsche's personal moral responsibility, but does not weaken the fact that, through Nietzsche, bourgeois German culture had put into motion one of the most serious of these guilt-ridden fulcrums, deliberately accepting horror itself. Even if all of Nietzsche's thought were cast under the sign of madness—and this would not constitute a moral accusation against him—the cultural guilt which Nietzsche chose as his guide would remain unchanged; he would continue to be radically faithful to the religion of death. One could make a discursive analogy with those devoted to Hitler: one might argue that Hitler was entirely mad, with the difference, nevertheless, that if in its devotion to Nietzsche German culture had accepted horror as part of a dangerous spiritual venture, Hitler's devotees grasped onto horrors which were far from the spirit. But this difference relates to intellectual standing, not moral guilt.

Adrian's great final confession, in the chapter of *Doktor Faustus* which precedes the epilogue, is followed

---

36 See Karl Kerényi, 'Nietzsche zwischen Literatur und Religionsgeschichte', *Neue Zürcher Zeitung*, 2 May 1965, pp. 4–5.

by his madness. What does this madness mean? Mann is quite exacting on this: 'He would not recover, but returned different from that which he had been, reduced to a burnt-out shell of his persona, which really had nothing to do with the man who was called Adrian Leverkühn. The word "dementia" originally meant nothing other than deviation from oneself, the estrangement of the self.'[37]

The pact with the devil, the deliberate acceptance of the horrific and the demonic, thus includes—up to a point—the loss of one's self, dementia as estrangement of the self, the becoming merely 'a man', void of individual personality and even of rationality. Once again, the novel employs psychoanalysis to provide images which define the demonic—an ambiguous function which we cannot describe as entirely positive. Whoever projects their own guilt onto genuine myth is disposed to subvert the humanistic equilibrium between subconsciousness and consciousness, and to abandon themselves entirely to the subconscious even up to the annihilation of conscious-ness itself. This is because the horror which the Faustian artist introduces into myth possesses a potent, fascinating power over the artist themselves. The face of their own moral guilt, projected onto a mythic dimension, is the face of the Gorgon, from which it is virtually impossible to flee. The guilty thus finds that they have subjected themselves to an incantation which they have themselves helped to create: an incantation which subdues the subjects of

---

37 Mann, *Doktor Faustus*, p. 670: 'Nicht zu sich kam er, sondern sich wieder als ein fremdes Selbst, das nur noch die ausgebrannte Hülle seiner Persönlichkeit war und mit dem, der Adrian Leverkühn geheissen, im Grunde nichts mehr zu tun hatte. Meint doch das Wort 'Demenz' ursprünglich nicht anderes, als diese Abweichung wom Ich, die Selbstentfremdung.' Woods translation, p. 729, modified.

Patera in Kubin's *The Other Side*, and this is also the incantation described in the opening of Mann's novella *Mario and the Magician*. The subjects of Patera have chosen their slavery: they themselves have contributed to the creation of the incantation which dominates them and to which they passively submit. And in *Mario and the Magician*, the young Roman who tries in vain to oppose the sorcerer Cipolla does not prevail precisely because he opposes the wizard through a passive resistance, with which he contributes to the efficacy of the incantation.

Adrian's Faustian pact thus represents the total abandonment to myth (which the artist has made horrific) and to the unconsciousness from which that myth emerges. The positive function of the subconscious, as the source of genuine myths, becomes negative and antihuman when myths are horrifyingly transformed, making them a vehicle for the destruction of man through the annihilation of consciousness. It is from the subconscious that the creative forces of his demonic art come to him, with as much potential for destruction as there is within the artist's person, rendering the artist merely a 'burnt-out shell of his persona', a receptacle of non-individual forces. Adrian's descent into madness is the sovereign power of the collective subconscious over the individual and of the subconscious over the conscious.

As such, Adrian seems to return to childhood, to the end of the process which he himself had emphasized, repeating in Pfeiffering the world of his own infancy. But it is not a beneficial return, just as Pfeiffering is not a genuine evocation of Buchel but only its artificial survival. This again reveals the broken relation with the past, born out of projecting one's own guilt onto myth, excluding every point of access to genuine myth, to true infancy. In the very first pages of the novel, Zeitblom alludes to the broken and artificial character of the 'repetition' of this childhood world: 'I never spoke with Adrian about any of this self-evident parallelism; I did not do so from the start, did not want to have done so later; but the phenomenon is something I never liked.'[38] And he sharply observes: 'The choice of a residence which reconstructs the earliest moments, this taking refuge in the oldest and set aside, in childhood, or at least in its exterior circumstances, can evidence an attachment, but still testifies to the oppressive aspects in a man's psychic life.'[39] Adrian's repetition of the childhood world is, therefore, equivalent to the recollection of 'Kaisersaschern's form of Germanism, Germany's own childhood. What continues in the childhood world throughout the most productive and demonic phase in Adrian's creative life represents an announcement of the end implicit in the Faustian pact. The conclusion of the pact, as we have seen, is to be signalled by the total dominance of the collective unconscious over individual consciousness: a phenomenon which appears to be equivalent to a return to childhood—but not to a true childhood as the site of the selection of genuine myths, but to the annihilation of man.

---

38 Mann, *Doktor Faustus*, p. 40: 'Ich habe über diesen ganzen, sich aufdrängenden Parallismus mit Adrian niemals gesprochen; ich tat es früher nicht und mochte es darum später nicht mehr tun; aber gefallen hat die Erscheinung mir niemals.' Woods translation p. 40, modified.

39 Mann, *Doktor Faustus*, p. 40: 'Eine solche das Früheste wiederhestellende Aufenthaltswhal, dieses Sichbergen im Altest-Abgelegten, der Kindheit, oder wenigstens ihren äusseren Umständen, mag von Anhanglichkeit seugen, sagt aber doch Beklemmendes aus über eines Mannes Seelenleben.' Woods translation p. 40.

That the Faustian pact does not entail a return to true infancy is also attested to in *Doktor Faustus* during Adrian's final tragic return to his mother. In his madness, Adrian attempts suicide when he learns that his mother is about to arrive; and then on the return journey to Buchel—to the *true* house of his childhood—he has a sudden outbreak of rage against his mother, only just kept at bay by the nurse.

It is not therefore a true childhood which is 'repeated' in Pfeiffering but its artificial and demonic repetition. Zeitblom notes that Adrian used to call the landlady at Pfeiffering 'mamma', but addressed her with the formal *Sie*—while, even when mad, he granted the informal *du* to his real mother. Zeitblom explains Adrian's hostility towards his mother, saying: 'I have reason to believe that in the depths of his spiritual dusk, there was nonetheless alive in Adrian a dread for this gentle degradation [the return to his mother after the "flight of Icarus"], an instinctive disrespect for her as the remnant of his pride.'[40] This reference back to the 'sin of hubris'—the demonic sin *par excellence*—rightly corresponds to the fact that Adrian's pseudo-infancy in Pfeiffering itself comprises a demonic element, the demonic result of the vitiated relation with the past; that the pseudo-infancy was the announcement of the final annihilation, and demonic inasmuch as it violently opposes the return to a true infancy.

Adrian's final fate is obscure and mysterious. It seems in fact that Mann, in the face of the horrifying Faustian destiny, wanted to evoke the perennial and positive

---

40 Mann, *Doktor Faustus*, p. 671: 'Ich habe Gründe zu glauben, dass in der Tiefe von Adrians geistiger Nacht ein Grauen vor dieser sanften Erniedrigung, ein instinktiver Unwille dagegen, als Rest seines Stolzes, lebendig war.' Woods translation, p. 730, modified.

potential which remains in human beings, and which in the Goethian *Faust* is shown through the return to the mothers. Despite the demonic framework of Adrian's pseudo-infancy in Pfeiffering, an entirely un-demonic figure is present in Frau Schweigestill, the 'other' mother: '*Schweige-Still*', Mrs 'Rest-in-Silence': this extreme refuge is even proffered to the man bound to the demon. At the end of Adrian's confession, the great words of hope and humanity are placed in Frau Schweigestill's mouth: 'But a good human understanding, believe you me, that's enough for anything.'[41]

Standing before the semblance of Adrian in the years of his dementia, the humanist Zeitblom has the impression of watching a trick of nature: the face of he who has lost all awareness seems to emanate the most profound spirituality. It is the victorious irony of the subconscious over consciousness, of dark forces over rationality. A trick of nature. But similar phenomena had already been spoken of at the beginning of the novel, and Adrian's mother had thus already recognized them as such tricks. Adrian's father explains that some moths seem to have a blue shade, 'as beautiful as a dream'; but that it is not their true colour, but the result of light refracted through the scaliness of their wings: 'Look for a while!—and I can still hear Frau Leverkühn say—so it's just a trick?'[42]

* * *

---

41 Mann, *Doktor Faustus*, p. 667. 'Aber a recht's a menschlich's Verständnis, glaubt's es mir, des langt für all's.' [The reference to Goethe is the 'Realm of the mothers' in *Faust, Part II*.] Woods translation, p. 526, modified.

42 Mann, *Doktor Faustus*, p. 23: 'Sieh an', höre ich noch Frau Leverkühn sagen, 'es ist also Trug?' Woods translation, p. 17, modified.

A musician's tragedy is emblematic of the 'tragedy of modern art'—according to the title of a celebrated essay by Georg Lukács—the kind effected in *Doctor Faustus*. Zeitblom's mistrust and love of music, evidenced in one of the first pages of the novel, is a symptom or reflection of this notion of music as the chosen path by which demonism enters into the kind of bourgeois society Mann inhabits. Zeitblom's reaction to music seems to harmonize with his love-hatred for Schopenhauer and Nietzsche. This notion, however, is also found in the thought of Herman Hesse, albeit with little attention to music itself and indeed with an added mistrust of music lovers. In *Steppenwolf*, Hesse writes:

> The German spirit is dominated by the matriar-
> chate, by earth-boundness and nature affinity in
> the form of the hegemony of music to an extent
> unknown in other people. We intellectuals,
> instead of fighting this tendency like men and
> rendering obedience to the spirit, the Logos,
> the Word, and gaining a hearing for it, are all
> dreaming of a speech without words that utters
> the inexpressible and gives form to the formless.
> Instead of playing his part as truly and honestly
> as he could, the German intellectual has con-
> stantly rebelled against the word and against rea-
> son and courted music.[43]

---

43 Herman Hesse, *Der Steppenwolf* (Frankfurt: Suhrkamp, 1969 [1927]), p. 113: 'Im deutschen Geist herrscht das Mutterrecht, die Naturgebundheit in Form einer Hegemonie der Musik, wie sie nie ein andres Volk gekannt hat. Wir Geistigen, statt uns mannhaft dagegen zu wehren und dem Geist, dem Logos, dem Wort Gehorsam zu leisten und Gehör zu verschaffen, träumen alle von einer Sprache ohne Worte, welche das Unaussprechliche sagt, das Ungestaltbare darstllt. Statt sein Instrument möglichst treu und redlich zu spielen, hat der geistige Deutsche stets gegen das Wort

Serenus Zeitblom, as an exponent of traditional humanism, plays his own instrument (the viola d'amore) 'truly and honestly'. But he too accuses music of having a nature contrary to the concept of the word:

> There is also that other language, perhaps more fervent but also wondrously inarticulate, the language of sounds (if one may define music as such), which does not seem to be included in the pédagogic and humanistic sphere, although I know very well that it played a useful role in Greek education and, more generally, in the public life of the *polis*. Even more, it seems to me indeed that, notwithstanding the moral and logical rigour by which it may give airs, it belongs to a spiritual world on whose unconditional fidelity in matters of reason and human dignity I would not wish to put my hand in the fire.[44]

'More fervent but also wondrously inarticulate', an art likely dangerous for 'matters of reason and human

---

und gegen die Vernunft froniert und mit der Musik geliebäugelt.' [English translation: *Steppenwolf* (Basil Creighton trans., Walter Sorrel revd.) (London: Allen Lane, 1963), p. 159.]

44 Mann, *Doktor Faustus*, p. 16. 'Auch jene andere, vielleicht innigere, aber wundersam unartikulierte Sprache, diejenige der Töne (wenn man die Musik so beyeichnen darf), scheint mir nicht in die pädagogisch-humane Sphäre eingeschlossen, obgleich ich wohl weiss dass sie in der griechischen Erziehung und überhaupt im öffentlichen Leben der Polis eine dienende Rolle gespielt hat. Vielmehr scheint sie mir, bei aller logisch-moralischen Strenge, wovon sie sich wohl die Miene geben mag, einer Geisterwelt anzugehören, für deren unbedingte Zuverlässigkeit in Dingen der Vernunft und Menschenwürde ich nicht eben meine Hand ins Feuer legen möchte'. [The German expression, meaning not wanting to take a risk, is a reference, especially in the mouth of the humanist Zeitblom, to the Roman legend of Mucius Scaevola putting his hand in the fire.] Woods translation, p. 15, modified.

dignity': within the framework of *Doktor Faustus*, these words assume a quite precise significance. Music is the language of the dark forces which Adrian evokes in projecting his own guilt onto myth: it is the language of the unconscious which in Adrian's story becomes potent with horror and the annihilation of consciousness, the enemy and destruction of man. Music is 'wondrously inarticulate', because within it one can recognize the inarticulate voice of the unconscious; while 'the word' is the result of a balance between consciousness and the unconscious, the creation of consciousness in which the genuine and vivifying forces of the unconscious intermix. In Halle, Professor Nonnenmacher lectures on the Pythagorean doctrine—and therefore of the pedagogic function in Greek music—in the very moment in which he proposes the bases of irrationalism and the power of dark forces. This means that music is also not in itself 'guilty' but, inasmuch as it is the voice of the unconscious, represents the danger of the final domination of the consciousness when the unconscious is roused in a horrific and transfixing way through the projection of human guilt onto myth.

Traditional humanism's extreme criticism of a vitiated relation with the past and with myth (a relation which was its very own) formed the 'gnostic' solution of the relation with the demonic: the idea of the god-demon, of the eternal and profound ambiguity of being. This ambiguity is the formal basis of Adrian Leverkühn's music, as understood by the humanist Zeitblom himself in relation to Adrian's *Apocalypse*, in which

> the demonic laughter at the end of the first part is entirely counterposed by the wondrous children's choir who, accompanied by a reduced orchestra, immediately begin the second part

[. . .] That which before was horror is as such transported, through the indescribable children's choir, into an entirely different place, the instrumentation and rhythm are indeed entirely altered; but in the yearning and whirring music of spheres and angels there is *not one note*, not a single one, which does not find its precise correspondence in the infernal laughter which has gone before.[45]

The possibility of representing this ambiguity through a musical system which, including in its historical genesis, consists in a parody of traditional musical structure, probably determined Mann's choice of the twelve-tone system for Adrian's music. Schönberg's teachings allowed the symbolic representation, on the limits of the crisis of bourgeois art, of the evocation in a demonic key of this 'primitive cosmological conception of a strict and devout spirit which rose its basic passion—mathematics, abstract proportions, number—to the principle of the world's formation and existence.'[46] These words, which refer to

---

45 Mann, *Doktor Faustus*, pp. 502–3: 'Denn das Höllengelächter am Schlusse des ersten Teils hat ja sein Gegenstück in dem so ganz und gar wundersamen Kinderchor, der, von einem Teilorchester begleitet, sogleich den yweiten eröffnet . . . Das zuvor vernommene Schrecknis ist zwar in dem unbeschreiblichen Kinderchor in eine gänzlich andere Lage übertragen zwar völlig umintrumentiert und umrythmisiert; aber in dem sirrenden, sehrenden Sphären- und Engelsgetön ist *keine* Note, die nicht, streng korrespondierend, auch in dem Höllengelächter vorkäme.' Woods translation pp. 397–8, modified.

46 Mann, *Doktor Faustus*, p. 126: 'dieser kosmologischen Früherkonzeption einer strengen und frommen Geistes, der seine Grundleidenschaft, die Mathematik, die abstrakte Proportion, die Zahl zum Prinzip der Weltenstehung und des Weltbestehens erhob.' Woods translation, p. 134, modified.

Pythagoras—thought pronounced by Zeitblom in relation to Professor Nonnenmacher's lessons—clarify that
which was the 'precedent', the past by which Adrian's art
entered into a deformed and demonic relation.

'The number and the numeric proportion as consti-
tutive totality of being and moral dignity': here is the
genuine counterpart of Adrian's musical demonism, now
dangerously transformed precisely for the ends of 'moral
dignity' and for man. It is not music, therefore, but music
contaminated by demonism—by man's guilt—which
serves as the vehicle of horror, emblematic of the crisis
of bourgeois art. Even before referring to Schönberg's system, Mann had recognized in Wagner the object of his
love-hatred. Wagner had been the author of the music
that accompanied the decadence of Buddenbrook; it is
Wagner who presides over the tragedy of bourgeois society in the novella *Wälsungenblut* ('The Blood of the
Wälsungs'), and the seduction of the death in the novella
Tristan. And in *Die Entstehung des 'Doktor Faustus'* (The
Origins of 'Doktor Faustus'), Mann recalls that during the
editing of the novel he could not hear enough of the
piano from *Tristan und Isolde*. Furthermore, is it worth
nothing that the cipher of *Hetaera esmerald* (B-E-A-E-$E\flat$)
derives from the solo of the French horn in Act 3 of
Tristan und Isolde: the theme of the hero's solitude.

But if in *Doktor Faustus* the memory of Wagner re-
emerges, and Schönberg's musical system is revealed
explicitly, there is another musician of whom Mann must
have thought in weaving together the biographical
threads and symbols of his drama. To clarify the identify
of this musician, we have to return to a letter which
Mann addresses in March 1921 to Wolfgang Born,[47] the

---

47 Letter of 18 March 1921, from Munich. In the figure of
Aschenbach there are also evident references to Platen. [Thomas

illustrator of an edition of *Death in Venice*, providing him with a unique revelation: the Christian name and physiognomy which he attributed to the protagonist of *Death in Venice*, Gustav von Aschenbach, were those of Gustav Mahler. Mann had decided to reveal this secret relation as Born, in drawing Aschenbach's face, had done so without forming an image in which one could recognize Mahler clearly.

Mann had known Mahler in Munich in September 1910, on the occasion of the first performance of the Eighth Symphony. He had subsequently sent the musician a copy of *Royal Highness*, together with a letter full of admiration: he wrote to him that the book 'is not at all suitable to represent that which I have correspondingly received from you, and must weigh less than a feather in the hands of the man in whom is embodied the most sacred and serious artistic will of our times'.[48]

'The man in whom is embodied the most sacred and severe artistic will of our times': these words could also refer, in a particular sense, to Adrian Leverkühn. For while the reference could be quite exact and it is worth considering the vice by which the Faustian musician undermines *a priori* the symbolic art: Adrian's artistic will is 'sacred' and 'severe' in its horrifying devotion to demonism. In this sense too, *Doctor Faustus* allows us to perceive some aspects of Mahler's work. Mahler experienced the tragedy of bourgeois art profoundly: with 'sacred' and 'severe' commitment, beyond that of suffering, he had drawn out

---

Mann, *Briefe. Band 1: 1889–1936* (Erika Mann ed.) (Frankfurt am Main: Fischer, 1962), pp. 184–6. Translated in Thomas Mann, *Letters of Thomas Mann, 1889–1955* (Richard and Clara Winston trans) (London: Penguin, 1975), pp. 100–2.]

48 Thomas Mann, Letter to Mahler, September 1910, from Bad Tölz; Mann, *Briefe. Band 1*, p. 88.

the almost exhausted substance of music borne in the sphere of bourgeois culture, including its most extreme possibilities. In sum, he had denounced the tragedy of bourgeois art, consuming its conventional substance and working from within his denunciation and his creative and destructive labours. Reflecting on Mahler's death in 1911, Schönberg said: 'Mahler was allowed to reveal just so much of this future; when he wanted to say more, he was called away. And so things cannot be entirely quiet yet; there must still be more battle and noise.'[49]

In discussing the 'message' contained in *Doktor Faustus*, we observed that Adrian's fate is a desperate one precisely because Adrian is a symbol of a society and a culture which is always entirely closed up within its own vices and guilt. But furthermore whoever participates in that society and that culture can, albeit dramatically, find escape in demonism and the restoration of pure bonds with the past, acquiring from this the genuine forces of creation. In order to achieve such a positive result it is necessary, nevertheless, to reject the guilty tendency of a civilization which has reached its own limits and broken away from them. This was exactly the position of Mahler, whose rebellion against bourgeois music—frequently manifested in parody—bears no relation to Adrian's icy irony which works against those same musical arts and is the utmost act of demonic pride. Even when he executes parody, Adrian does not do so on a moral level higher than that of the bourgeois society and culture

---

49 'Soviel durfte Mahler von dieser Zukunft verraten; als er mehr sagen wollte, wurde er abberufen. Denn es soll noch nicht ganz still werden; es soll noch Kampf und Lärm weiter sein.' Arnold Schönberg, *Stil und Gedanke* (Frankfurt: Fischer, 1976[1912]), p. 24 [English translation: *Style and Idea* (Dika Newlin trans.) (New York: Philosophical Library, 1950), pp. 35–6, modified.]

against which his parody rebels. Adrian's parody is enacted with an icy and demonic laughter; the symbol of the pride of whomever has abandoned collective guilt, falling into the abyss alone.

Confronting this proudly nihilistic attitude, Mahler condemns the consumption of structures of bourgeois music but without ever rescinding his desire for artistic renewal through a necessarily moral renewal; and the sanity of this moral proposal allows him to once again draw on the genuine sources of myth without reflecting the horrific elements flowing out from within it. Mahler turned to folk music and myth throughout his life, finding an element of purity and vitality within these in order to enliven his works. The utilization of traditional musical themes became ever-more tragically evident as Mahler made the vital and renewing forces that he drew from a popular, primordial past break into the old structures. He experienced a phenomenon of healing that allowed him to deal with genuine elements of the past, from the very start, leaving behind that which myth freely brought forth from his own psychology. In a second moment, thanks to a faculty of memory which was also a faculty for revival, he 'recognized' the mythic elements of popular tradition that might be woven into his creative work. As such, he was able to draw productively on *Des Knaben Wunderhorn*, finding the symbols which poured forth from within him spontaneously in its collection of survivals from the past,

'Like a sound of nature': the celebrated line which Mahler occasionally added to his scores so as to refer to the 'primordial quality' for which he searched both in the creative forces and mythic images born out of his being, and in the survivals of the past which tradition posed to him and which—in an intimate and genuine relation with myth—he was ready to grasp in all their authentic value.

Making traditional instruments sing 'like a sound of nature' meant for him not only the revelation of the limitation and depletion of such instruments, but also that in the utmost depletion such instruments reached the overcoming of their limits and returned, at least for a moment, to a primordial purity. The void in Mahler forced Romantic music to fall back not only into annihilation but also freedom, and therefore the ideal conditions for enlightenment. In Mahler's symphonic works, the musical form of Romanticism undergoes a kind of strengthening which we might describe as 'physical', including the introduction of non-traditional instruments into the orchestra: in approaching the monstrous and gigantic orchestra invoked by Berlioz, Mahler again took on a parodic attitude—but a desperate parody that includes the hope that traditional form, in being forced to the limits of its own nature, can reach through to primordial sources.

In Mahler's work, the recourse to myth and parody through traditional musical forms and means announces innocence and a regained primordial character. Such parody also allows for the regaining of innocence when it turns against morally unacceptable elements, and when the soul of the parodist is not confined to the desire for destruction. The traditional accusation of banality turned against Mahler's musical motivations, according to which Mahler merely vainly amplified banal musical ideals, collapses when we realize that in this case *banal* means *primordial*, in a double sense: primary elements traced through traditional music, and primordial human experiences taken from the sources of myth. Adrian performs an analogous operation, even if in an exclusively nihilistic manner, in *Doktor Faustus*: 'There are in these [compositions], notwithstanding the highest level of musical development, before a background of utmost tension, "banalities", naturally not in the sense of sentimentality of an outpouring of pleasure, but rather banalities in the sense of a technical primitivism: naivety, or apparent naivety.[50]

In a conversation on the future of music in Chapter 31 of *Doktor Faustus*, Adrian seems for an instant to abandon demonism for a humanist renewal:

> The future of music will see in art, and art will in its turn see in itself, the handmaiden to a community which will embrace much more than 'education' and will not so much have as be a culture. We can imagine it only with courage, and yet it will come to pass, and naturally so: an art without suffering, spiritually healthy, not solemn, not sad, but faithful, an art standing with humanity.[51]

These words shock Zietblom to the core, who represents a final humanistic tradition that ignores such concepts. But they can also be suited to the concept of 'popular music' according to Mahler, and as such to the

---

50 Mann, *Doktor Faustus*, p. 242: 'Es gibt darin, auf entwickeltster musikalischer Stufe, vor einem Hintergrund äusserster Spannungen, 'Banalitäten'-natürlich nicht im sentimentalen Sinn oder in dem schwunghafter Gefälligkeit sondern Banalitäten in Sinn eines technischen Primitivmus, Naivitäten oder Schein-naivitäten also'. Woods translation, p. 263, modified.

51 Mann, *Doktor Faustus*, p. 429: 'Die Zukunft wird in ihr, sie selbst wird wieder in sich die Dienerin sehen an einer Gemeinschaft, die weit mehr als 'Bildung' umfassen und Kultur nicht haben, vielleicht aber eine sein wird. Wir stellen es uns nur mit Mühe vor, und doch wird es das geben wird das Natürliche sein: eine Kunst ohne Leiden, seelisch gesund, unfeierlich, untraurig-zutraulich eine Kunst mit der Menschheit auf und du . . . .' Woods translation, p. 466, modified.

notion of a music which will overcome the fracture between art and the masses typical to the bourgeois era, so as to rediscover primordial and collective forces and emotions.

Theodor W. Adorno wrote that in Mahler's works 'the inferior music irrupts Jacobinically into the higher. The self-righteous gloss of the middling form is demolished by the inordinate clamour from the bands in military chapels and palm court orchestras'.[52]

Such a notion of 'inferior music' seems nonetheless analogous to that of the 'banality' typically cited by Mahler's detractors: the primordial elements, to which the music in Mahler's works traces back, can also seem to emanate from the 'bands in military chapels' but this depends precisely on the depletion of the traditional musical means by which these primordial elements are brought into contact with each other. Bourgeois music is not ready to embrace these primordial elements without profoundly modifying their structures. Mahler's work does not reach that point of modification, for 'things cannot be entirely quiet yet; there must still be more battle and noise'; his work demonstrated the inevitable necessity for renewal and simultaneously obtained a great energy from traditional music, that also represents the beginning of its catharsis, compelling it to ring out 'like a sound of nature.'

---

52 Theodor W. Adorno, *Mahler. Eine musikalische Physiognomik* (Frankfurt: Suhrkamp, 1960), p. 52: 'Jakobinisch stürmt die untere Musik in die obere ein. Die selbstgerechte Glätte der mittleren Gestalt wird demoliert vom unmäßigen Klang aus den Pavillons der Militärkapellen und Palmengartenorchester.' [English translation: *Mahler: A Musical Physiognomy* (Edmund Jephcott trans.) (Chicago: University of Chicago Press, 1992), p. 35, modified.]

In Mahler's work, myth and the primordial element of nature thus reach towards an identification by allowing the recognition of myth within genuine popular musical elements developed by the artist, and the primordial nature in the mythic images in the *Lieder* texts and the symphonies. Furthermore, if the relation of the artistic with myth were truly genuine, it would be inevitable that genuine myth become a voice of nature echoing within man.

Under this aspect, in Mahler's creative life, genuine myth is revealed as a healing power for those artists who, with humility and purity, allow it to pour forth spontaneously. Myth was the healer, and without any of its horrifying aspects, even in the most tragic moments or renewal executed by the artist; he made the parody productive rather than nihilistic, and revealed the antagonist dialectic of the deformed survivals of the past as symbolized through 'Kaisersaschern'. The symbol of this dialectic seems, in Mahler's Symphony No. 3, to be Zarathustra's 'Midnight Song' which rings out with a melody developed from a reference to the popular *Paloma*, almost as if Nietzsche's pain and voice were cured through a primordial force, the voice of nature transformed into human song.[53]

Letting the mythic flow pour out spontaneously, a flow which springs from the subconscious and derives from a vital and creative impulse, is both good and just; only the projection of one's guilt onto that flow represents a truly culpable act, the abandonment of consciousness to the horrific images which spring forth from within it, even up to the point of annihilation. Only the morality of the devil is thus truly diabolical in *Doktor Faustus*,

---

53 See Ugo Duse, 'Origini popolari del canto mahleriano', *L'approdo musicale* 16–17 (1963): 113.

when he says to Adrian, referring back to Goethe: 'Whatever he in his classic days could have had without us, today only we are able to offer.'[54] For the artist of the bourgeois age, demonism is inevitable only if he does not refuse the guilt and limitations of civilization which surround him and if, with all humility, he allows the voice of nature to speak, while maintaining the lucidity of his own moral conscience.

* * *

Our research into the demonic aspects of the relations between myth and artist in twentieth-century German culture cannot disregard the works of Rainer Maria Rilke, even if we are here dealing with a poet who—as with Gustav Mahler, who we have already discussed—never belonged to the German nation. Our expression 'German culture', however, implies a linguistic and not a political distinction, and the criteria of German linguistic unity seems to us more innocent and acceptable that any notion of a 'Germanism' like that on which the *Anschluß* was established, far more reprehensible than any notion which we employ here.

Rilke's work presents difficulties for our point of view, ones more serious than we have met up till now, as so far we have only examined the personality of a symbol of demonism (Adrian Leverkühn), whose guilt is only of an emblematic evidence, and of an artist (Gustav Mahler) whose spiritual story was carried out under the sign of a mythic 'healing'. In approaching Rilke, we find ourselves confronted with an artist in whose activity myth surfaces at times in a genuine and serene semblance, at others in

---

54 Mann, *Doktor Faustus*, p. 316: 'Was der in seinem klassischen Läuften allenfalls ohne uns haben konnte, das haben heutzutage nur wir zu bieten.' Woods translation, p. 343, modified.

that of horror, generating a dense and mysterious forest of images and illuminations, as ambiguous and mysterious as the poet's own moral outlook.

Rilke began a commentary on *The Duino Elegies* of which, unfortunately, there remains no trace; only a few letters by the poet provide some clarifications for the frequent and undeniable obscurities of a supremely mysterious work—even if not an inaccessible one. Rilke's esotericism is entirely idiosyncratic, implying a cursory overcoming of the ciphers and symbols within the dynamic process of poetry, so that a reality emerges in the space left open by these obscure images, one which the poet did not intend to subject to any definitive symbolic process. In other words, one part of the poems of *The Duino Elegies* is essentially evocative, and its esotericism is only a very provisional instrument by which Rilke allowed himself to provide an unmediated instrument for his own voice, the handling of fragmentary and partial references for whoever is absorbed in the experience of reaching for the supra-sensible. We insist on saying '*part* of the poems of *The Duino Elegies*', because the poem is not entirely evocative, nor entirely esoteric. Alongside the points which correspond to evocations and visions there are poetic fragments in which Rilke reached for and showed a genuinely *human* consciousness, with all the limitations and positive aspects which this adjective brings with it.

The Duino Elegies are a forest of mythic images which can, without doubt, be connected to the most disparate of traditions, but which came from or were experienced by Rilke in his personal mythological aura, or used by him as the wreckage of the past, independent from their historical roots. It is important to note that up to this point Rilke was never a mythologist in the sense of a historian of mythology: his historical interests were very partial and, in a certain sense 'superficial', for they were always determined by the desire to weave traditional material into his creative life. This method of choosing and developing traditional material means, of course, that Rilke did not always work with the awareness of what might arise from it; in his case, Mahler's claim is apt: 'The artist shoots in the dark, not knowing whether he hits or what he hits.'[55]

Among the images of *The Duino Elegies*, that of the angel, in terms of magnitude and gravity (in the literal sense of 'weight') stands out, or better of the angels. In a letter to his Polish translator, Witold von Hulewicz,[56] Rilke explained that the angels of the *Elegies* were not meant to be a reference to images of Christian angels but rather, if anything, to Muslim angels. This indication—as approximate as it is—confirms the impression which one receives upon reading the First Elegy, in which the angels appear as gigantic figures, just as Gabriel appeared to Muhammad, filling up the sky above the hill. The Muslim tradition does not claim, however, that Muhammad was filled with terror in front of this giant apparition, but emphasizes instead the substantially beneficent nature. Rilke's angel is, rather, from the very first, *terrifying* ('schrecklich'); he cannot hear the man's cries, and is real enough to be able to destroy the man's partial reality if he were to push at it from close behind. One of the principal

---

55 Alma Mahler, *Gustav Mahler: Memories and Letters* (Basil Creighton trans.) (New York: Viking, 1946), p. 94.

56 Letter of 13 November 1925, from Muzot. [Rainer Maria Rilke, *Briefe. Band 2: 1914–1926* (Ruth Sieber-Rilke and Karl Altheim eds) (Wiesbaden: Insel Verlag, 1950), p. 711. English translation: *Letters of Rainer Maria Rilke, Volume 2: 1910–1926* (Jane Bannard Greene and M. D. Herter Norton trans) (New York: W. W. Norton, 1947), p. 373.]

components to Rilke's anguish in the First Elegy is exactly the limited, unstable reality of man: the man of 'when we feel, we evaporate',[57] does indeed 'evaporate' outside of himself in the very moment of sensation, which is also his own natural form of expression and consciousness.

We have already spoken of the broken relation with the past and with myth which is shown in German culture and manifested through the religion of death. Rilke's angel seems without doubt to be a demon born from the deformation of genuine myth, pertaining to that kind of mutated relationship. The anguish which pervades the first elegies evidences, nonetheless, that Rilke did not feed off any satisfaction in the religion of death but, rather, was unable to escape its horrific imagery. This fact—this difficulty in freeing oneself from the horrors of deformed myth—is nonetheless a symptom of the poet's own guilt, for one does not inherit horror unless one is, in some way, active in arousing it. And Rilke, with his esoteric abandonment, with his deliberate and recurrent abandonment of himself into hidden zones of the psyche, granting them with a momentary domination over his entire consciousness, is also in some way culpable.

As such, the terrifying angel extends his sovereignty over the first elegies—at least the first six—while an entire cosmology and biology emerges unstoppably before it, which might seem to be merely the ravings of anguish, if it were not for their construction in a poetic form that, in its fragmentary character, in its games of mirrors, reveals a personality of previously inaudible power and intellectual richness: a spirit shocked by all forms of terror, forced into ever-more terrifying evocations, and granted the faculty to reach for horror upon horror without losing its

---

57 *Duino Elegies*, II, Line 18: 'Denn wir, wo wir fühlen, verflüchtingen.'

own purity of song. Even those fragments of the elegies which announce the most painful victories of horror over the poet do not reveal any yielding in the aesthetic quality of his song. Rilke managed this exceptional unity of *The Duino Elegies* through his will to reduce every mythic image which contained horror to rubble, to sterile and incomprehensible survivals of the past: in the exact moment of gathering such an image into the peaks of horrific evocation, Rilke reduces it to rubble, removing its vitality and power, drawing on its poetic technics. Apologists for an esoteric Rilke have generally considered these images as living evocative instruments in the poet's hands: on the contrary, these images are in reality the horrific evocation imposed upon him but which he manages to 'sterilize', to remove of their horrific life, to reduce to rubble in the instant in which he gathers them into his song. For Rilke, to sing is the only means of not allowing oneself to be dominated by horror; indeed, in his song he possesses an instrument which can bend to each and every will, and which has the power to reduce every image generated through horror to the level of mute, chaotic rubble.

The first elegies are composed from this rubble, in which Rilke provisionally flees horror, sterilizing the images which are borne from within it, thus surviving into evocation, as well as from passionate human lamentation. The weapon which sterilizes and reduces horrific imagery to rubble is the miraculous faculty to remain human, of suffering humanly, here without doubt evidence of humility. *Doktor Faustus* shows us, indeed, that the great weakness in front of which the demonic attacks consists precisely in *superbia*, in the pride of man, the belief in the possibility of being more than just a man, even in suffering.

This same faculty, which is faithful to man even in the great agony imposed by demonism, allowed Rilke to counterpose a notion of profoundly human death to the demonic religion of death. Announced from the very first elegies, which reference the bond binding the dead to the living as an objective norm of the cosmos, this notion of death pervades the final, Tenth Elegy, from which the terrifying presence of the angel is now absent. Painful images of women—the Laments—accompany the young dead man to the feet of the 'mountains of primal grief', where the 'fountains of joy' spring forth.[58] Human pain, and no longer horror, signals the acceptance of death into experience which is 'another face' of life but also its terrifying opposite. The victory over horror is manifested in Rilke's work as the overcoming of human agony when confronted by death, which itself becomes a component of human life. Death is the experience of the invisible which completes the visible in daily life as two symmetric halves of the same fruit, made whole by them and allowing the experience of unity. Life cannot estrange itself from death nor death from life, for the one is the completion of the other. Horror is estranged from this unity, and indeed this unity and its force of reality is juxtaposed to such horror, borne out of an imperfect consciousness, i.e. through a deformation of myth.

It is important to note that Rilke's esotericism, which included the poet's anti-human guilt, is finally purified in the Tenth Elegy, forming the means of restoration. Rilke's anti-human abandonment, in which he can synthesize his participation in the guilt of a bourgeois art that favours sinking into the abysses of demonic subjectivism rather than embracing a collective sentiment of humanity, are

---

58 See Furio Jesi, 'Rilke e l'Egitto. Considerazioni sulla X Elegia Duinese', *Aegyptus* 44(1–2) (1964): 58–65.

overcome thanks to the poet's fundamental humanism, one that outlives weaknesses and failures, and which—throughout these same failures—functions as a means of healing, giving rise to the most human of suffering, void of demonic pride. But this victory of humanism coincides with the genuine assertion of myth, that is, with the poet's access to myth void of both horror and anguish. Wherever esotericism becomes a means of humanism it is no longer truly esoteric because genuine, human myth is a source of spiritual life that involves the whole community within it.

* * *

A fundamental objection, not entirely against the ethical standpoint which has dominated our discussion up till now, as much as against the precision of our language, can be found in the work of Ludwig Klages. Up till now we have spoken of myth, subconsciousness and consciousness, making exactly that error identified by Klages in the language of Freud and Jung, which is to freely make use of spatial metaphors, those of the *flow* of myth and its *sources* in the subconscious.[59] Klages' scholarship substituted the dualism of consciousness-subconsciousness for that of spirit-soul, without, of course, maintaining an intrinsic identity for each pair of opposites. It has been shown that on the basis of Klages' thought, one can 'correct' Freud and Jung's thought, through formulating a psychoanalytic system which could be called 'Klagesian' (naming a school after someone who was, paradoxically, unyieldingly opposed to psychoanalysis). Such 'Klagesian' alterations to Freud and Jung's teachings substantially consist in a different notion of the relation between

---

59 See the comment by Albino Galvano in *Per un'armatura* (Turin: Lattes, 1960), p. 88ff.

consciousness and subconscious, in which one becomes
the active elaboration, in a destructive sense, of the content provided by the other, and in their 'hostility' and
extraneity from such elaboration. There would not be,
however, a 'surfacing' of images from the subconscious
to consciousness but, rather, the antagonism between the
subconscious and conscious 'intentions', with the alternating dominance of one or the other in the events of a
human life.

We ought say immediately that our acceptance of the
terms of *flow* and *emergence* of myth are not entirely
dependent on a deliberate adhesion to Freud and Jung's
language, as much as the influence exercised on our
thought by a sentence from Rilke: 'He who pours himself
out as a spring shall find Recognition.'[60] That would likely
be enough to redeem our 'error' in Klages' eyes for to
'pour oneself forth like a spring' could also be understood
as a negation of the *Spirit* as Klages meant it, and as a
return to the 'maternal underworld' which Klages would
identify in the work of Stefan George (even if in an open
and disharmonious contrast with the poet's own opinion).[61] Klages, nonetheless, might return to denounce us

---

60 Cited in Carl Gustav Jung and Karl Kerényi, *Einführung in das Wesen der Mythologie. Gottkindmythos. Eleusinische Mysterien* (Amsterdam: Pantheon, 1942) [English translation: *Science of Mythology: Essays on the Myth of the Divine Child and the Mysteries of Eleusis* (R. F. C. Hull trans.). New York and London: Routledge, 2002[1942], p. 5. The line is from Rilke's *Sonnets to Orpheus*: 'Wer sich als Quelle ergießt, den erkennt die Erkennung'. Rainer Maria Rilke, *Die Sonette an Orpheus* (Frankfurt: Suhrkamp, 1955).]

61 Klages speaks of George as a prophet of 'the original place of the soul' ('Urheimat der Seele'), determining the recombination with the 'maternal underworld' ('mütterliche Unterwelt'): Ludwig Klages, *Stefan George* (Berlin: Bondi, 1902). See also Mario Pensa, *Stefan George: Saggio critico* (Bologna: Zanichelli, 1961), p. 3 and p. 6.

if he were to learn of our interpretation of Rilke's artistic experience and our concept of the healer as achieved by the poet through a humanistic balancing of spirit and soul. We believe, however, that Klage's own ideas correspond to a stage of the illness which Rilke tried to heal. The notion of the spirit according to Klages, in which it intrinsically brings with it destruction and death, seems to us exactly the kind that belongs to those who refuse humanism and the values of the collective, or at least recognize them only in the indiscriminate predominance of 'dark forces' and in the consequent annihilation of consciousness. Following an analogous line of thought to those who consider philosophy the *ancilla theologiae*, we believe that philosophy must be the *ancilla humanitatis*, that is, it must be the instrument of moral judgement rather than that of pure and abstract 'research'. We claim, as the basis of such a morality, a humanism which we are still willing to believe is empirical wherever it pertains to the safeguarding of elements which can guarantee the survival of man, love and freedom today. We recognize in this empiricism, nonetheless, a particularly profound value, for we believe that it allows us to recognize that which truly suited man—adducing, as evidence of this faith of ours, that notion of 'earthly' happiness by which the paladins of philosophy are estranged from indiscriminate research. We have to confess that it is not clear to us how such 'happiness' can correspond to the 'good' and to 'truth' on a metaphysical level; but we must also recognize that an irrepressible intuition, albeit quite obscure, forces us to exclude the possibility that metaphysical 'good' and 'truth' can negate this earthly happiness.[62]

---

62 We find a similar attitude in Mircea Eliade, in relation to the rejection of history implicit in the ever-renewed time of myth: 'It is not our part to decide whether such motives were puerile or not,

This obscurity—which we do not hesitate to criticize—seems to us to correspond to a mystery, for which
we find it appropriate, paradoxically, to utilize Klages'
thought (whose own profundity and singular genius, on
the other hand, we would never dare to deny). We use the
word *mystery* in the sense it is given in the history of
Greek religion (and therefore we refer ourselves to a cultural tradition which also survives in Klages): in the
Greek world, *mystery* also historically included the
mourning for lost knowledge; but this history teaches us
that there those who are devoted to mysteries through an
undeniably critical conscience, those who feel it morally
necessary to place themselves on the same level as those
devotees who are, instead, ignorant of such mourning.
This most likely reveals the human depth and validity of
the Eleusian experience, beyond the mourning for consciousness which history identifies in the origins of the
Eleusian cult: whoever, in the classical epoch, initiated
themselves into Eleusis desired access to an experience
beyond that of pure and indiscriminate research. Instead
they opted to be a healer of man, with the ability to guarantee survival, love and freedom.

Survival: projected onto the afterlife, this concept can
perhaps justify indiscriminate philosophical research,
perhaps even capable of sacrificing the 'earthly' experience for the certainty of an afterlife; Klages thought of the

---

or whether such a refusal of history always proved efficacious. In
our opinion, only one fact counts: by virtue of this view, tens of
millions of men were able, for century after century, to endure great
historical pressures without despairing, without committing
suicide or falling into that spiritual aridity that always brings with
it a relativistc or nihilistic view of history.' Mircea Eliade, *Le mythe
de l'éternel retour* (Paris: Gallimard, 1949), p. 223 [English
translation: *The Myth of the Eternal Return* (Willard R. Task trans.)
(New York: Harper and Row, 2005[1959]), p. 152].

afterlife in his notion of 'obscure forces', threatened by the destructive actions of the spirit. Every morality founded on such an afterlife is a religious morality; but we prefer to remain faithful to a religion of man while being aware that we are not providing a theological apparatus any less flawed from a philosophical point of view. At the same time, this does not prevent us from benefiting from Klages' thought, precisely in our notion of a humanistic equilibrium between consciousness and the unconscious. Klages' dialectic between spirit and soul correctly corresponds, at least from a structural point of view, to our concept of the humanist alternation between the victory of unconsciousness and of consciousness. At the base of that empiricism which we have already declared we will follow, we believe that a victory of unconsciousness—the 'delirious' state of the artist to which Schönberg alludes in a celebrated essay[63]—does not exclude the expansion of consciousness. Rather, we believe that the physiological, biological and psychic unity of man allows consciousness to enrich itself even in defeat, and that the conciousness of the artist is a human 'organ' capable of benefiting positively from the enrichment gained by man through that other 'organ', unconsciousness. Consciousness and unconsciousness thus appear for us intrinsically antagonistic, but are in reality 'collaborators', so long as one and the other do not reach a definitive self-annihiliation.

Klages and his psychoanalytic interpreters consider consciousness to be more than only an instrument for the elaboration of 'content'. For while unconsciousness and consciousness both make up parts of man—and we do not believe that the components of man can naturally act as his own destruction—it seems to us that the phenomenon of the elaboration of the content provided

---

63 See below, p. 63ff.

to unconsciousness enriches consciousness itself inasmuch as the content itself is particularly rich. That is, consciousness tends to identify itself with unconsciousness—and unconsciousness with consciousness—when the objects and 'content' pregnant with 'humanistic values' are the object of a conscious elaboration. Such 'humanistic values' are, for us, those mythic realities which the will of man abandons in order to accept them as enrichments of man: those genuine myths, that is, which spring forth from the depths of the psyche, a psyche whose genuineness is determined by the human ability to make use of the myths themselves. How such an ability is the criteria of absolute ethical validity remains for us—as we have already said—a mystery.

The word 'mystery' has become imprecise and worn out ever since it lost its original technical role in the context of Greek religiosity. Mystery is, in our quite specific context, that which one does not recognize but also that which one cannot communicate through a certain language. This means that, as such, a reality becomes mysterious only in a relative sense, with respect to a given language; and precisely this, to us, seems the case with the antinomy we have observed between philosophy as *ancilla humanitatis* and the laws intrinsic to philosophizing. We are not claiming that philosophical language is unable to embrace the pure and simple proclamation of belief in happiness, love, etc., as a worthy element of faith; rather, we are claiming that, today, Western philosophical language evidences such an inability. That historical metamorphosis by which myth was able to be technified and distanced from its original purity has very likely contributed to the determining of this situation in an important way. For those who defend a philosophy as an *ancilla* to nothing, and those who support the technification of myth (Sorel, for example), today find themselves on opposing barricades, both realizing, in different terms, the consequences of a distancing from a form of thinking and feeling that pertains to a primordial communion with the flow of myth. It is this that renders images and names accessible, ones that are intrinsically valid *within* philosophical thought, just as—though necessarily only through definition—the postulates of logic are.

Is it possible, and not only a utopian desire, to return to such a condition? One of the principle aims of our discussion here is precisely the study of this problem. When Hegel wrote that in the 'free development of the spirit . . . all superstition, and all faith which remains restricted to determinate forms of intuition and representation, is degraded into simple moments and features over which the free spirit, not considering them in and for themselves as sacrosanct conditions for its own exposition and configuration, exercises its sovereignty',[64] he meant, fundamentally, how that which we have defined as 'mystery' remains latent, and that a lack of consciousness is not

---

64 G. W. F. Hegel, *Vorlesungen über Aesthetik. Band 2* (Berlin: Duncker and Humblot, 1843), p. 233: 'besonders bedarf der heutige große Künstler der freien Ausbildung des Geistes, in welcher aller Aberglauben und Glauben, der auf bestimmte Formen der Anschauung und Darstellung beschränkt bleibt, zu bloßen Seiten und Momenten herabgesetzt ist, über welche der freie Geist sich zum Meister gemacht hat, indem er in ihnen keine an und für sich geheiligten Bedingungen seiner Exposition und Gestaltungsweise sieht'. [English translation: *Aesthetics: Lectures on Fine Art, Volume 1* (T. M. Knox trans.) (Oxford: Clarendon Press, 1975), p. 606, modified.] It is interesting to consider, beyond this interpretation of this thought by Hegel, that given in Theodor W. Adorno, *Philosophie der neuen Musik* (Frankfurt: Suhrkamp, 1975), pp.˙21–2 [English translation: *Philosophy of New Music* (Robert Hullot-Kentor trans.) (Minneapolis: University of Minnesota Press, 2006), pp. 14–15].

absolute enough to determine an absolute agnosticism. The 'free spirit', rather, lives among such linguistic mysteries or limitations, and as its mere unifying existence is enough to guarantee the possibility of access to the purity of myth, our discussion will aim only to experience the reality and truth of such an existence in its phenomenological presence.

CHAPTER 2

Thence it became clear to me that the work of art is like every other complete and perfect organism. It is so homogeneous in its composition that in every little detail it reveals its truest, inmost essence. When one cuts into any part of the human body, the same thing always comes out—blood.[1]

The notion of the work of art implicit in the words of Arnold Schönberg poses a fundamental problem for relations between those elements participating in the genesis of this 'complete organism'. The citation is taken from Schönberg's essay 'The Relationship with the Text' ['Das Verhältnis zum Text'] dedicated to the relation between music and text in works of art which, as with opera or

---

1 Arnold Schönberg, 'Das Verhältnis zum Text' (1912) in *Gesammelte Schriften 1. Stil und Gedanke. Aufsätze zur Musik* (Berlin: Fischer, 1976), pp. 3–6. The essay has been published many times in Italian ('Il rapporto col testo'), most recently in P. Chiarini, *Caos e geometria. Per un regesto delle poetiche espressioniste. Con la collaborazione di F. Lo Re e I. Porena* (Florence: Libreria Antiquaria SEAB, 1964), p. 169. [German: p. 5. 'Mir war daraus klar, dass es sich mit dem Kunstwerk so verhalte wie mit jedem vollkommenen Organismus. Es ist so homogen in seiner Zusammensetzung, daß es in jeder Kleinigkeit sein wahrstes, innerstes Wesen enthüllt. Wenn man an irgendeiner Stelle des menschlichen Körpers hineinsticht, kommt immer dasselbe, immer Blut heraus.' English translation: 'The Relationship to the Text' in *Style and Idea* (D. Newlin trans.) (New York: St Martin's Press, 1975), pp. 1–6; here, p. 4.]

Lieder, interweave music and word; in this essay, Schönberg also refers to aspects of that problem which touch more closely on literature and the figurative arts, citing Karl Kraus in calling language 'the mother of thought', and Wassily Kandinsky's book *Concerning the Spiritual in Art* [*Über das Geistige in der Kunst*] 'in which the road for painting is indicated and the hope arises that those who inquire into the text and its material, will soon exhaust their questioning.'[2]

The conclusion of Schönberg's essay is the refusal of the attitude of those who would have it that the linguistic elements in a work of art are components of a rational design: a rationally meaningful one. He claims to have penetrated the depths of the reality of those lyrics of Stefan George that he used for his own *Lieder*, 'intoxicated by the opening sound of the first words of the text, without troubling myself in the slightest about the further course of the poetic processes, without grasping them in the slightest during the delirium of composing.'[3] Schönberg, nevertheless, never entirely excludes rationality from the process of understanding the work of art, observing that, having written the songs with George's texts in a 'delirium', some days later he 'found the rationality' in the poetic content. His rationality had been singularly strengthened through this creative delirium, bringing him to a greater

---

2 Schönberg, 'Das Verhältnis zum Text', p. 5: 'in welchem der Weg für die Malerei gezeigt wird und die Hoffnung erwacht, dass jene, die nach dem Text, nach dem Stofflichen fragen, bald ausgefragt haben werden'; Newlin translation, p. 4, modified.

3 Schönberg, 'Das Verhältnis zum Text', p. 5: 'berauscht von dem Anfangsklang der ersten Textworte, ohne mich auch nur im geringsten um den weiteren Verlauf der poetischen Vorgänge zu kümmern, ja ohne diese im Taumel des Komponierens auch nur im geringsten zu erfassen'; Newlin translation, p. 3, modified.

ability to understand that which otherwise would have been comprehended only superficially.

It is not surprising that a musician—and a German musician at that—might theorize the supra-rational nature of artistic experience in this manner, for Schopenhauer had already himself spoken of music in his own analogous theoretical effort: 'The composer reveals the most intimate essence of the world and expresses the most profound wisdom, in a language which their reason cannot comprehend, like a magnetic sleepwalker who provides explanations for things about which, on waking, he has no idea.'[4] In recalling Schopenhauer, we find ourselves again within the realm of the discussion we began in the preceding chapter in relation to music and its demonic variations. Schönberg's words encourage us to examine that element within the artist's creative experience that empowers rationality so as to allow it to participate in an awareness of the 'poetic content'. No doubt Schönberg's approach towards rational knowledge in the artistic sphere was polemical, justified by the situation of the years in which he wrote (the essay cited is from 1912); neither does he entirely exclude rationality; nor, above all, does he remove the work of art from the life of human consciousness: the creative experience is 'delirious' and somnambulistic, but the fruit of that delirium—the 'complete and perfect organism'—enriches human existence without depriving it of consciousness. In order to create,

---

4 'Der Komponist offenbart das innerste Wesen der Welt und spricht die tiefste Weisheit aus, in einer Sprache, die seine Vernunft nicht versteht; wie eine magnetische Somnambule Aufschlüsse gibt über Dinge, von denen sie wachend keinen Begriff hat.' Cited in 'Das Verhältnis zum Text', p. 3.; Schopenhauer, *Die Welt als Wille und Vorstellung* (Munich: Georg Müller, 1911), p. 307. Newlin translation, p. 1, modified. [By 'magnetism' Schopenhauer intends a form of hypnotism.]

artists must abandon themselves to delirium; but such delirium is an exceptional state, running in parallel to waking life: it is not to be opposed as a negating element but integrated along with the richness of its products.

Schönberg's irrationalism—and Kandinsky's—is neither nihilistic nor does it negate consciousness as a part of man: Schönberg does not propose a utopian vision of society founded on delirium but, rather, in speaking of delirium, speaks only of the artist's experience. His problem, and that of the best part of his contemporary culture, is also that of the insertion of the artist—with his delirious and somnambulant experiences—into a society of men who must live in the state of consciousness on which everyday reality is founded.

The resolution of such a problem depends necessarily on knowledge of the suprarational element in which the artist participates during their delirium. In the previous chapter, we tried to exclude the idea that this element is demonic—at least in the horrific sense attributed to this word by Serenus Zeitblom. We can, nonetheless, deepen our knowledge by studying the metamorphoses of a mythic image constant to German culture of the last hundred years, and which acts as a useful mirror on the course of spiritual cure and sickness of artists.

Schopenhauer compares the composer to a 'sleepwalker who provides explanations for things about which, on waking, he has no idea.' We can trace this image of the sleepwalker immediately to that of Kundry, the character in *Parsifal* periodically dominated by the demonic force of the magician Klingsor, who puts her into a state of magically induced hypnotism or somnambulism; in this state, she serves him with her beauty in winning over the paladins of purity. Kundry's laughter under the bewitching influence of Klingsor seems to resound in Adrian Leverkühn's laughter in *Doktor Faustus*, and thus also the book that the composer creates under demonic influence, in a somnambulant state—like a blind tool, susceptible to the solicitations of dark forces.

The analogy between Kundry and Leverkühn might seem to confirm the demonic nature of the supra-rational element which the artist accesses during creation; but the course of the metamorphoses followed in the mythic images collected by Wagner in the figure of Kundry can also lead to a very different conclusion. In the second act of *Parsifal*, Kundry appears in Klingsor's kingdom among the flower maidens, of which she is in a certain sense a sublimation: the songs of the flower maidens, as with those of the Sirens, are expected to demonically enchant Parisfal, whose seduction is entrusted to Kundry. The image of the flower maidens in its human-vegetation hybridity reveals mythic sources, those in which woman and vegetation are identified in the character of the Hellenic *kore* (not only a Hellenic source).[5] This singular hybridization recurs, after Wagner, in the European figurative arts with a frequency symptomatic of a constant— if at the same time not always pure—recourse to myth. Already in *Parsifal*, on the other hand, the flower maidens are demonic images, in itself enough to attest to the deformation imposed by Wagner on the genuine myth. But with some decades after *Parsifal*, the name of the flower maiden reappears, with a mythological purity and

5 An expedition of the Frobenius Institut to Seram Island (Indonesia) has discovered images of *korai* genuinely analogous to those of Greece. See Adolf Ellegard Jensen and Hermann Niggemeyer (eds), *Hainuwele: Volkserzählungen von der Molukken-Insel Ceram* (Frankfurt: V. Klostermann, 1939). See also Kerényi, 'Kore' in Jung and Kerényi, *Einführung in das Wesen der Mythologie*. [English translation: 'Kore' in Jung and Kerényi, *Science of Mythology*, pp. 119–83; here, p. 154.]

genuineness, in Mann's 1905 play *Fiorenza*.[6] Fiore, the beloved courtesan of Lorenzo the Magnificent, dominates the events not so much as a protagonist of determinate scenic activity but, rather, as a symbol of a superior reality. Superior to the conflict between Lorenzo and Savonarola, distant from both the competitors and their desires, Fiore lives out a reality which could be accused of corrupting men only by those who, like the Savonarola of the play, passionately distort and debase that reality, constricted as he is from accessing it. Fiore represents an apparition of genuine mythology, like Aphrodite as depicted by Botticelli or the Homeric hymn to the Goddess transcribed in the *Stanze* of Agnolo Poliziano. Like Aphrodite and Kore, Fiore is both virgin and violated; her fate is analogous to that of the sacred prostitute of antiquity, perennially virginal though always violated by a god; and for this reason she always remains removed from Lorenzo, dying and preoccupied with the seduction of his city.

The passage from *Parsifal* to *Fiorenza* involved a metamorphosis which corresponds to a purifying access to myth. Already in *Parsifal*, Wagner had avoided the profound difficulty in making the image of the women coincide exactly with that of the demon of seduction, and had evoked the portentous actions of Klingsor, emphasizing the hypnotic, involuntary nature of Kundry's culpability. With *Fiorenza*, however, one finds a real revelation: the accusation made against the woman derives from a limitation, from a failure in the awareness of the accuser. Blossoming forth from primordial depths, the woman participates in the purity of genuine myth, but where the myth is no longer included as genuine, where

---

6 See on this proposition: Karl Kerényi, 'Thomas Mann zwischen Norden und Süden', *Nere Zürcher Zeitung*, 4 July 1955, p. 3.

it deforms 'through power', the image of the woman changes in the view of the technifier and tends to become an emblem of sin and horror. The problem of the mysterious identity between Fiore and Florence is formed through the phenomenon of the technification of myth: whoever wants to possess Florence, and therefore deform the myth to this end, cannot possess Fiore—that is, genuine myth.

Language, Karl Kraus says, is the 'mother of thought'. When Schönberg speaks of the sonority of the words of a *Lied*, he does not only refer to the phonetic value recognized in those words by those who conceive of it simply as an instrument for rational communication. He alludes also to the more profound resonance of the word, drawing on its supra-rational worth and therefore also on its mythical substrate. Word and image, in the sense of their most profound and supra-rational value, constitute the reality of the feminine figures blossoming from within the sources of myth in German art. The supra-rational aspects of such images, even when they stand on the level of genuine myth, no doubt constitute the cause not of horror but of agitation for the artistic conscience. The most explicit consequences of this feeling—a standing in wonderment before the mystery, an abandonment to enchantment—appears in Thomas Mann's novella *Der Kleiderschrank* (The Wardrobe): the dark, enchanting, feminine image found by the protagonist of the novel within that of an unknown city within the wardrobe of a rented room, emerging from the remote depths of the human psyche. The wardrobe's doors—which he opens every evening to rejoin the phantom woman—represent an anti-portal to the great beyond, a glimpse out from behind the canvas, the back wall of the wardrobe.

The novella's esotericism—if one can speak of such esotericism—is of a very particular quality; objectively, one can say that there is no symbolism in the novel, that everything is exactly that which it represents: the revelation comes from a daily reality, barely covered by a half-slumberous veil. The mythic appearance is improvised and deprived of every symbolic emblem: a nude woman who narrates stories that drown out reason, as in sleep. Only the name of the protagonist, Albrecht *van der Qualen* (of the torments) conceals a deep and revelatory symbolism; Gustav von Aschenbach and Adrian Leverkuhn could also bear that surname, also being men *of torment*; as such it seems that Mann wanted to emphasize the 'predisposition' or destiny of the artist to endure epiphanies from the deep.

The novella ends without any real conclusion: one only has the impression that the narrator distracts himself from the flow of myth like someone who awakes and then finds themselves confusing dreams and reality. In the work of Mann there is only one similar, even if perhaps unique, finale:[7] at the end of the demonic summoning, a silence follows that coincides with the voices of daily reality. At the same time, the novella is deeply cautionary and does not evade a certain pedagogy by the author: myth, the supra-rational lives through 'men of torment', separated from their daily life only by a door which opens easily. That which lies beyond that door is enchanting and obscure, the truth which they understand beyond that door cannot be repeated in words, so long as the words follow no more than a faculty of rational communication. The lived experience beyond that door can perhaps be expressed only in music or in words which resound like

7 See also Georges Fourrier, *Thomas Mann: Le message d'un artiste-bourgeois (1896–1924)* (Paris: Les Belles Lettres, 1960), pp. 73–4.

music. It is perhaps such words which Mann heard when, during the genesis of *Doktor Faustus*, he never tired of listening to *Tristan und Isolde* on the piano.

The profound agitation aroused in the artist by the mythical female image is also captured in *Buddenbrooks*. It is impossible to overestimate the significance of the figure of Gerda, Thomas Buddenbrook's 'unusual' wife. In choosing her, the final adult heir of the bourgeois house reveals his 'difference' from his ancestors, and thereby his predisposition towards death. Gerda introduces a disturbing element into the life of the family: music (for which none of the Buddenbrooks have any tendency), an action that coincides with decadence and death.

The violence and suggestion by which the figure of Gerda imposes itself on Mann's characterization is clearly also an attempt to mollify or ironically exorcize the enchantment, simultaneously showing the tragic abyss which separates her from the bourgeois world. ' "Tiptop," the guys said with a strike of the tongue, this being the latest expression from Hamburg for a really fine choice, thus treating her like a make of red wine, a cigar, a lunch, or a credit rating.'[8]

But using mythological language, Gosch (as mediator) makes a statement all the more accurate for its irony: 'What a woman, my lords! Hera and Aphrodite, Brunhilde and Melusina in a single person.'[9] And Tony Buddenbrook is enchanted by her sister-in-law, but obscurely aware of

---

8 Thomas Mann, *Buddenbrooks* (Frankfurt: Fischer, 1951), p. 305: ' "Tipptopp", sagten die Suitiers und schnalzten mit der Zunge, denn das war der neueste hamburgische Ausdruck für etwas auserlesen Feines, handelte es sich nun im eine Rotweinmarke, um eine Zigarre, um ein Diner oder um geschäftliche Bonität.'

9 Mann, *Buddenbrooks*, p. 306: 'Welch ein Weib, meine Herren! Here und Aphrodite, Brünhilde und Meulsine in einer Person.'

the destructive power which she brings with her introduction into bourgeois life, 'she reiterated that she had
always hated Gerda, but that she for her own part (and
her eyes were filled with tears) had always repaid that
hatred with love'.[10]

On the other hand, there is a moment in *Buddenbrooks* in which Mann gives into the enchantment of the
revelation: and this is the woman of the myth, the
enchanting feminine figure of *Der Kleiderschrank* who
takes shape in the shadows. Tony and Thomas

> without thinking about the lamp, were suddenly
> left in the evening darkness. There the door to
> the corridor opened and, enclosed in the twi-
> light, before both of them, in a flowing, crum-
> pled snow-white *piqué* housedress, stood an
> upright figure. The thick red hair framed the
> white face, and in the corners of the brown eyes
> which lay so close to one another, a blue shadow
> gathered. It was Gerda, the mother of the future
> Buddenbrooks.[11]

In order to fully understand the tragic and revelatory
significance of these final words, it is necessary to recall
that in reality Gerda was not the mother of 'future

---

10 Mann, *Buddenbrooks*, p. 304: 'beharrte Tony störrisch dabei,
dass Gerda sie immer gehasst habe, dass sie aber ihrerseits -und
ihre Augen füllten sich mit Tränen- diesen Hass stets mit Liebe
vergolten habe.'

11 Mann, *Buddenbrooks*, p. 315: 'Ohne an die Lampe zu denken,
hatten sie den Abend hereinbrechend lassen. Da öffnete sich die
Korridottür, und von der Dämmerung umgeben stand vor den
beiden, in einem faltig hinabwallenden Hauskleide aus schnee-
weissem Pikee, eine aufrechte Gestalt. Das schwere, dunkelrote
Haar umrahmte das weisse Gesicht, und in den Winkeln der nahe
beieinanderliegenden braunen Augen lagerten bläuliche Schatten.
Es war Gerda, die Mutter zukünftiger Buddenbrooks.'

Buddenbrooks'. Her only son, Hanno, died as a youth. Transported into the environment of bourgeois society, the woman of myth cannot be a mother: Kore remains uniquely and infernally virginal. It is not by accident that in the final pages of *Buddenbrooks*, Tony commits a naive faux-pas in speaking of the dead Hanno: 'And I always wanted the best for him—he sobbed.—You cannot imagine how much I wished him well . . . More than all of you . . . oh, forgive me Gerda, you are his mother . . .'[12]

In the novel, the arc of the presence of the woman of myth entered into bourgeois society is thus followed right to the end. Even the maternity of the mysterious mythic figure is an obscure and precarious fact: the product is the figure of a young man, Hanno Buddenbrook, whom Mann would recognize as the closest to his heart, perhaps even more so than Tonio Kröger. In the image of Hanno, the autobiographical element of Mann's art seems to reach its deepest level or—in the sense of Faust's 'dark gallery'—its highest. We would contend that Mann had, at least for an instant, identified his self with that of this mysterious adolescent, according to a phenomenon that includes, fundamentally, the projection of one's self onto a nothingness. Mann's autobiographical identification is a return not only to infancy but also to non-existence, the memory of which survives in true infancy. Hanno Buddenbrook is a sliver of life deprived of a future: a negative image of historical reality, almost like a hollowed-out mould which nonetheless has the capacity to contain and remodel a future reality in its own image, a reality from which it is inherently estranged. Hanno is born from the fusion between the mythic woman and the final

---

12 Mann, *Buddenbrooks*, p. 315: '"Ich habe ihn so geliebt," schluchzte sie . . . "Ihr wisst nicht, wie sehr ich ihn geliebt hat . . . mehr als ihr alle . . . ja, verzeih, Gerda, du bist die Mutter . . ."'

representation of bourgeois society: an intercourse that generates life and at the same time determines nothing but death. The bourgeoisie cannot survive this intercourse with the mythic image, nor can it transmit its blood into a future life through such intercourse. But the adolescent who is born—an adolescent chosen to die— is the hollowed-out mould of a life yet to be born out of the marriage of myth and a renewed humanity.

In the first pages of his essay 'Goethe, eine Phantasie' ['Goethe, A Fantasy'], Mann evokes the image of an asphyxiated newborn on 28 August 1749, brought into the world in a bourgeois house in Frankfurt, 'black all over and apparently dead.'

> After a little while the grandmother behind the bed was able to exclaim to the sobbing woman: 'Elisabeth, he lives!' It was the voice of one woman to another, an instinctive, homely message, nothing more. And yet, were that cry to be delivered to the world, to all humanity, it would contain the greatest of joys, as indeed it does today, after two hundred years, and will preserve this through all that comes . . .[13]

This moment of death which signals the entrance of Goethe into life, represents the painful, laborious detachment from the hollow form of the adolescent destined for death, on behalf of a being 'predestined for an

---

13 Mann, *Neue Studien*, p. 11: 'Geraume Zeit währze es, bis die Grossmutter hinterm Bett hervor der seufzenden Wöchnerin zurufen konnte: 'Elisabeth, er lebt!' Es war ein Ruf von Frau zu Frau, animalische frohe, häusliche Nachricht, nichts weiter. Und doch hätte er der Welt, der Menschheit gelten sollen, und doch hat er noch heute, nach zwei Jahrhunderten, vollen Freudengehalt und wird ihn wahren durch alle kommenden . . .'

extraordinary life'.[14] Even though born into a bourgeois household, right from the first he was marked by a faculty of serene and human connection with the mysterious forces of myth, a destructive element within bourgeois society. Through a long and dark history, generations of bourgeoisie have been subjected to the influence of these forces and finally produced the child who constitutes the positive equivalent to Hanno Buddenbrook:[15]

> ... for an ancient house does not replicate
> the demigod, nor the monster ...

The demigod, the hero: in the final act of *The Valkyrie*, Brunhild is condemned by Wotan to be violated by any ordinary man; but in the end she manages to convince the god to place her in a sleep within a circle of flames which will can be crossed only by a *hero*, that is, the only one worthy of taking her virginity. And the great courtesan Fiore refuses the overtures of Pier de Medici as unworthy, declaring that she belongs only to a *hero*. What is this hero? Mann replied: a man 'of torment' capable, despite these torments—the circle of fire—to approach the purity of myth. Albrecht van der Qualen is thus a new Siegfried who, in the mysterious feminine figure of the 'wardrobe', finds his Brunhild and joins with her. While for Albrecht van der Qualen the torments lead to the enchanting feminine apparition of *Die Kleiderschrank*, for Gustav von Aschenbach they lead him to a homosexual passion—thereby sterile and mortal; for Adrian Leverkuhn, they are the prelude to his full embrace of the demonic with the Little Mermaid or Hyphialta. These, therefore, are the inherent dangers of the artistic condition: sterility and guilt, horror and death.

---

14 Mann, *Neue Studien*, p. 11: 'Dem Menschenkinde ... war ein ungeheurer Lebensbogen vorgeschrieben'.

15 See above, p. 17n16.

But to this dangerous darkness one can juxtapose the serene power of the poet who, at the age of 66, sang 'Suleika', and at 74 still dreams of wedding a 16-year-old woman, praising her creative force up till the song of Marienbad. He is without doubt the 'hero': the darkest creations of his being, those completed in the epoch before his birth, carry with them a latent penetration of the forces of genuine myth into bourgeois humanity; but as he himself at the end of his life sees, with deep, objective introspection, that the greatness of genius does not depend only on the dark forces which move in him but, rather, on the moral qualities of conscious activity which must be respected and empowered even if genius remains fundamentally unaware of this final capturing of its own greatness: 'The organs of mankind, through practice, teaching, reflection, success, failure, assistance and resistance, and ever more reflection, unconsciously bring together in free activity the acquired with the inherent, producing a unity which astonishes the world.'[16] This means that the artist, the genius, comes to the realization of his own greatness, behaving as a man among men, recollecting the experiences of his life through a filter of humanity.

This, the true message of the great artist of the bourgeois era, stands in contrast to the gravity of the crisis into which German culture and society fell when the hero was estranged from humanity: all of the horrors to which

---

16 'Die Organe des Menschen durch Übung, Lehre, Nachdenken, Gelingen, Misslingen, Fördernis und Widerstand und immer wieder Nachdenken verknüpfen ohne bewüsstsein in einer freien Tätigkeit das Erworbene mit dem Angeborenen, so dass es eine Einheit hervorbringt, welche die Welt in Erstaunen setzt.' Goethe to Humboldt, cited in Mann, *Neue Studien*, p. 13 (*Goethes Werke: Briefe. Band 4* [1982], p. 480).

the ancient Siegfried has been subjected. The gravity of this crisis, however, is also clearly there in the testimony of those who, like Mann himself, attempted a process of healing. From this point of view, it is the pedagogic writers who are the most lucid witnesses to the epoch's sickness, and its guilt. A work like *Death in Venice* does not concede any escape to those artists who remain intertwined with the guilt of their sickened society; at the same time, it cannot negate Mann's respect for—and also perhaps participation in—the spiritual life story of Gustav von Aschenbach. But this is a self-confessional, cathartic kind of participation, and excludes any moral approval. Certainly, even the great pedagogues and teachers of German culture of our century have lived through the painful experience of guilt for which they should thus be placed under watch; but they have also arrived at a process of healing, and the memory of their guilt was merely one element of a more vivid and emotive participation in the tragic lives of other guilty parties.

In an exemplary manner this was also Rilke's fate, in whose work the feminine image which we have observed in Wagner and Mann returns and emerges through singular metamorphoses. During his journey to Viareggio in 1899, Rilke composed the drama *The White Princess* (*Die Weisse Fürstin*) which, as with Mann's *Fiorenza*, is set in the Renaissance with a female protagonist. Rilke's Renaissance is nonetheless an image of the dangerous and guilty aspects of that culture which Mann denounces in *Fiorenza*, juxtaposing it to the genuine mythic figure of Fiore. Unlike Fiore, however, the White Princess is an emblem of the deformations of myth—myth that she undeniably opens herself up to, even if under the sign of fear and torment.

The White Princess is a virgin, and her virginity is partly manifested through maintaining mythological memories—the ancient documents of which were nevertheless completely unknown to Rilke. The Princess, in fact, remains a virgin for eleven years for love, notwithstanding the violence and passion of her legal husband, who, in the moment preceding the action of the drama, removes himself and disappears. One of the aspects of the virginity of the mythic Kore consists exactly in her being married to a god and thus in maintaining her virginity even in marriage. The studies carried out both on the non-classical, Indonesian Kore and on the Greek *Kore* who merges with Isis have shown images of a Kore wedded to a god who distances himself from her and then disappears, almost as if to confirm the importance of her virginity.[17]

In Rilke's drama, the Princess is finally left alone for a day by her husband, and waits for her lover with her sister on the seashore. But, before he arrives, a messenger announces that a plague is coming to the country. Then, in the same moment in which the lover's ship appears on the sea, a group of friars in black masks approach the Princess: it is death which comes, and the Princess, overcome with terror, does not manage to give the signal with her scarf to her lover, to give consent to his landing. The ship vanishes and, while the Princess remains frozen, from the window of the cottage where the sister is preparing the nuptial bed for the Princess and her lover, a thin, fair figure gives a slow nod, like a goodbye.

At every moment, *The White Princess* reveals the 'sickness' from which Rilke managed to free himself only much later: the true sickness of a culture that idolizes and fears death. In the play, Rilke constructs the emergence of a figure of the virgin in which the element of love is

---

17 See p. 67n5.

fatally united with that of death. Already in *Florentine Diary* [*Florentinischer Tagebuch*], he had evoked the figure of a maiden 'who dies from love' in the image of a farm girl beloved by Giuliano de Medici, who dies in giving birth to his son. Analogous visions of lover and death, in which death is a horror inevitably intermixed with love, are signalled throughout Rilke's young works: one thinks of tales such as *The Grave-Gardner* [*Der Grabgärtner*], a horrific erotic-necrophilic pastiche; *Lady Blaha's Maid* [*Frau Blahas Magd*], a story of infanticide, in which maternity appears as a monstrous consequence to the loss of virginity; and, above all, *Fragment*, which announces some of the motives destined to assail the poet for a long time:

> It is a fantasy about a dead girl, whose virginal body death does not touch, taking the life that is still in her from her face. Unable to bear the sight of her pinched features, the hero lays two frosty red rosebuds over her eyes. They open and blossom; and at the end of the day George has two great red roses in his hand, heavy with the life of one who had never given herself to him.[18]

The date of composition of *Fragment*, along with certain biographical documents, help to connect this story to events experienced by Rilke among the artists of Worpswede, especially with the two young women Clara Westhoff (who would become his wife) and Paula Becker. These connections allow us to understand the extent to which the poet was dominated by the image of the mythic woman, denied to him because he could not access its genuine reality. The figure of inviolable virginity thus emerges from Rilke's mind, a figure which accepts death

---

18 Eliza Marian Butler, *Rainer Maria Rilke* (Cambridge: Cambridge University Press, 1946), p. 102.

rather than being violated by a man. And this singular acceptance of mythic flow reveals an incapacity to embrace myth in its genuine form within the poet—myth deprived of horror, filled with the wealth of human experience. For Rilke, death remains a monstrous, looming, enchanting and fearsome reality: he subjects himself to this enchantment and rejects humanity: he would rather kill the virgin off than see her violated.

The artist's solitude which Rilke theorizes in *The Diaries of a Young Poet* [*Briefe an einen jungen Dichter*] remains the refusal of humanity at the same time as it contains elements of the poet's cure, on the basis of which the artist's solitude will become a painful experience of individualism. It is the experience of those who suffer loneliness in order to access a revelation which, in the final *Duino Elegy*, will be an element of collective salvation. The figure of a maiden 'killed' by a poet who wants to save her virginity at any cost and monstrously justifies such a murder through the notion of a death 'proper to a virgin'—through that which the virgin would herself carry out—finds a strict, cautioning riposte in the words of Goethe. On Walpurgis Night, Gretchen appears to Faust:

> *Faust.* Mephisto, can you see
> That lovely child, far off, alone there,
> Travelling slowly, so painfully,
> As if her feet were chained together.
> I must admit, without question
> She's the image of my sweet Gretchen.

> *Mephistopheles.* Forget all that! It has no beneficial role.
> It's a magic image, lifeless, an idol.
> Encountering it will do no good:
> Its fixed stare stops human blood,

And then one's almost turned to stone:
Medusa's story is surely known.

Faust. Those are the eyes of the dead, truly,
No loving hand has closed their void.
That's the breast Gretchen offered to me:
That's the sweet body I enjoyed.

Mephistopheles. It's magic, fool: you're an easy
one to move!
She comes to all, as if she were their love.

Faust. What delight! What torture!
I cannot break my gaze from her.
Strange, around her lovely throat,
A single scarlet cord adorns her,
Like a knife-cut, and no wider!

Mephistopheles. That's right! I see it too: and note,
She could also carry her head aloft,
Since Perseus did cut it off . . .[19]

---

19 *Faust, Part I*, ll. 4183–4208. Johann Wolfgang von Goethe, *Faust Parts I and II* (A. S. Kline trans.) (Poetry in Translation, 2003; available at: http://bit.ly/2KKigMy), translation modified.

Faust. Mephisto, siehst du dort
Ein blasses, schönes Kind allein und ferne stehen?
Sie schiebt sich langsam nur vom Ort,
Sie scheint mit geschlossnen Füssen zu gehen.
Ich muss bekennen, dass mir deucht,
Dass sie dem guten Gretchen gleicht.

Mephistopheles. Lass dass nur stehn! Dabei wird's niemand wohl.
Es ist ein Zauberbild, ist leblos, ein Idol.
Ihm zu begenen, ist nicht gut:
Vom starren Blick erstarrt des Menschen Blut,
Und er wird fast in Stein verkehrt;
Von der Meduse hast du ja gehort.

Faust. Fürwahr, es sind die Augen eines Toten,
Die eine liebende Hand nicht schloss.

The identification of Gretchen with Medusa reveals Goethe's great 'descent' into the history of mythology. Medusa is a horror born from the deformation of mythic virginity, just as Persephone (Kore) probably signifies 'the killing by Perseus'. The virgin who Rilke leads to death rather than the loss of her virginity is none other than Medusa: the petrifying gaze, the same gaze which Odysseus is afraid to see emerge from the depths of Hades.

This context of horror and death in which Rilke is steeped, and his idolification of the appearances of ingenuine myth, is also the site of the great elegy *Requiem For a Friend* [*Requiem für eine Freundin*] which the poet composed soon after the death of Paula Becker. Becker had been one of the two virgin women the poet met in Worpswede—to whom he probably refers in the *Fragment*. When she married, and finally died in childbirth, Rilke's illness engendered its most horrifying and horrifically astonishing production, for in the *Requiem* he accuses the dead woman of having accepted violation and therefore having refused her true death, and her groom—the violator—of having determined a death which was 'not hers', not that of a virgin. 'Wo ist ein Mann, der Recht hat

---

  Das ist die Brust, die Gretchen mir geboten,
  Das ist der süsse Leib den ich genoss.

Mephistopheles. Das ist die Zauberei, du leicht verführter Tor!
  Denn jedem kommt sie wie sein Liebchen vor.

Faust. Welch eine Wonne! Welch ein Leiden!
  Ich kann von diesem Blick nicht scheiden.
  Wie sonderbar muss diesen schönen Hals
  Ein einzig rotes Schnürchen schmücken,
  Nicht brieter als ein Messerrücken!

Mephistopheles. Ganz recht! ich seh' es ebenfalls.
  Sie kann das Haupt auch untern Arme tragen;
  Den Perseus hat's ihr abgeschlagen . . .

auf Besitz?' ('What man has the right to possession?'):[20] this delirious accusation resounds like the utmost symptom of Rilke's sickness, incapable of human feeling, coinciding with the epiphany of the horrific image of the deformed *Kore*, seemingly contaminated by death.

This is the ultimate female fantasy of Germany, similar to the fantasy of the woman who acts as harbinger of the Hohenzollern's tragedies or to the dark-haired woman who assails Marcel Proust: for Rilke, the appearance of Paula Modersohn-Becker opens up a seemingly incurable wound. It is she again who appears in the female phantoms of *The Notebooks of Malte Laurids Brigge*, and again, in the triple identity of Teresina, Raimondina and Polissena—the phantoms of Castle Duino (Rilke's stay at the residence constituted the cradle of the great elegies). A violated Kore, a horrific Kore: unable to live in Hades as sovereign, she will be exorcized by Rilke through his startling lyrics on Alcestis and Eurydice, in which genuine myth emerges to heal the poet. Alcestus, in Rilke's version, offers herself to death in the place of Admeto on the marriage night, a virgin destined for death through marriage;[21] and Eurydice walks the roads of the dead without being able to participate in the conditions of the living—not even that of

---

20 Rainer Maria Rilke, 'Requiem: Für eine Freundin' in *Sämtliche Werke. Band 1* (Frankfurt: Insel, 1955), Line 217.

21 The identity of Alcestus/Kore, intuited by Rilke, has also been verified by scholars. See Paula Philippson, *Origini e forme del mito greco* (Turin: Bollati Boringhieri, 1949) [Oroginal German: *Untersuchungen über den griecheschen Mythos. Genealogie als Mythische Form. Die Zietart des Mythos* (Zurich: Rhein, 1944)]; Furio Jesi, 'The Thracian Herakles' (Benjamin Egli trans.), *History of Religions* 3(2) (1964): 261–77.

desire.[22] But not even these mythic images, truly and supremely pure, can definitively liberate the poet from his torments. He remains exposed to esoteric experiences which tie him in mystifications, overwhelming him. He tries bizarre 'psychic shudders' in a haunted, deserted area of Venice which has never been rediscovered. He attempts a plethora of mystifying occult experiences. In short, he subjects himself, painfully, to all the metamorphoses of the mythic virgin, metamorphoses born from the observer's broken gaze, transformed through frustrated desire, like that of Savonarola for Fiore in Mann's *Fiorenza*.

After the horrors of such difficult conception, such as those which reach their apex in the essay on dolls, Rilke finally found a glimmer of salvation. The great, unfinished elegies loomed over him like the towers of an almost unreachable castle: and then the castle was reached. When, in the solitude of Muzot, Rilke reached the end of the *Duino Elegies*, he found a serenity he had never experienced: for the first time in his tormented existence, an emblem of serene being and true purity seems to win out. The Eighth Elegy sadly concludes:[23]

> Just as they
> will turn, stop, linger, for one last time,
> on the last hill, that shows them all their valley—,
> so we live, and are always taking leave.

---

22 This is also the opposite of the friend 'returning' from the beyond.

23 A. S. Kline translation. Rilke, *Duino Elegies*, VIII, ll. 72–5:

> Wie er auf
> dem letzten Hügel, der ihm ganz sein Tal
> noch einmal zeigt, sich wendet, anhält, weilt,
> so leben wir und nehmen immer Abschied.

Referring to the elder Lament, the true and wondrous image of the shadowy virgins responds in the Tenth Elegy:[24]

> But the dead must go on, and in silence the elder
>   Lament
> leads him as far as the ravine,
> where the fountain of joy
> glistens in moonlight.

After a long and painful wandering, Kore finally allows the poet to contemplate her true face: the genuine face of myth.

The song finally reaches its true, immortal sound:[25]

> Strike the earth: it resounds dull and earthly,
> softened and augmented by our goals.
> Strike the star: it will uncover you!
> Strike the star: invisible numbers
> fulfil themselves . . .

At a solitary tomb in Raron, the terrifying roses which flower over the eyes of the dead virgin of *Fragment*

---

24 A. S. Kline translation. Rilke, *Duino Elegies*, X, ll 96–9:

> Doch der Tote muss fort, und schweigend bringt ihn die ältere
> Klage bis an die Talschlucht,
> wo es schimmert im Monschein:
> die Quelle der Freude . . .

25 Rainer Maria Rilke, 'Musik' (1925) in *Ausgewählte Werke, Bd. 1. Gedichte* (Leipzig: Insel, 1948), p. 363:

> Schlag an die Erde: sie klingt stumpf und erden,
> gedämpft und eingehüllt von unsern Zwecken.
> Schlag an den Stern: er wird sich der entdecken!
> Schlag an den Stern: die unsichtbaren Zahlen
> erfüllen sich . . .

[Jesi interprets 'eingehüllt' (concealed) as 'aumentato' (augmented)].

again reveal their shadowy nature; now mysteriously calm after their horrific and painful ordeal:[26]

> Rose, oh pure contradiction, the joy
> in being nobody's sleep, under so many
> eyelids.

* * *

The image of the virgin who must not be violated, tragically assailing Rilke's artistic life for so long, is also to be found at the beginning of the century in one of Mann's fundamental writings, that is, in the novella *Tristan*. From this point of view, the letter written by the protagonist of the novella, the author Detlev Spinell, is quite revealing, addressed as it is to the husband of a woman who had enchanted him. In the letter, the 'bourgeois' husband appears in the semblance of a demonic violator—certainly not a divine one!—of the virgin who he ought only to have contemplated. In the garden of her paternal home, the young woman remains with her female friends:

> Seven virgins seated in a circle around the fountain; but among the hair of the seventh, the first, the last, the setting sun seems to secretly weave a shimmering sign of supremacy . . . That image was a terminus, Sir; must you come and destroy, to follow it up with vulgarity, with brute suffering? . . . You gazed upon her, this mortal beauty: you gazed upon so as to lust after her. Nothing of reverence, of restraint, touched your heart in confronting that peaceful sanctity. It was not

---

26 The epigraph dictated by Rilke for his own tomb in the cemetery of the church at Raron:

> Rose, oh reiner Widerspruch, Lust
> niemandes Schlaf zu sein, unter soviel
> Lidern.

enough for you to look on; you had to possess,
to use, to profane her . . .[27]

The preceding references allude to the mythic nature
of the female image emerging in the figure of Gabriele
Klöterjahn; later, having described the scene of the young
women in the garden to her, Spinell tells her:

'There was a golden crown, not very apparent
but full of meaning, perched twinkling on your
hair'.

'No, nonsense. There was no crown.'

'On the contrary: it shone secretly. I saw it,
I saw it clearly in your hair, as I was in one of
those bushes, hidden away for hours . . .'

'God knows what you saw. In any case, you
weren't there; in fact it was the man who is now
my husband who emerged from the bushes, in
the company of my father . . .'[28]

---

27 Thomas Mann, *Tristan* (Berlin: Fischer, 1903), p. 83: 'Sieben
Jungfrauen sassen im Kreis um den Brunnen; in das Haar der
Siebenter aber, der Ersten, der Einen, schien die sinkende Sonne
heimlich ein schimmerndes Abzeichen der Oberhoheit zu weben.
. . . Dies Bild war ein Ende, mein Herr; mussten Sie kommen
und es zerstören, um ihm eine Fortsetzung der Gemeinheit und
des hässlichen Leidens zu geben? . . . Sie sahen sie, diese
Todesschönheit: sahen sie an, um ihrer zu begehren. Nichts von
Ehrefurcht, nichts von Scheu berührte Ihr Herz gegenüber ihrer
rührenden Heiligkeit Es genügt Ihnen nicht, zu schauen; Sie
mussten besitzen, ausnützen, entweihen . . . .'

28 Mann, *Tristan*, p. 66:

'Eine kleine goldene Krone, ganz unscheinbar aber
bedeutungsvoll, sass in Ihrem Haar und blinkte . . .'

'Nein, Unsinn, nichts von einer Krone . . .'

'Doch, sie blinkte heimlich. Ich hätte sie gesehen,
hätte sie deutlich in Ihrem Haar gesehen, wenn ich in

While on the one hand the golden crown on the head of a chosen virgin is a typical attribute of Kore ('the moon and Nereus' fifty daughters dance, goddesses of the sea and the endlessly flowing rivers, in honour of the maiden with the wreath of gold and of her holy mother'),[29] on the other hand, the future husband who emerges from the bushes and surprises the young girls can appear as a grotesque parody of the figure of hell that overcomes Kore and her companions at the lake of Pergusa.

As is the case with Rilke, *Tristan* does not fail to denounce the maternity *imposed* upon the virgin. Gabriele Klöterjahn dies through an abundance of force in maternity:

> And now indeed your dreaming will lead you astray, and conduces you away from the wild garden towards life, towards brutality; and giving to you its ordinary name, and making of you a married woman, a housewife, eventually a mother ... She, with eyes like fearful dreams, gives birth to a child: and to this being, who perpetuates the vile existence of its progenitor, is transmitted all of reserves of blood and life faculties she possesses; and she dies.[30]

---

einer dieser Stunden unvermekt im Gestrüpp gestandend hätte.'

'Gott weiss, was Sie gesehen hättem. Sie standen aber nicht dort, sondern eines Tages war es mein jetziger Mann, der zusammen mit meinem Vater aus dem Gebüsch hervortrat . . . .'

29 Euripides, *Ion,* Line 1078. [English translation: *The Plays of Euripides* (Edward P. Coleridge trans.) (London: G. Bell and Sons, 1910), modified.]

30 Mann, *Tristan*, pp. 85–6: 'In der Tat, Sie lenken ihren verträumten Willen in die Irre, Sie führen sie aus dem verwucherten Garten in das Leben und in die Hässlichkeit, Sie geben ihr Ihren

Here is a denunciation of the masculine violator that corresponds to the letter of Rilke's in *Requiem für eine Freundin*. But if in *Requiem* Rilke emerges sincerely and openly, in *Tristan* the accuser is not Mann but the figure continually parodied by the author—the artist. As always, Mann wants to place himself on a different level: to observe his characters, showing their lives without ever identifying himself with one of them.

In *Tristan*, however, the image of the woman appears pregnant with virginity and death if observed from a determinate standpoint, that of Detlev Spinell, the artist. This is the basic situation. The female figures of nearly all of Mann's work cannot be understood without being aware of the problem created by the author regarding the figure of the 'artist' and his relations with the rest of mankind.

We put the word 'artist' in quotation marks because in Mann's works it is only a parody of artists that appears: a parody intertwining human types who, while not being exactly artists, share certain revealing characteristics with artists. One could not call 'Little Herr Friedemann' an 'artist'; he pertains to an ancient merchant family and distinguished himself from the bourgeois citizens. 'He managed to play the violin discreetly, and every beautiful and soft note which emanated from the instrument brought him joy. Similarly, through much reading, over time he had acquired a literary taste which he shared with no one else in the city.'[31] But above all, Herr Friedemann held a

---

ordinären Namen und machen sie zum Eheweibe, zur Hausfrau, machen sie zur Mutter. . . . Sie, mit den Augen, die wie ängstliche Träume sind, schenkt Ihnen ein Kind; sie gibt diesem Wesen, das eine Fortsetzung der niedrigen Existent seines Erzeugers ist, alles mit, was sie an Blut und Lebensmöglichkeit besitzt, und stirb.'

31 Thomas Mann, *Der kleine Herr Friedemann* (Berlin: Fischer, 1898), p. 15: 'Er selbst spielte allmählich, obgleich er sich ungemein

certain deformation in common with other artists—evidenced by his crippled body—one that puts him in a condition of inferiority, meaning indeed that people on the street greeted him 'in that pitying, friendly manner to which he was by now accustomed'.[32] That the condition of the artists corresponds to a kind of impairment and deformation in the confrontation with the bourgeois being is clear in *Tristan*, in which an actual artist appears, Detlev Spinell, who earns the nickname 'rotting suckling',[33] revealing a monstrous return to infancy. But this precarious condition, of 'tolerance' by the bourgeois world, relates again to another 'non-artist artist', the protagonist of *Der Bajazzo* [*The Clown*], born into a bourgeois family but also a born 'clown': skilful in parody, quick at recalling music, intolerant of the order of bourgeois life. More tragic still is the figure of the 'non-artist artist' Christian in *Buddenbrooks*: a lover of theatre like Herr Friedemann, incapable of following a respectable bourgeois career, rich in theatrical gifts, frail, and attentive to a thousand latent flaws within himself: he is the parodical image of a 'man of torments'.

In their relationships with women, these ambiguous characters—whether artists or 'artists'—meet at every turn female images not disposed to concede themselves to them: virgins who ought never to have been violated (in *Tristan*); inaccessible virgins (in *The Clown*); demonic

---

merkwürdig dabei ausnahm, die Geige nicht übel und freute sich an jedem schönen und weichen Ton, der ihm gelang. Auch hatte er sich durch viele Lektüre mit der Zeit einen literarischen Gaschmack angeeignet den er wohl in der Stadt mit niemandem teilte.'

32 Mann, *Der kleine Herr Friedemann*, p. 15: 'mit jener mitleidig freundlichen Art begrüssten, an die er von jeher gewöhnt war.'

33 Mann, *Tristan*, p. 55: 'der verweste Säugling'.

women who attract, hunt and bring death (in *Little Herr Friedemann*). As Mann says: they have no good relation to life.

Demonism and the horrific deformation of myth is always a negation of life and humanity. Such negations dominate the best part of German culture in the first years of the twentieth century: the female images which arise from the *humus* [earth] of that culture are monstrous and demonic flowers like the flower-maidens of *Parsifal* or the serpent-women of whom images remain in the figurative arts and especially in art nouveau jewellery. This particular sector of art, dominated by precious materials according to a secret relation between gold and demon which is the negative and deformed inverse of the mythic, Pindar-like relation between gold and the great beyond, invoke images of flower-maidens even beyond Germanic culture—although with explicit reference to *Parsifal*—in the orchid-women of René Lalique: emblems of the night in Eugène Feuillatre's creations and again by Lalique in his Baudelairian owls; depictions of serpents in Lalique's reptilian knots, and especially in the motif of the celebrated *serpent kiss* in a famous brooch by E. Dabault.[34] Charles Van Lerbeghe had already sung of the serpent kiss:[35]

---

34 See the catalogue of the exhibition *Le bijou 1900* (Brussels, 1965).

35 Charles van Lerberghe, 'La Faute' in *La chanson d'Eve* (Paris: Mercure de France, 1904):

> Sois absous par ma bouche
> de toute trahison
> et de toute malice
> mon beau serpent, et glisse
> en paix, comme un rayon,
> parmi ces roses.

Be absolved on my mouth
from every infidelity
and from every spite
my beautiful serpent, and slide
in peace, like a sun ray
among the roses.

This hybrid serpent-woman—also evoked through a celebrated bracelet by Georges Fouquet made for Sarah Bernhardt—refers directly to the subject of *Tannhäuser*: the seducers of the realm of Venus periodically transform themselves into serpents, revealing their demonic nature according to a tradition also reflected in *Il Guerin Meschino* [The Wretched Guerin] in the image of the Apennine Sybil. To these one might also add, though a deforming, parodical mirror, Lulu in Frank Wedekind's *Erdgeist* [Earth Spirit]: in the drama's prologue, she appears as the 'serpent' led before her handler:

> *Handler.* Hey, August!—bring our Serpent in! (*A stage-hand with a big paunch carries out the actress of Lulu in her Pierrot costume, and sets her down before the handler.*) Here is the personification of evil: here is the being born to stir up trouble, to entice, seduce, poison and to kill . . .[36]

In this climate of horror one can also rightly evoke the definition of the handler in Flaubert's *Dictionnaire*

---

36 Frank Wedekind, *Erdgeist*, Prologue: He, Aujust! Bring mir unsre Schlange her! (*Ein schmerbäuchiger Arbeiter trägt die Darstellerin der Lulu in ihrem Pierrotkostüm aus den Zelt und setzt sie vor dem Tierbändiger nieder.*) Sie ward geschaffen, Unheil anzustiften, zu locken, zu verführen, zu vergiften—zu morden, ohne dass es einer spürt. [English translation: *Erdgeist, Earth-Spirit: A Tragedy in Four Acts* (Samuel Atkins Eliot trans.) (New York: Albert and Charles Boni, 1941), p. 9, modified.]

des idées reçues: 'Emploient des pratiques obscènes', a definition which also seems to be confirmed within the German context through a depiction by Max Beckmann, portraying a handler in a showy uniform—whip in hand—and a reclining woman in a pink dress.[37] Wedekind's female image is, on the other hand, the mirror of the deformed metamorphoses of the mythic virgin. Just as Lulu leads her lovers to death, so too Kadidja in the play *Die Zensur* ['The Censor'] mortally falls into the great beyond, as with the Indonesian Kore who slowly sinks into the earth: in the final scene of the play, Kadidja throws herself off a balcony, killing herself in front of her lover, slowly falling ever further down—until only her head is visible—into the great beyond. And this is also the case, finally, with Carlotta Corday, the mythic virgin who appears naked and standing, a vision imbued with death in Edvard Munch's famous painting.[38]

The image of Lulu is the extreme survival of the mythic virgin within German culture, albeit monstrously deformed. It is the emblem of a misunderstood sexual force, deprived of its mythic genuineness.

In the finale of Wedekind's *Die Büchse der Pandora* [Pandora's Box], Lulu is killed by Jack the Ripper—who was played in the scene by Wedekind himself. This horrifying character speaks English, not German.[39] His presence is a clear, cowering self-confession by artists in general, transformed into the woman's killer, just as Rilke had transformed himself in the works of his youth. But, unlike Rilke, Wedekind unites both pain and parody within the deformed image of the mythic virgin.

---

37 Marx Beckmann, *Zirkuswagen* [The Circus Caravan] (1940).

38 Edvard Munch, *La morte di Marat* [The Death of Marat] (1907).

39 In relation to his transformation of language, see below, pp. 154–5.

This monstrous virgin is the horrific survival of the female phantasms of Romanticism, now made unnatural; she is barren and fascinated by murder, like Klarisse in Musil's *Der Mann ohne Eigenschaften* [The Man Without Qualities], and dressed in Pierrot's costume, the white, funereal shroud of the corpse of romanticism, which will find its singer in the Schönberg of *Pierrot lunaire*:[40]

> Homewards to Bergamo
> Pierrot now returns:
> Weakly the green horizon
> Is dawning in the East.

It is no accident that in 1905 Hugo von Hofmannstahl composed for Gertrude Eysoldt—the then-celebrated 'Lulu' of the Deutschen Theater—a programme of declamations 'of poetry which all carry the same tone: a lament on the solitude of the artist, on the abyss which separates the beauty of art and the beauty of life.'[41]

* * *

In confronting these considerations one might perhaps object that the moralistic intention of us as observers impedes us from penetrating the depths of the most mysterious metamorphoses of the mythic virgin, those which—while apparently being horrific—open up dark experiences for artists, of an importance difficult to

---

40 The final verse of Giraud's penultimate lyric [in Hartleben's translation] appears in Schönberg's text for *Pierrot lunaire*: (original English translation).

> Nach Begamo, zur Heimat,
> kehrt nun Pierrot zurück,
> schwach dämmert schon im Osten
> der grüne Horizont.

41 See Mayer, *Thomas Mann*, p. 27.

evaluate. Certainly, genuine myth is also a mysterious reality, as its application to creative activity. When artists like Schönberg speak of a delirious creative condition, it is reasonable to ask ourselves if we have not gone too far into ethical considerations, retreating from every experience that lies beyond reason and consciousness, confusing horror for that anguish which so frequently cannot be avoided in the confrontation with mythic images.

We not believe, however, that this criticism can find much justification. We have great respect for that which Leo Frobenius calls 'commotions' and considered a determinate force of civilization. Images such as that of Fiore or the Laments of the Tenth Elegy blossomed in the minds of Mann and Rilke at the apex of a devastating, profound commotion that reverberates in the reader and before which we are struck by awe and respect. We nevertheless hold·that only genuinely mythic figures contain those elements and values worthy of study devoted to and capable of enriching the human soul. Other images, those which appear before the eyes of an artist taken over by illness, are like feverish hallucinations, intrinsically deformed and lacking any depth. Their obscurity and their seeming mystery derives only from the annihilation of reason and of consciousness inherent to the manifestations of human sickness, and especially to the sickness of anti-humanity. These deformed images are simply masks and projections of human wrongs, the investigation of which is a kind of pathology. Demonology cannot be a form of human science, nor even a humanistic science, without falling into Manicheism. When man falls into the illness of anti-humanity, he deprives his own existence of any depth: phantasms appear to him which are merely epiphanies of nothing. And the nothing ceases to be profound and becomes entirely unreal when man's sickness transforms itself from being a continuous dialectic into an imperious ruler, wielding sovereign power over existence.

In the final pages of Hermann Broch's *Der Tod des Vergil* [*The Death of Virgil*], Virgil, on death's door, opens himself up to the primordial unity of being and welcomes all matter, every object becoming a thing in itself:

> And one glimpses in the middle of the shield of the world, in infinite depths, glimpsed there within the infinite life of mankind, glimpsed for the last and indeed for the last and yet as for the first time: peace without war, the human countenance in a peace without war, one glimpses the image of a boy in his mother's arms, united with her in a sorrowful, smiling love. Thus he saw this, he saw the boy, he saw the mother, and to him they were so very familiar, so that he was almost able to call them, even without being able to place their names.[42]

The poetry of the fourth eclogue of the *Bucolics* thus becomes the language of being, revealing its objectivity in the instant in which the poet's individuality is weakened.

---

42 Hermann Broch, *Der Tod des Vergil* (Zurich: Rhein, 1947), p. 531: 'Und in der Mitte des Weltenschildes ward es erblickbar in unendlichster Tiefe, dort ward es erblickbar inmitten unendlich menschlichen Seins und Hausens, erblickbar zum letzten und doch auch zum ersten Male: der kampflosen Friede, das menschliche Anlitz in kampflosem Frieden, erblickbar als das Bild des Knaben in Arme der Mutter, bereint mit ihr zu trauernd lächelnder Liebe. So sah er es, so sah er den Knaben, so sah er die Mutter, und sie waren ihm so überaus vertraut, dass er sie fast zu benennen vermochte, freilich ohne ihre Namen zu finden.' [English translation: *The Death of Virgil* (J. S. Untermeyer trans.) (New York: Pantheon Books, 1945), p. 480, modified. Henceforth, Untermeyer translation.]

Broch's concluding vision possesses a mythological depth which renders it worthy of Virgil. In his 'final and first' epiphany, 'Virgil' is also the mother: one spies in this image the ancient unity of mythic figure of Kore who is also Demeter, just like the unity which emerges in the final verses of *Faust* and guarantees salvation. In the finale of *Faust*, Gretchen appears as the saviour—juxtaposed to the Gorgon phantom of the Walpurgis Night but unified through the grace of the 'Mater gloriosa'.

The problem of the value of Broch's religious experiences attempts to confront a fundamental element in the metamorphoses of the women of myth, one that counts all the more when the relation between the artists and that mythic image also becomes an unmediated relation to the divine. The establishment of such a relation is, on the other hand, a general phenomenon that recurrs throughout relations between German artists and the flow of myth. In Broch's case, an artist's religious experience does not always distance him from socially and historically constituted religions; and while in *The Death of Virgil* he seems to refer directly to Christianity, in subsequent works he faithfully returns to his Judaic origins and seems to refer to Hasidism. Other artists, however, and especially Rilke, accepted the genuine myth of the women as an element of relation with the divine within a strictly personal religion. Rilke himself, above all in relation to the *Duino Elegies*, was much preoccupied in exhorting the interpreters of his work to not read it in a Christian sense.

These two attitudes, in the acceptance of mythic images according to the scheme of either constituted or personal religions, once again propose a problem outlined by Karl Jaspers in relation to Hölderlin's religiosity. The total estrangement from any constituted religion seemed to Jaspers to bear witness to a fracture between artists and the surrounding world and, as such, represent a morbid element, an early symptom of the poet's madness.[43] One can juxtapose Jasper's thesis with that advanced by Kerényi's essay on Hölderlin,[44] in which the absolute individualism of the poet's religious experience finds justification in being an experience carried out exclusively in the world of poetry. Hölderlin's relation with the divine takes place within poetry, and therefore is personal inasmuch as it pertains to the solitary life of the poet in his journey towards the purity of myth which is nonetheless also a journey towards a most profoundly collective language—and guarantor of that collectivity.

Kerényi also emphasizes the fact that Hölderlin's Hellenism is not a true Hellenism but, rather, the image of its revival of mourning within the poet. This mourning does not stop Hölderlin from entering into a devoted relation with gods, but puts him into a situation which—in the most dramatic form—can become that of the false priest expelled from the temple.[45]

---

43 Karl Jaspers, *Arbeiten zur Psychiatrie, Band 5* (1921); the essay on Hölderlin is translated in Karl Jaspers, *Strindberg and Van Gogh* (Oskar Grunow and David Woloshin trans) (Tucson: University of Arizona Press, 1977).

44 Karl Kerényi, 'Hölderlin und die Religionsgeschichte' in *Hölderlin-Jahrbuch* (Tübingen: Siebeck, 1954), pp. 11–24. See also in relation to Jaspers' thesis: Alessandro Pellegrini, *Hölderlin, Storia della critica* (Florence: Sansoni, 1956), pp. 103–07 and 207ff.

45 Kerényi examines in particular the hymn 'Wie wenn am Feiertage . . .' which—it seems important for us to note—was the only one of Hölderlin's lyrics included by St George in his anthology of poetry from the century of Goethe (1910).

One finds a similar kind of mourning in the *Duino Elegies*, when Rilke evokes the images of Hellenism:[46]

> Did you all not stand astonished before the
>   human gestures of the Attic steles'
> Were not love and distance laid so lightly on
>   the shoulders
> as if made of material other than our own?
> Think of the hands, how they were freed from
>   weight,
> even while power remained in the torso.
> These masters knew: so long as we are here,
> this is ours, ours to touch:
> the gods weigh upon us strongly still.
> But that is the gods' affair.
> Oh if only we too could find a pure, measured,
>   subtle, human
> strip of fruitful land, our own between stream
>   and rock.

---

46 Rilke, *Duino Elegies*, II, ll. 66–79:

> Erstaunte euch nicht auf attischen Stelen die Vorsicht
> menschlicher Geste? war nicht Liebe und Abschied
> so leicht auf die Schultern gelegt, als wär es aus anderm
> Stoffe gemacht als bei uns? Gedenkt euch der Hände,
> wie sie drucklos beruhen, obwohl in den Torsen die
>   Kraft steht.
> Diese Beherrschten wußten damit: so weit sind wirs,
> dieses ist unser, uns so zu berühren; stärker
> stemmen die Götter uns an. Doch dies ist Sache der
>   Götter.
> Fänden auch wir ein reines, verhaltenes, schmales
> Menschliches, einen unseren Streifen Fruchtlands
> zwischen Strom und Gestein. Denn das eigene Herz
>   übersteigt uns
> noch immer wie jene. Und wir können ihm nicht mehr
> nachschaun in Bilder, die es besänftigen, noch in
> göttliche Körper, in denen es größer sich mässigt.

> For our own heart always transcends us, as
>   those do.
> And we can no longer gaze upon it through
>   images
> which might soothe it
> nor in a divine body
> where it tempers itself all the more.

This is the finale of the Second Elegy. Emerging from depths submerged by 'antiquity', the mythic images arouse agitation and mourning; but if the poet welcomes them in with purity and abandon, they can cure him, showing themselves to be eternally alive and healing. In the Tenth Elegy, the myth no longer arouses mourning but an active participation in its reality of salvation: certainly, it is inevitable that this no longer pertains to Greek myth but to a flow of myth contemporary to and embraced within the poet. This healing is not determined only through the definitive, complete realization of the relation to the divine within the poetic experience, but also through the poet's refusal of those terrifying, idolized angels so feared in the Rilke's youthful work as well as in the First Elegy. A similar return to the human, inasmuch as a poet can be, is also a fact of poetry; but such recognition must not lead one to believe that Rilke's return to the human belongs to the category of 'delirious' experiences which participate in the origin of the work of art: it is fundamentally the result of an act of conscience and of will (the conscience and will of a poet are also components of poetry).

A poet's relation with the divine, even in its apparently more individualistic sense, cannot be excluded from his consciousness, and pertains only to the sphere of delirium: otherwise it would be the same as that spiritual locus in which consciousness and reason are annihilated by 'dark forces', thus a relation to the demonic rather than the divine. But it is exactly this kind of participation of consciousness in a relation with the divine which allows mythic images to give rise to a language that works towards collectivity, and thus the religious experience apparently furthest from constituted religions is also that most imbued with the value of collectivity.

Das Glasperlenspiel [The Glass Bead Game], Herman Hesse's great novel, provides a serious warning in relation to this, in which two religious communities appear opposed to each other: one is a Catholic monastery, the other an ascetic community of artists and spiritual devotees, dedicated with great concentration and seriousness to its 'games'. In the future in which the novel takes place, relations between the Catholic church and this community of 'spiritual game players' are good enough, even if reliant on a mutual distance. A more profound relation between the religious experiences participated in by members of each community is finally reached by the protagonist of the novel, the *Magister ludi* Knecht, whose final and authentic dogma also represents, nonetheless, a critique of the ideals of the community of 'game players' without, at the same time, signifying an adhesion to Catholicism. Educated for decades in an attempt to establish ever-closer relations with vital images and survivals of the past—the material of the 'games'—Knecht feels it necessary to go a step further, leading this devotee of the spirit to a profoundly collective religious experience and one which, above all, renders him conscious of the value as such of collectivity, even in his more solitary life.

Knecht takes over from Thomas von der Trave in his great responsibility as *Magister ludi*: a transparent name under which one can easily recognize Thomas Mann. Knecht is therefore the inheritor to the highest aspect of

Western humanism—but he was also for a long time the disciple of an incarnation of Eastern wisdom. In all of Hesse's work, that phenomenon of love for the philosophical and religious doctrines of the Far East reaches its highest level here, one which characterizes part of the German culture of modernity without remaining on the level of a necessary spiritual dignity. But in *Das Glasperlenspiel*, Hesse went beyond the moral of his *Siddharta*, or at least the moral led to a synthesis between East and West which emphasizes the theme of collectivity. In the metamorphoses that signify the flow of myth and solitary meditations, Hesse exemplified the great words of Novalis that he quoted in *Die Morgenlandfahrt* [*Journey to the East*]: 'Where are we going? Always home.'[47] The access to myth, enacted with purity of heart and awareness, is always a return to the human. East and West are opposite ends of the 'years of education': the goal of that education is the return to the human, the collective and the totality.

* * *

Some critics have emphasized Thomas Mann's *Die vertauschen Köpfe* [*The Transposed Heads*] as a parody of Hesse's *Siddharta*. This observation is valid so long as it does not neglect the noble character of Mann's polemical approach, and the respect—something not exclusive from parody—that Mann had for Hesse's thought. Certainly, the courtesan Kamala in *Siddharta* seems like a sister figure to Fiore in *Fiorenza*: at the end of her life, she moves towards the Buddha, dying, announcing her overcoming

---

47 Herman Hesse, *Die Morgenlandfahrt. Eine Erzählung* (Frankfurt: Suhrkamp, 1951), p. 17: 'Wo gehen wir denn him? Immer nach Hause' [Novalis, *Heinrich von Ofterdingen* (Vienna: C. F. Schade, 1827), p. 209.]

of the art of love and of the religious experience implicit in the figure of Aphrodite. The metamorphoses of the mythic woman in Hesse's work are always signalled by the artist's profound anxiety, simultaneous with a revelation of their own internal structures: in *Der Steppenwolf*, the protagonist is 'healed', or at least moves towards a cure, through the enigmatic figure of Hermine, who rejects him while satisfying him sexually by offering him a kind of emanation or double of herself in Marie, a figure who lives an exclusively erotic life. The anxiety generated by the emergence of this Kore has forced the artist to split her figure into two images, one which refuses him and one which offers herself to him. This is therefore still the ancient Kore, virgin and violated according to the profound paradox of myth which also dominates the relation of love and death: Hermine in fact asks Harry to kill her.

The same idea of the secret relation between love and death—once quite obvious in the Eleusinian mythical tradition—re-emerges (without any hope of a cure) in Oscar Kokoshka's play *Mörder, Hoffnung der Frauen* [*Murder, The Hope of Women*] as well as in Kokoshka's drawing published in the first pages of the journal *Der Sturm*[48] which contained the script. Here, a naked woman appears trampled and held down by a man with a dagger raised. Hesse's splitting of Hermine and Marie in *Der Steppenwolf* attests to the writer's anguish faced with the woman of myth, a figure he could not allow himself to gather within a unified identity of both healer and lover. This partial division of the sexual element from the healing forces inherent in the image of the woman becomes an inexorable fracture in Kokoshka's work, one that does not necessarily exclude the artist's conscious abandonment to a state of delirium in which the

---

48 *Der Sturm*, 14 July 1910.

sexual components of the mythic woman appear as an enchanting abyss—even if not 'healing' in any humanistic sense.

Kokoschka's attitude is, furthermore, emblematic of that part of Expressionism disposed to recognize the weakness of humanistic forces and the mysterious power of destructive ones. A truly symbolic figure of a naked woman appears on the poster for Erik Heckel's *Die Brücke* exhibition of 1911 (designed by Max Pechstein), just like the two naked women flanking the *Mitgliedskarte* for *Die Brücke*, designed in the same year by Karl Schmidt-Rotluff.[49] This is a 'public' recognition of the power by which the figure which once emerged in 'Lulu' now, in an anti-humanistic sense, dominates the efforts of those who propose a profoundly human renewal of the figurative arts, and of those who stand outside social scruples. But if the poet of a more politically engaged Expressionism, Johannes R. Becher, limited himself to rendering homage to the mythic woman identified in Red Rosa/Red Rose,[50] —i.e. Rosa Luxemburg—(in a final and transformed survival of the flower-maiden!), then the artists of *Die Brücke* do not hide from themselves that by this point the woman represents for them an insoluble and consequently tragic paradox. In the instant in which they call on the woman as a source of healing, she appears to them as 'Lulu', an abyss not only from the masculine standpoint,

---

49 Bernard Samuel Myers and Elke Kaspar, *Malerei des Expressionismus. Eine Generation im Aufbruch* (Cologne: DuMont, 1957), p. 113 and p. 116.

50 J. R. Becher, 'Hymne auf Rosa Luxemburg' in *Menschheitsdämmerung. Symphonie jüngster Dichtung* (Kurt von Pinthus ed.) (Berlin: Rowohlt, 1920), pp. 285–7, reprinted as numbers 55/56 in the series *Rowohlts Klassiker der Literatur und der Wissenschaft* (Hamburg: Rowohlt, 1959).

an emblem of death and lust such as Emil Nolde's 'Maria Aegyptiaca',[51] looming 'behind the back' of every man— such as the naked woman rising behind the figure of Kirchner in his self-portrait in soldier's uniform[52]—but also from the feminine point of view: few images are so unsettling for a woman as the figure of the naked woman covering her face with an arm and hair in Munch's painting.[53] This figure alludes to the drama of recognizing a mysterious and destructive force in oneself that alienates the feminine being from its genuine mythic reality, attributing a terrifying supremacy to those elements of that image that lead to seduction and death without rebirth. For the woman who recognizes herself in such images, they reveal horrors, such as the attempted paternal incest suffered by Clarisse in Musil's *The Man Without Qualities* or the demonic lover who appears as if in a nightmare with the face of a clown, in Karl Hofer's ink drawing *Loving Couple*.[54]

However, when the man and woman subjected to such horrors become a 'couple', this prepares them for the experience of their 'shame', being the exposure of their sexual bond to the eyes of the world. Kirchner depicted a 'couple in front of men',[55] in which a naked man and woman are surrounded by grinning faces who recall particularly the moment in Broch's *The Death of Virgil* when Virgil is overcome by the image of his embrace with

---

51 Emil Nolde, *Legende der heiligen Maria Aegyptiaca* [Saint Mary of Egypt] (1912).

52 Ernst Ludwig Kirchner, *Selbstbildnis als Soldat* [Self-Portait as a Soldier] (1915).

53 Edvard Munch, *Liegender weiblicher Akt* [Reclining Female Nude] (1914). [Jesi notes this as being from 1905.]

54 Mayer, *Thomas Mann*, p. 86.

55 Ernst Ludwig Kirchner, *Das Paar vor den Menschen* (1924).

Plozia, opening him up to ironic and accusing stares: 'Without the green-dark foliage having cleared in the slightest, the bed was exposed on all sides and at the mercy of all glances; the glances were not to be warded off, nor were the scornfully outstretched fingers, most of them adorned with rings, pointing from all sides towards the couch.'[56]

Was this vision of such painful distress the product of illness, a vision which in its pathos distorts the woman of myth until it makes of her an emblem of destruction? We cannot conclude otherwise. There was an antidote, however, for this illness, so profoundly rooted in German culture, a cure which comes not through any formal tranquillization but through the return of pain into to its elementary human character. Käthe Kollwitz's drawings and engravings bear witness to this, in which woman is a constant protagonist of human pain, but never loses her maternal nature even while she is in paroxysms of the pain itself. Kollwitz's work, with its countless widows and suffering mothers, constitutes a fascinating counterpart to the images of suffering in which the woman is only 'Lulu', lover and the harbinger of death. For Kollwitz's women, death's constantly looming presence is a force which is intrinsically alien to femininity, a threatening enemy who strikes mothers in the instant in which they give way in the utmost defence of their children. Rather than a prerogative of femininity, here death is its opposite.

---

56 Broch, *Der Tod des Vergil*, p. 332: 'Ohne dass die gründunkle Laube sich im geringsten lichtete, war das Bett weithin ausgestellt und allen Blicken preisgegeben; unabwehrbar die höhnisch ausgestreckten Finger, die sich, vielfach ringgeschmückt, von allüberall her auf das Lager richteten'. Untermeyer translation, p. 412.

Without doubt, Kollwitz's approach contains its polemical moment, arguing against the destructive eroticism of those subjected to 'Lulu's enchantments: in all of his work, the erotic elements appear in second place. And as much as there is no lack of imagery of couples (more peaceful than those evoked by Kirchner and Broch), women usually appear alone, with their children, a bastion against death. This too might seem a limitation, for it blocks any adhesion to those mysterious, symbolic forces of the dark Eleusinian lover; but such a limitation has a polemical significance of great moral value, for it constitutes a rejection of every erotic satisfaction—at the cost of losing a certain enlightenment—determined by the will to salvage humanity. Kollwitz's mothers, pregnant with humanity, represent an important counterweight to the aerial interpretation of woman as witches, flying through the aether, as depicted by Goya in an aquatint entitled 'They Flew' for the series *Caprichos*, perhaps a version of the Germanic 'woman-of-death'. For Goya, however, this was a direct reference to an engraving by Max Klinger—Kollwitz's first teacher—entitled *In der Gosse* [*In the Ditch*], representing the image of a woman in white suspended over the edge of a ditch by a shadowy, grinning crowd.

The newspapers record that in May 1902 a party was held in the Secession Building in Vienna, in honour of Klinger: at the centre of the great hall decorated with frescos by Klimt, Klinger's 'Beethoven' was unveiled, and when the artist arrived, the chorus of Beethoven's Ninth Symphony blasted out, arranged for wind instruments by Gustav Mahler. The evocation of the sovereign claim to humanism celebrated in the 'Ode to Joy' provides adequate confirmation of the will to adhere to suffering shown by Klinger (in approximating himself to the great genius) provided a worthy prelude to the work of his pupil, Kollwitz, who situated the theme of the survival of man and the overcoming of 'Lulu' within the mother's pain. The myth, in other words, would not be genuine—that is, human—if it did not allow people to draw upon it in the moment in which the defence of the human is at its most urgent and definitive. Only genuine myth can allow both Kore and Demeter to become a single 'mater dolorosa' if evil assumes the appearance of a sterile eroticism.

* * *

Hesse's Hermine and Kamala can be juxtaposed to Sita, the protagonist of Mann's *The Transposed Heads*: she too—as Hans Mayer has noted—lives almost exclusively in the erotic sphere:[57] his most profound and complete character sketch is not a psychological picture but the description of a naked young girl. For as much as her actions are apparently marginal in the events narrated: Mayer claimed that *The Transposed Heads* is not the story of Sita but of her two husbands; she constitutes the basic ruling figure of the narration, the element which renders the discord between spirit and body dramatic, and which also raises itself up beyond this discord. The observation accompanying her first appearance in the novel, surprised while bathing—'It must have been no different for Pramlocha, the young celestial maiden sent by Indra to the great hermit Kandu . . . '[58]—is fundamentally an echo

---

57 Mayer, *Thomas Mann*, pp. 243–4.

58 Thomas Mann, *Die vertauschten Köpfe* in *Ausgewählte Erzählungen* (Stockholm: Fischer, 1945), p, 533: 'Nicht anders konnte des Himmelsmädchen Pramlotscha gebildet gewesen sein, das Indra zu dem grossen Asketen Kandu geschickt hatte.'

of the eternal astonishment and commotion of man before the woman in whom the divine maiden is always concealed:[59]

> Oh queen, hear my pleas. But ought I call you a
> Goddess
> or a human woman?

The figure of Sita does not represent the discord between eroticism and moral revelation that rules Kamala, nor a scission between desire and rejection, between healing and eroticism, which Hermine symbolizes. Rather, the serene language of the parody relates entirely to the appearance of the woman of myth. Even if the goddess Kali allows one to name that woman 'a stupid goat,'[60] her language is that of the gods, and the gods are certainly not spellbound by myth! Sita subjects herself to the will of the goddess devotedly when the latter enforces respect for the laws of life's continuity: the mythic figure is also subjected to the norms of existence, so long as that figure is not a demonic conqueror of man, and reveals itself 'humanly' to man. Sexual desire arouses the discord between body and spirit but Sita is not merely that desire; rather, she surpasses it through her 'divine' beauty and femininity.

The Transposed Heads is a much less 'oriental' story than *Siddharta*, for inasmuch as elements of ancient oriental tradition emerge from it,[61] they have a mythological

---

[English translation: *The Transposed Heads* (H. T. Lowe-Porter trans.) (London: Secker and Warburg, 1941), p. 28.]

59 These are the first words Odysseus speaks to Nausica: *Odyssey, Book VI.* [Homer, *Odyssey* (A. T. Murray trans.) (London: Heinemann, 1919), translation modified.]

60 Mann, *Die vertauschten Köpfe*, p. 565: 'dumme Ziege'. Lowe-Porter translation, p. 80, modified.

61 Karl Kerényi, 'Die goldene Parodie', *Neue Rundshau* 67 (1956): 549–56; here, p. 549.

structure estranged from any topographical or chronological determinants. It may thus quite rightly be called
a 'game' worthy of the *Magister ludi* Thomas von der
Trave, but it escapes any accusation of sterility thanks to
the powerful evocation of myth through Mann's parodic
language, a language which works through a wondrous
and humanistic function of mythic 'tranquillization', or,
better still, the revelation of the serene and human forces
within genuine myth. It is precisely this function of language that allows the most genuine quality of Mann's religious experience to be recognized within the story. The
apparently 'playful' tone of the narrative ought not to distract one from its profound gravity; it is enough simply
to take heed of the story's opening line—'It is hoped that
the listener will follow the example of the narrator's own
firmness, for it takes almost more courage to tell such a
story than it does to listen to it'[62]—along with the constant references by Serenus Zeitblom, in *Doktor Faustus*,
to the anguish which dominates the activity of the narrator. To narrate the events of a man's life and the appearances of myth is always a turbulent undertaking, no
matter what—as well as wondrous; and, in Mann's case,
always bears witness to a religious experience too.

> By the time that memory ascends in the souls of
> men, like a sacrificial vase filled slowly from the
> bottom, whether with intoxicating liquor or with
> blood; like the womb of severe religious obser-
> vance opens itself up to the seed of the distant and

---

62 Mann, *Die vertauschten Köpfe*, p. 519: 'Es wäre zu wünschen,
dass die Zuhörer sich an der Festigkeit des Überliefernden ein
Beispiel nähmen, denn fast mehr Mut noch gehört dazu, eine
solche Geschichte zu erzählen, als sie zu vernehmen'.

primordial, and the homesickness for the Mother surrounds the old symbols with shudders . . .[63]

The solemnity of the opening lines of *The Transposed Heads* does not renege on the parody which simultaneously pervades these words. Mann's parody is above all in its emotional 'reserve' which does not negate such emotions but allows the artist to access them humanistically, without the risk of annihilating them. The religious experience of which he speaks acts as a consistent testimony to a man's act of religion: not in the sense of man's idolization but of the *human* relationship with the divine.

The parody, however, when exercised by a truly humanist artist, also works against the language of men, not in the end to destroy it, or to show it to be ineffective, but to reveal the detachment between man and the god, the only condition in which man can access the divine. Mythic images are not angelic intermediaries between man and god, but the human reality enriching man's consciousness, allowing it to enter into a relationship with the divine.

* * *

The truly 'golden'[64] parody with which Mann opens his own creative experience to the flow of myth can be significantly countered by the hard, grim parody which Bertolt Brecht evokes in *Saint Joan of the Stockyards* [*Die*

---

63 Mann, *Die vertauschten Köpfe*, p. 519: 'Zu der Zeit, als Erinnerung in dem Seelen der Menschen emporstieg, wie wenn ein Opfergefäss sich vom Fusse her langsam mit Rauschtrank füllte oder mit Blut; als der Schoss strenger Herrenfrömmigkeit sich dem Samen der Ur-Vor-herigen öffnete, Heimweh nach der Mutter alte Sinnbilder mit verjüngten Schauern umgab . . .' [The Italian translation used by Jesi omits that the shudders are 'verjüngten', i.e. rejuvenated.]

64 This is Kerényi's expression: 'die goldene Parodie'; see p. 109n61.

heilige Johanna der Schlachthöfe] through the figure of Johanna Dark, an extreme, desolate version of the woman of myth.

With Johanna we seem to conclude an arc of metamorphoses which began with the figure of Kundry: Johanna also advances herself as the moral imperative of 'serving', but more of the knights of purity than the meek and disinherited; not those who understand and practice goodness, but those whom the tragic conditions of existence have conduced to forget about it and even to subordinate it, at any cost, to the satisfaction of the most basic necessary elements of human life. Johanna is by now entirely alien to the forces of seduction which represent the negative element in Kundry; she is, at least in her intentions, the healer of the evils of man, but does not possess the strength nor the tranquil presence of the feminine figures of myth as evoked by Mann.

Must we conclude then that through Johanna, Brecht deformed the image of the divine maiden? This is only true to a certain extent. Effectively, in *Saint Joan of the Stockyards*, Brecht provided a deformed image, but a deformation imposed by him on the figure of myth is a 'flaw' (*colpa*) or a symptom of illness in which he does not confine himself; rather, he denounces it in a tone of self-confession:[65]

---

65 Bertolt Brecht, 'An die Nachgeboren' (To Those Born After) in *Hundert Gedichte* (Berlin: Aufbau, 1958):

> Dabei wissen wir doch:
> Auch der Has gegen die Niedrigkeit
> Veryerrt die Züge.
> Auch der Zorn über das Unrecht
> Macht die Stimme heiser. Ach, wir
> Die wir den Boden bereiten wollten für Freundlichkeit,
> Konnten selber nicht freundlich sein.

And so we know:
hatred against baseness
still distorts the face.
Ire against injustice
still makes the voice go hoarse. Alas! We
who wanted to prepare the earth for kindness
were not able to be kind.

In Brecht's drama, however, the figure of the deformed mythic woman is destined for failure in her mission as a healer. Johanna, while dying a martyr, does not manage to achieve her goal because her deformity consists in an abasement of the mythic image at the level of being human among human beings. And this figure, in this manner so painfully 'humanized', lives among men in a world dominated by baseness, in which personal initiative no longer suffices but, rather, collective strength is necessary in order to overpower wickedness. Losing a good part of her mythic features, the woman also loses the value of collectivity implicit in the genuine myth: Johanna attempts in vain to bring the abattoir workers with her, but no one can follow her right to the end. This failure, along with Brecht's self-confession, shows how, by now, for the dramaturg, myth could only be evoked in negative terms, through allusions to mourning and pain. The deformity of myth which appears in *Die heilige Johanna der Schlachthöfe* does not derive, therefore, from a determinate will of demonic negation of genuine myth, nor from an illness in which the artist finds horrific refuge: she is merely the consequence of a sickness which pervades the world and the artist, which painfully recognizes this deforming force within it. But to recognize this sickness and deformity in this way is, in the same instant in which its inevitability is accused, also to denounce its horror: it is already an act of overcoming.

The explicit references to religious experience in Brecht's drama are characteristic of the same attitude of refusal of Christian religion as inapplicable to the salvation of men, due to the same illness which deforms the figures of myth. This attitude, however, does not exclude —or, rather, on the contrary, actually implies—the mourning for a religion of salvation; Brecht's response was not merely superficial when he was asked which literary work had influenced his development the most: 'The Bible; don't laugh . . . '[66]

The contemporary presence in German culture of a work such as *Saint Joan of the Stockyards* and *Fiorenza* or *The Transposed Heads* (the contemporaneity is not absolute, but Mann's two works were undertaken in an arc of 1906–40, into which Brecht's drama intervened, 1929–30) poses an antimony through which to assess the validity of one or the other artistic experience. Nevertheless, as we are dealing here with poetry, it would be useless to juxtapose them in a polemic in terms of validity. Brecht executed his religious experiences in the field of art as much as Mann did, both quite aware of the moral implications of aesthetic creation. For as much as there was probably never a particularly keen human sympathy between the two artists, they did not hesitate to combine their forces against Nazism. The journal *Mass und Wert*, the organ of German exiles edited by Mann, published Brecht's writings on more than one occasion; and the relation of a German artist to Nazism is the best litmus test of their work's humanistic health.

The profound difference which separates Mann's truly radiant mythical woman from the desolate figure of

---

66 Cited in Ernst Schumacher, *Die Dramatischen Versuche Bertolt Brechts 1918–1933* (Berlin: Rütten and Loening, 1955), p. 559. See also John Willett, *The Theatre of Bertolt Brecht* (London: Methuen, 1959), p. 88. [Jesi used the Italian by Ettore Capriolo.]

Johanna ought not be confused with any moral difference between Mann and Brecht. Both artists dedicated their creative experiences to respect for man, and such respect is the necessary basis of morality. From the religious point of view, their relations with the divine were divergent, yet both lived intimately solitary human lives as well as profoundly participating in the value of collectivity. Both lived outside any constituted religion; in fact, both produced important critiques of the constituted religions of their era. And yet both were religious spirits. This claim might be disturbing, particularly in Brecht's case, for those who have fundamentally accepted Marxist teachings. The concept of religion is, however, so vast and profound as not to be susceptible to the limitation of the doctrines of parties. Even from the standpoint of the orthodox Marxist, one commits no heresy by defining Brecht as a 'religious spirit', if one remembers the lesson by which a master of the history of religion such as Raffaele Pettazzoni redeemed his own weakness and political errors: 'Religion is any faith that has had its martyrs.' Philology teaches that *martyr* means witness, and a painful witness, who engages all of their humanity in the adhesion to a faith. That this faith must be noble is implicit in the fact that the martyr engages all of their humanity in it: it is, in fact, impossible to engage all of one's humanity in an abject doctrine or a phantasm.

We thus return to the image of the 'man of torments', *van der Qualen*, whom Mann evokes as the revelatory emblem of the artist. Both Mann and Brecht were, without doubt, 'men of torments', for the moral discipline of art inevitably implies 'torments', forcing the artists to enter into contact with seductive, 'shadowy forces' and to impose the bridle of humanism upon them.

One can observe, in relation to this, that throughout his work Mann never evoked the image of the artist as he truly was: neither Detlev Spinell, nor Gustav von Aschenbach, nor Adrian Leverkuhn are entirely Thomas Mann. A profound moral necessity opposed the filter of parody in defence against every possible narcissism. His autobiographical writings are intimately mixed with parody where they touch on the artistic life of the writer. The most profoundly autobiographical work, *Felix Krull*, remains autobiographical due to it being the very apogee of parody. This parodic approach constantly intervenes to exclude the dangers of indulging in the most personal of culpability as is inherent in self-analysis.

The figure of the artist, or at least of the man of genius, signals two distant points of a parabola in Brecht's work: Baal and Galileo. Both are men imbued in the weaknesses of humanity, but the tragic and solitary artistic experience of Baal concludes itself in the noble collective work of Galileo. Galileo represents a non-hero inasmuch as he does not sacrifice any human weakness for an extra-human heroism. Nevertheless, he is a 'man of torments' whose work is to be a healer for collectivity.

Galileo's human weaknesses are not a consequence of the illness which deforms the woman of myth in the figure of Johanna, an illness that can lead to the consideration of such weaknesses as guilt. Brecht instead attempts to overcome evil and to calmly evaluate the weaknesses of Galileo; in the same moment in which he condemned society for forcing men to be heroes, in *Der gute Mensch von Sezuan* [*The Good Man of Sezuan*] he evoked the image of a divine maiden who we can recognize as an extreme metamorphosis of the divine Fiore. The maiden, Shen Te, is also a prostitute, and the only one to welcome the travelling gods into her house. A serene healer, she is also tormented by a discord which in the end manages to split up her individuality—that of Brecht himself—into being good and into being evil by necessity. In his self-confession, Brecht thus reflects on his access to myth, and once again identifying the illness which forces man to be evil. But in *The Good Man of Sezuan*, the deformity imposed by the illness respects at least one aspect of the mythic image and saves the serene side of Shen Te, imposing itself instead only on the 'evil' face of Shui Ta. The religious experience contained in the drama includes, nonetheless, an almost Epicurean estrangement from the gods, who are only judges and who, in the moment in which they could help in some determinate fashion, ascend into the clouds. Man stands alone before good and evil: that is Brecht's lesson. The figures of myth can only confer a great truth on human experience, but the choice between good and evil depends on man. Even if this message does not exclude the illness which prohibits the pure and tranquillizing access to myth, it nevertheless bears witness to a genuine humanism.

* * *

Throughout the course of Mann's spiritual life, the image of the artist cannot be set asunder from that of Goethe. The final, mysterious and profoundly *hermetic* meeting (in the mythological sense of the word) between Goethe and Charlotte in *Lotte in Weimar* contains an idea whose profundity lies in unifying the fates of Mann and Goethe, and revealing the intimate religious component of the mature Mann's access to Goethe. The reason for this eternal return is appropriately the prelude to the final revelation, which Goethe reserves for the Lotte of *Werther*; a reason more mysterious than any other, which intertwines the obscurity of human destiny and which penetrates it with a moral intuition approaching the divine. 'Once I burnt myself up for you, and I burn myself into spirit and light for you always,' Goethe says to Lotte.

You know that metamorphosis is most intimate and dear to your friend, his greatest hope and deepest desire—a game of metamorphosis, changing face, in which the old man changes into an adolescent, from adolescent into boy, a simple human face, in which the course of life's ages changes, where youth magically reveals itself from within old age, and old age from youth . . . .[67]

The metamorphosis of the mythic image thus reveals itself as the metamorphosis of man, and the power of the healer inherent in myth becomes an intrinsic element of humanity. Myth is man's past. In this light, the dedication to Faust acquires a value of moving illumination.[68] All that which passes through and arouses the commotions of the human soul, with which man has drawn on the past of his being, with which he draws on myth, is the healing reality and dominating force of the present. Thus religion anoints a chrism of grace on Faust's renewed youth. Even when myth is forcefully subjected to horrific deformations, the respect for man can lead to truth across pain and mourning, for man in his integrity is able to

---

67 Mann, *Lotte in Weimar*, p. 449: 'Einst verbrannte ich dir und verbrenne dir allezeit zu Geist und Licht. Wisse, Metamorphose ist deines Freundes Lienstes und Innerstes, seine grosse Hoffnung und tiefste Begierde,—Spiel der Verwandlungen, wechselnd Gesicht, wo sich der Greis zum Jüngling, zum Jüngling der Knabe wandelt, Menschenantlitz schlechthin, in dem die Züge der Lebensalter changieren, Jugend aus Alter, Alter aus Jugend magisch hervortritt . . . .' Lowe-Porter translation, p. 452.

68 'Ihr naht euch wieder, schwankende Gestalten / Die früh sich einst dem Trüben Blick gezeigt', ll. 1–2. ['Again ye come, ye hovering Forms! I find ye, / As early to my clouded sight ye shone!' J. W. Goethe, *Faust: A Tragedy* (Bayard Taylor trans.) (London and New York: Ward and Lock, 1889).]

reunify the past with the present by drawing on myth, myth that weds past and present in the purifying light of primordial reality.

The image of the 'men of torments' resurfaces:

Then a departure will no longer be anything but a taking leave, taking leave for ever, the death struggle of feelings, and the hour will be heavy with tremendous pain, pain like that which likely precedes death for a while, and which is dying if nonetheless still not death. Death, the final flight into the flames—into the all-as-one, how could it also not be simply a metamorphosis? In my resting heart, sweet pictures, may you rest—and what sweet moment it will be, if one day we awaken together![69]

The woman of myth has laid bare her mortal aspect and in the same moment redeemed man from death. This experience, intimately religious, free from sickness and guilt, releases whoever has not turned their back on man and the most serious cause of evil—the dedication to, or nightmare of, death.

---

69 Mann, *Lotte in Weimar*, p. 449: 'Dann wird das Verlassen nur noch Abschied, Abschied für immer sein, Todeskampf des Gefühls, und die Stunde grässlicher Schmerzen voll, Schmerzen wie sie wohl dem Tode um einige Zeit vorangehen, und die das Sterben sind, wenn auch noch nicht der Tod. Tod, letzter Flug in der Flamme,—im All-Einen, wie sollte auch er denn nicht nur Wandlung sein? In meinem ruhenden Herzen, teure Bilder, mögt ihr ruhen—und welch ein freundlicher Augenblick wird es sein, wenn wir dereinst wieder zusammen erwachen.' Lowe-Porter translation, p. 452.

CHAPTER 3

A basic foundation of the bourgeois spirit is a tendency to organize life within a microcosm, in which social relations reveal the presence of solid walls: those of the house, the family business, eventually of the city. This tendency towards a restricted, autonomous community corresponds to the notion of a collectivity that leaves the interests of the individual intact, engaged in the organization of life in such a way as to erect solid barriers between oneself and things—the external world. It is natural that the decay of society and of bourgeois culture has led to a desperation to again enclose oneself within surrounding walls, confronted with the menacing advance of those forces that have always been excluded from the 'serene' microcosm, corresponding to the intrinsic weakening of that microcosm's internal defences. It is inevitable, however, that the greatest spirits of bourgeois culture have deepened this microcosmic experience with 'sympathy' and sentiment, forcing itself to live through this experience right till the end so as to be able to thus eject the deteriorating features from it and—at least as instruments of instruction—to resurrect those elements usable for a renewed humanism. This was Mann's attitude when he spoke in a positive sense of Lübeck 'as a form of spirit',[1] and when he identified the emblem of demonism in Kaisersaschern. In doing so, the 'praeceptor' of bourgeois

---

1 See the title of Thomas Mann's essay *Lübeck als geistige Lebensform: Die Entstehung der Buddenbrooks* (Lubeck: Quitzow, 1926).

Germany did not fail in his great mythological activity: the city is a mythic image of ancient and profound tradition in Western culture, assuming both celestial and infernal privileges depending on whether evoked by St Augustine or Baudelaire. In a series of famous essays, Franz Altheim and his students[2] have, however, clarified the historical and psychic bases of that *square* city which Jung connected to the Eastern *mandala*, symbolizing the foundation of the personality.[3] Their research has shown the existence of an image behind the appearance of the bourgeois city, one that is inherently resistant to classist qualifications: a genuinely mythical image, and therefore profoundly and uniquely human.

While Mann, accepting his own bourgeois quality in the same instant in which he overcame the bourgeois tradition, reached for this image of Lübeck as healer and cure, as a form of spirit, his brother Heinrich, polemically rejecting his bourgeois heritage, ended up settling on the image of the horrific, despicable city of *Professor Unrat*, which includes, even in its very details, a negative and dark equivalent of the Lübeck in which both Tonio Kröger and the Buddenbrooks live. On the other hand, the radical refusal of the bourgeois tradition brought with it, for Heinrich Mann, a certain loss of contact with the obscure forces which emerge from the substrates of the city; the roads taken by professor Unrat are dark and desolate, but in these the horror does not emanate from the houses, the shadowy entrance halls and deserted crossroads, as in the Prague of the Bohemian novelists, from Kubin to Kafka and Meyrink. The bearer of this horror is

---

2 See Werner Müller, *Kreis und Kreuz* (Berlin: Widekind, 1938).

3 The problem recurs in the majority of Jung's writings. As an introduction to this problems, see the introduction by Kerényi to Jung and Kerényi, *Science of Mythology*.

a man: the deformed and vitiated professor Unrat. The horror rises above all human guilt, not extra-human threats, pressing down from the skies, whether celestial or infernal. This approach is undoubtedly humanistic, exactly because it refuses the descent into the infernal depths of the bourgeois world—closing one's eyes to the monstrous symbols evoked by human guilt, and concentrating only on that great deal of guilt which remains attached to man—leading to a lesson less expansive and profound than that implied in Thomas Mann's writing. Mann, in fact, did not hesitate to enter into contact directly with those symbolic creations—living beings of spectral, autonomous life—of bourgeois guilt, evoking, in contrast to his Lübeck, that which most fundamentally reveals the destructive energy inherent to the bourgeois city: Venice—the 'Mediterranean Lübeck'—the city of Wagner's death and of Rilke's mysterious 'psychic shudders'.

The mythic nature—that is to say, a profoundly human nature—of the image of the city defines its emergence in the works of artists estranged from the bourgeois world and engaged in an open polemic against it. Its appearance, however, precisely through being an epiphany of the mythic image, also stirs up emotions of love and torment in the soul of the Expressionist artist, those who participate in the problematics connected with the survival or refusal of the bourgeois city.

The city evoked by such artists is no longer the bourgeois microcosm surrounded by walls and populated by a well-defended aristocracy and faded images of the popular classes. Their city is not Lübeck but, above all, Berlin: the city of the great periphery, over-ridingly populated by a proletariat in misery and revolt. Arnolt Bronnen recounts his arrival in Berlin in the winter of 1921–22:

What names the streets have! There were the dreams of holidays of entire petit bourgeois generations, from Rosenheimer to Aschaffenburger, from Munchener to Freisingestrasse. They lack nothing from the treasured geography of southern Germany. The names, however, deceive as much as dreams: in reality there is nothing but the icy wind. Not a single shelter for the solitary traveller caught in the middle of the billows, caught between the four-storey barracks for rent . . .⁴

Berlin was by now the city of the poor and rebelling: 'in reality there was nothing but the icy wind', Bronnen's words re-echo the final condemnation of the bourgeois city as declared by Brecht:⁵

> Of these cities all which will remain is that which
>> passes
> Through them: the wind!'

In a city such as this, the living image of myth nourishes itself on love and terror. In 1914, Ludwig Meidner wrote in 'Anleitung zum Malen von Grossstadtbildern' [Instructions for Painting the Great Cities]: 'We must communicate in the end how to paint the place in which are were born, them metropolises which we love with an infinite love.'⁶ But Georg Heym, one of the purer, more

---

4 Arnolt Bronnen, *Tage mit Bertolt Brecht. Die Geschichte einer unvollendeten Freundschaft* (Vienna: Henschel, 1960).

5 Bertold Brecht, 'Von armen B. B.' in *Gedichte, 1918–1929* (Frankfurt: Suhrkamp, 1960), p. 147: 'Von diesen Städten wird bleiben: der durch sie / Hindurchging, der Wind!"

6 Ludwig Meidner, 'Anleitung zum Malen von Grossstadtbildern', *Kunst und Künstler* 12 (1914): 312–14; reprinted in P. Pörtner (ed.), *Literature-Revolution 1910–1925. Band 2: Zur Begriffsbestimmung der 'Ismen'* (Darmstadt: Luchterhand, 1961), pp. 164–9.

authentic poets of Expressionism, sung of the city's demons, monsters who weighed heavily, dark and gigantic over the isolated, bringing together the urban buildings and skies in grim horrors of Apocalypses.[7] Love and terror signal the relation between Expressionists and the city, the chosen place for their human life: the place which also, through its spectral, spellbinding structures, mythically transfigures the misery and the revolt, mutating them into apocalyptic symptoms. The representation of Berlinerstrasse, Dresden, in a lithograph by Karl Schmidt-Rottluff, is flanked by the serene, summery—as well as profoundly emotional and disturbing—image of Dresden painted in 1922 by Kokoschka.[8] But across from this ambivalence over love and terror stands Georg Grosz's revelatory and terrifying vision, dominated by a twilight that confers a tone of definitive tragedy to the notion of 'the twilight of humanity' celebrated through the homonymous anthology of Expressionist lyrics published by Kurt Pinthus in 1920.[9]

For the artists of Expressionism, the city became a battlefield. In the years immediately following the First World War, the city is a place of struggle, in which the moment in time reaches the highest level through the streets, the great symbols of the battle waged for the victory of a humanity aware of the terrifying threat weighing

---

7 One might refer, for example, to the words of 'Die Dämonen der Städte' (1911) in Georg Heym, *Umbra vitae. Nachgelassene Gedichte* (Leipzig: Ernst Rowohlt, 1912).

8 Schmidt-Rottluff's lithograph is reproduced in Bernard S. Myers, *The German Expressionists: A Generation in Revolt* (New York: Frederick A. Praeger, 1957), p. 110; the painting by Kokoschka is in Cologne, in the Wallraf-Richartz Museum. [This is *Dresden Neustadt III* (1921), now in the Museum Ludwig.]

9 See p. 104n50.

down upon it: 'with the same rage of feeling from one side came an echo: "Down, down, down!" which radiated outwards even beyond the street corners. A moment later came the strength of another cry. "Long live Liebknecht!" Everyone ran towards a point where a cab had stopped. Inside was Liebknecht. He had to speak.'[10] Thus Erwin Piscator bore witness to the climax of those days, in which one fought without losing even a moment.

* * *

Hinkemann, 'cripple', is an appropriate name for a veteran whom the war has wounded irremediably: the aquatints of Georg Grosz's album *Ecce Homo* are populated by images of such amputees who pass through the streets of Berlin immersed in the twilight of the Apocalypse. Ernst Toller gave the name *Hinkemann* [*Cripple*] to the tragedy he wrote in the Niederschönenfeld prison in 1921–22 after the failure of the communist revolution in Munich. The war has wounded the 'crippled' protagonist of the tragedy in the very vitality of his body and to the depths of his soul; he is a veteran unable to survive in the world to which he has returned because his old bonds with that world have been broken. The images of the period before the war only apparently return around him: he can take nothing but horror and suffering from these because the war, beyond its wounds to his body, has wounded that which rooted him vitally to the past. For the veteran there is no return: this conclusion is already implied in the sentence placed by Toller as an epigraph to the opening of the tragedy: 'Whoever has no power to dream, has no

10 Erwin Piscator, *Das politische Theater* (Berlin: Adalbert, 1929), pp. 18–19. [English translation: *The Political Theatre: A History, 1914–1929* (Hugh Rorrison trans.) (London: Eyre Methuen, 1980).]

power to live.'[11] The veteran no longer has the power to dream because the war has cut his innermost roots of dreaming, depriving him of his past. Solitary and desolate, for him 'every tree can bear paradise, every night hell.' In the tragedy, the figure of the woman who could be his cure—Hinkemann's wife—is only an image of suffering and weakness; the mutilation has also afflicted Hinkemann sexually, and his wife betrays him with a man who has the transparent name *Grosshahn*, 'big cockerel'.

The war has broken the relationship between man and the genuine, salvational forces of myth; unable to find the past once more, the veteran was irremediably alienated from the sources of myth which would allow an element of continuity between past and present.

Twenty-seven years later, at the end of the Second World War, the general situation was very accurately evoked by Wolfgang Borchert in his play *Draussen vor der Tür* [Outside the Door].[12] Borchert died at 26 in 1947 from tuberculosis contracted during the war, making his own fate conform with the tragic destiny of the veteran deprived of a future.

Toller's *Hinkemann* ends with the veteran's wife committing suicide and his own desolate survival: *Draussen*

---

11 It is interesting to put Toller's epigraph next to a citation of Giacomo Leopardi in his *Diaologo di Torquato Tasso e del suo genio familiare*: 'At that rate, since men are born and live for pleasure alone, whether of the body or of the mind, if moreover pleasure is found solely or chiefly in dreams, it will be right that we shall resolve to live for the sake of dreaming: a thing which in truth I cannot consent to do.' [*Translations from Leopardi* (Robert Calverly Trevelyan trans.) (Cambridge: Cambridge University Press, 1941), p. 53. Original in Leopardi, *Tutte le opere*, *Volume 1* (Florence; Sansoni Editore, 1969).]

12 Wolfgang Borchert, *Draussen vor der Tür* in *Das Gesamtwerk* (Hamburg: Rowohlt, 1959), pp. 99–168.

vor der Tür begins with an attempted suicide by the veteran, Beckmann, in the waters of the Elba, which nonetheless reject him, pushing him out and back to life, violently imposing on him all the other attempts. Like Hinkemann, Beckmann is destined to survive, but also to find every link with the past broken; the 'stations' of his return demonstrate to him that his wife has cheated on him, that his parents have chosen suicide, that his wartime commander is only all the more a monstrous puppet. For a long while, Beckmann is encouraged from despair by 'Other', the mysterious character who walks alongside him, symbolizing the survival of his hope in human solidarity and the possibility of a true return. 'Men are good!' Other claims, repeating the belief of Expressionism. But at the end of the play even Other disappears and with him, God: Beckmann is alone; no one replies.

In the play's prologue, Borchert wrote:

A man returns to Germany. And there he lives his life as if in an amazing film. Throughout the events he keeps having to pinch himself, to check whether he's awake or dreaming. But then he sees everywhere around him other people are living out the same adventure, and then he realises that this must actually be reality . . . [It is a film] about a man who returns to Germany, one of many. It's about one of those people who return home but also don't, because for them there is no being home any more. Their being home is outside the door. Their Germany is outside, in the night and the rain, on the streets.[13]

---

13 Borchert, *Draussen vor der Tür*, p. 102: 'Ein Mann kommt auch nach Deutschland. Und da erlebt er einen ganz tollen Film. Er muss sich während der Vorstellung mehrmals in den Arm kneifen, denn er weiss nicht, ob er wacht oder träumt. Aber dann sieht er,

Thinking of those words of Novalis we have already cited—'Where are we going? Always home'[14]—we can read Borchert's final message in this tragedy. Novalis' 'always going home' refers to a direction towards the primordial and the *humanly* primordial, that which orients the experiential flow of whoever lives in communion with the past within him, and therefore also in communion with genuine myth. The war had broken this bond in the lives of those veterans represented by Beckmann. Borchert's recourse to the language and images of Expressionism seems justified by the deformity of those images which the experience of the First World War had already manifested in emblems of the veterans' own vitiated mythology. This same aspect of Beckmann, that of the face deformed through the lenses of the gas mask— which he always wore, no longer possessing any others— recalls that aspect of the tragic protagonists of Karl Kraus' *Die letzten Tagen der Menschheit* [The Last Days of Mankind]. Indeed, Kraus' apocalyptic vision includes characters named merely as 'a male gasmask' or 'a female gasmask', which say: 'We have right to neither face nor

---

dass es rechts und links neven ihm noch meht Leute gibt, die alle dasselbe erleben. Und er denkt, dass es dann doch wohl die Wahrheit sein muss. Ja, und als er dann am Schluss mit leerem Magen und kalten Füssen wieder auf der Strasse steht, merkt er, dass es eigentlich nur ein ganz alltäglicher Film war, ein ganz alltäglicher Film. Von einem Mann, der nach Deutschland kommt, einer von denen. Einer von denen, die nach Hause kommen und die dann doch nicht nach Hause kommen, weil für sie kein Zuhause mehr da ist. Und ihr Zuhause ist dann draussen vor der Tür. Ihr Deutschland ist draussen, nachts im Regen, auf der Strasse.' [Original translation, but see Wolfgang Borchert, *The Man Outside* (David Porter trans.) (New York: New Directions, 1971) p. 82].

14 See p. 102n47.

gender. Life fled among the corpses and maggots . . . .'[15] Beckmann too has no right to sex nor gender: his face is a mask of war, and when, already having been cheated on by his wife, he picks up a girl on the beach at Blankensee, he fails to find comfort even in this feminine image. The young women has a phantom husband who has also returned mutilated from the war; in sleeping with her, Beckmann would incur the same guilt as that entailed by his own wife.

Beckmann is thus inexorably 'outside the door': the young woman who wants to comfort him calls him 'fish, little fish',[16] but this aquatic symbol, which could simultaneously be a primordial emblem of infancy—indeed, of pre-natal infancy—acquires a tragic meaning for whoever, like Beckmann, has tried to drown themselves. When he throws himself into the river, the Elba takes him in its waters and then expels him from them like a mother: for Beckhmann this is apparently a second birth, and a second birth seems exactly the fate of the veteran who returns again to the world; but in reality such a birth is only a deformed image of actual birth or of a genuine rebirth. Such rebirth does not include any access to the true and complete life of man, but only an existence among 'corpses and maggots'. The play ends with a dance of death in which Beckmann—before remaining alone— sees all the characters of the 'stations' of his return for the last time: his wife, the young woman, her husband, the colonel, the theatre manager who he calls on in order to try and survive at least by parodying himself.

---

15 Kraus, *Die letzten Tagen der Menschheit*, p. 275: 'Wir haben kein Recht auf Geschlecht und Gesicht. Das Leben verbracht zwischen Leichen und Larven.'

16 On the mythic basis of the fish as symbol of primordial infancy, see pp. 164–5.

Being 'outside the door' is the condition of the veterans of both the world wars; but, in the Expressionist literature of the first decades of the century, the 'sons' are also 'outside the door' in relation to their 'fathers'. The great conflict between 'sons' and 'fathers' is witnessed in the play *Der Sohn* [The Son] by Walter Hasenclever, in which the Son is cut off from a genuine existence through the discipline imposed on him by the Father:

> Down there, profound, magnificent without
>   comparison
> enchanted nights exist, which never come to me
> here in this gloomy room which beheld my
>   childhood.

The crisis of society and bourgeois culture, which also implies a serious crisis for relations with myth, is shown in this tragic discord between father and son, which can only end in death. As the veterans of the two wars, the Son also tries to kill himself; but, unlike the veterans, he manages to overcome the barrier erected by patriarchal society. With an act of violence—which nonetheless includes the Father's death—the Son seems to stop being 'outside the door'. He runs away from the paternal home, entering the world with courage—pushed forward by an enigmatic Friend who will re-emerge in Other in *Draussen vor der Tür*—inciting all the 'sons' to revolt against the 'fathers', and in the process seems to find the capacity of accessing our sources of existence. While for Beckmann the home is 'outside the door', the Son's return is greeted through the words:

> Now you are here again—and at your
> Feet homeland and wonderland are intermixed

'Homeland and wonderland': here again is Novalis' 'always going home', in the sense of an eternal return to the sources of myth. The Son is welcomed on his return by a woman—the Governess—whom he had never managed to love when he was subjected to his father, but who now appears as a healing figure. At the same time, the Son says to the Governess:

> Remember that young man who wanted to
>   abandon you?
> Oh, you don't believe that I have returned to
>   you . . . ?

For the Son, neither rebellion nor activity are means for a total salvation:

> I know that activity demands sacrifice:
> My heart overflowed . . . and now is empty.
> Being and birth—once in one's womb
> Could not sustain its love for me,
> I am too poor. The world has abandoned me.
> And my body is dragged along
> a weight of a heavy conscience, in a painful lack
>   of love . . .'*

---

* [The following German text from Walter Hasenclever, *Der Sohn* (Stuttgart: Reclam, 1994[1917]) was not provided by Jesi:

Act 1, Scene 2:

Dort unten, tief und herrlich ohnegleichen
sind Wundernächte, die mich nie erreichen
im dumpfen raum, der meiner Kindheit sah.
Nun bist du wiederhier—und dir zu
Füssen vermischt sich Heimat mit dem Wunderland.

Act 5, Scene 3:

Kennst du den Knaben noch, der dir entschwindet?
O glaube nicht, ich kehrte dir zurück. [. . .]
Ich weiß, daß Taten nur durch Opfer werden:
mein Herz war übervoll jetzt ist es leer. [. . .]
Geburt und Dasein—einst in Ihrem Schoß—
mich würde Ihre Liebe nicht mehr tragen,
ich bin zu arm. Die Erde ließ mich los.
Ins schmerzlich Ungeliebte,
in die Schwere des tief Erkannten treibt mein Körper hin.]

Neither the governess, nor the prostitute Adriane whom the Son meets during his rebellion, represent feminine images pregnant with the all-redemptive force of myth. The activity of the revolt itself excludes the Son from that love which is the very condition of pure and healing access to myth. Thus one can understand how, with a distance of more than 20 years, Borchert relentlessly excluded the 'sons'—now 'veterans'—from accessing a fully human and serene existence, and how he had sacrificed even those brief flashes of myth which emerged in certain moments in the Son's experience. Myth became inaccessible in its healing purity; the will to rebel shows itself unable to modify the course of German history; the veteran Beckmann is truly 'outside the door'.

Borchert's final message is nevertheless not nihilist. *Outside the Door* is followed by an epilogue, given the significant title 'And then there is only one choice!' [*Dann gibt es nur eins!*]:

> Listen, man at the machine and man in the workshop! When tomorrow they command you to no longer make pipes and pans, but only helmets of steel and machine guns, then there is only one choice: say NO! Listen, shop girls and secretaries! When tomorrow they command you to stuff the grenades and mount projectiles for ballistic missiles, then there is only one choice: say NO! [. . .] All this will come to pass, tomorrow, perhaps tomorrow, perhaps this very night, perhaps this night itself—if, if, if you don't say NO![17]

---

17 Borchert, *Das Gesamtwerk*, p. 318: 'Du Mann an der Maschine und Mann in der Werkstatt. Wenn sie dir morgen befehlen, du sollst keine Wasserrobe und keine Kochtöpfe mehr machen—sondern Stahlhelme und Maschinengewehre, dann gibt es nur ein Sag NEIN! Du. Mädchen hintern Ladentisch und Mädchen in Büro. Wenn sie dir morgen befehlen, du sollst Granaten füllen und

Thus Wolfgang Borchert found once more the passion and struggle of those years in which the city of Berlin had become a battle site. Even if the battle waged by Rosa Luxemburg and Karl Liebknecht led to defeat, it was not a definitive one. In the case of Luxemburg and Liebknecht, the martyrs provided a weak victory, but Borchert's work evidences the fact that the battle is still in motion. The city is not a place of perennially being 'outside the door'. If one 'will say NO', the city too will return to being the serene mythic image of collective life on which the individual is founded.

Such a lesson was already implicit in Bertolt Brecht's play *Drums in the Night* [*Trommeln in der Nacht*]. Again, the subject of this drama is the return of a veteran, Andreas Kragler. But Kragler, immersed in the nocturnal city, disturbed by the drums of the Spartacist revolution destined for failure, is far more oriented towards the future— towards victory—than Hinkemann was in Toller's play. Brecht's drama overcomes the failure of Spartacism, substituting Kragler's attitude for the confused emotion of honour through which Liebknecht and Luxemburg die, for Kragler abandons the nocturnal drums in order to go home with the woman who had left him and who he has now finally won back: 'The noise will be over tomorrow morning, but I will be in bed, reproducing myself so as not to die.'[18] In *Galileo*, Brecht taught that a civilized world

---

Zielfernrohre für Scharfschützengewehre montieren, dann gibt es nur eins: Sag NEIN! [. . .] all dieses wird eintreffen, morgen, morgen vielleicht, vielleicht heute nacht schon, vielleicht heute nacht, wenn-wenn-wenn ihr nicht NEIN sagt.' Original translation, but see the David Porter translation, p. 268.

18 Bertolt Brecht, *Trommeln in der Nacht* (Munich: Drei Masken, 1923), Act 5, p. 204 : 'Das Geschrei ist alles vorbei, morgen früh, aber ich liege im Bett morgen früh und vervielfältige mich, dass ich nicht aussterbe.'

does not force men to be heroes; in *Drums in the Night*, Brecht, if always in imperfect terms, admonishes that victory over horror is entrusted to those who refuse heroism by surviving the mortal battle. Survival itself is already a victory against those who idolize death.

In *Drums in the Night*, the stage directions reveal a nocturnal city, immersed in the apocalyptic lights of battle: 'From the window one sees the red moon. When the door opens: wind.'; 'A suburban street. From top left to bottom right the walls of a cottage, of red brick. Behind, the city in starlight. Wind'; 'Wooden bridge. Cries. A great red moon.' 'The city in starlight':[19] we are truly on the threshold of an Apocalypse which draws on the greatest depths of German culture; the stars which illuminate the city are also those evoked by Nietzsche as well as an extreme, pathetic reflection of Kant's starry infinity.

Thus, the artists who tragically oppose themselves to the survivals of bourgeois culture are invoking mythic images such as that of the city, drawing on the very depths of humanity. As Bronnen wrote:

> Outside, the starving, freezing city played itself out in a sporadic buzz of the noise of the tram, betrayed by the bosses who tear at the night, upturned by strikes, assemblies, demonstrations, stock market manoeuvres, rhetorical riots. Everything therein is condensed in the injections which the patient Brecht, a sharp, keen actor-spectator, gave himself, with a cynicism like a cut from a jagged blade. 'The play really

---

19 Brecht, *Trommeln in der Nacht*, stage directions at the opening of Act 2: 'Im Fenster roter Mond. Wenn die Tür aufgeht: Wind.'; of Act 3: 'Rote Backsetinmauer einer Keserne, von links oben nach rechts unten. Dahinter in vewestem Sternenlicht die Stadt. Nacht. Wind.'; of Act V: 'Holzbrücke. Geschrei, grosser roter Mond.'

would be like drums, if all this were in there,' Bronnen observed. 'Very well then,' Brecht agreed, 'I'll put that in there.' 'When?' asked Bronnen. 'It's already there,' Brecht replied.[20]

TThe city had thus transformed from being the entrenched site of the bourgeoisie into a site of battle against them. But shadowy forces run through that field without pause, and Brecht opposed them with Kragler's humanism, a humanism which was merely the will for human survival. At the point in which the image of myth had become the site of struggle, it had also morphed, for true humanists like Brecht, into the prophetic rubble of the future, an emblem of a society alien to eroticism while proving itself a human environment all the same.

The bourgeois city, in its extreme and horrific metamorphoses, represents the place in which man finds himself 'outside the door'. But myth posseses regenerative forces, ones that survive the modifications of a bourgeoisie in agony. The city of myth stands under starlight. Within it, false astral emblems become merely papier-mâché furnishings; Andreas Kragler 'hurls the drum at the moon, an electric light. Drum and moon end up in the river, which is dry.'[21] But the astral bodies themselves, those which light up the towers of Lübeck 'like a kind of spirit', stand watch over the *civitas hominis*, and reflect down a starry infinity upon it. While 'the man walks to the woman, they go home.'

* * *

The image of the apparently 'celestial' city began to reveal its 'infernal' aspects in the same moment in which the

---

20 Bronnen, *Tage mit Bertolt Brecht*, p. 25.

21 Brecht, *Trommeln in der Nacht*, Act 5, p. 204: 'schmeisst die Trommel nach dem Mond, der ein Lampion war, und die Trommel und der Mond fallen in den Fluss, der kein Wasser hat.'

programmatic cry of Expressionism echoed emptily within it: 'Man is good!' In *Outside the Door*, the voice of Other endlessly repeats this cry, until eventually he gives up; for the veteran, the city has becomes the place in which he always remains 'outside the door': a papier-mâché world which only just conceals the semblances of both apocalypse and hell. Hell is, on the other hand, a place in which man—in Brecht's words—is no longer of any aid to his fellow man; human guilt is the primary cause of the transformation of the flow of myth through which the city becomes infernal, just as the vision of the 'houses of Hades' fill the gods themselves with terror. The city is hell also in the sense of a regression into the depths of being, in which man can no longer find himself at ease, lacking those defences that the strength of genuine myth and its humanistic use once guaranteed. The streets, the walls, the skies of the hellish city which has revealed itself to the veteran are no longer real images of the human city but dramatic scenes which are easily torn through, revealing behind them, within the gashes, either terrifying abysses of obscurity or terrifying walls. The architectonic structures constructed by man give way to forms which only partially resemble such structures, just as larvae and ectoplasm resemble man, and such forms juxtapose themselves to those created by him, almost as if they were proliferations of an unregulated nature, now horrifying in their anti-human character.

The crisis through which man finds himself perennially 'outside the door', in every environment of his actions, also breaks the balance of relations between man and nature, because in this manner man is most 'outside the door' in the places in which nature has not been subjected to man's interventions. The infernal city assumes the appearances of a monstrous nature, enemy to man. Such a nature is present also in the peripheries, in the countryside, rendering the entire habitable world hostile to him. The supremely humanistic function of genuine myth is the harmonization of man with nature, almost, indeed, with the biological substratum of being. When such a function is lessened through myth's deformation— when it is no longer genuine—man finds himself surrounded by horrors which assail him from all sides, even from 'within' his own self.

* * *

We have said that the city reveals its infernal nature when Expressionism's profession of faith is shown to echo emptily within it. At the end of the First World War, Thomas Mann juxtaposed to this cry of 'man is good!' with the events of a being who is undeniably 'good', but not a man: Bauschan, the canine protagonist of the prose 'idyll' *A Man and His Dog* [*Herr und Hund*]. Bauschan's sudden, overwhelming delight, but above all his troubles, his waiting in vain, his fears, his disappointments are the leitmotiv of the story which unfolds on the margins of the city, in an area recently reclaimed from the swamps to be transformed into a garden city; but the building bubble has burst, the projected roads retuned to being overrun with vegetation, and the signs announcing the names of such roads are rusting and half rubbed out. It is no accident that all the names are those of writers: Stifter, Opitz, Flemming, even Shakespeare . . . It is a kind of *civitas litterarum* in which the structures of bourgeois society have attempted in vain to imprison the reality of nature; and the sole consequence of such an effort has been the emergence of images of pathetic, fascinating destruction, which include more dangerous symptoms, just as the hidden zones remained damp and marshy.

Bauschan's master remains full of good will towards the project of building villas and shops in the area, and as such of finding a calm balance between nature and the lives of men; but the economic moment has rendered such attempts vain (attempts which, on the other hand, had been executed by businessmen up to the point of subjecting nature to the condition of a spectacle, a landscape, to man's apparent advantage). Bauschan's master carries himself with a serene melancholy along the pathways of the projected city, which will soon fall under the full power of a thriving and disorderly nature, thanks to the high humidity of the marshlands. This is essentially the same melancholy aroused in Thomas Mann by the images of bourgeois decadence, which in *A Man and His Dog* nevertheless assumes the redemptive profundity of a disturbed vision, intertwining the primordial relation between man and nature but not resolving it either through a benevolent nature nor in that of the good man. If we want to find a literary parallel for the environment of *A Man and His Dog*, on the one hand we can think of the dead cities invaded by jungles in Kipling's works, and on the other to Renzo's overgrown vineyards in Manzoni's *The Betrothed*: one the symbol of the morally difficult relation of Western colonial civilization with the deeper images of Eastern tradition (transformed into emblems of death); the other an evocation of a primordial guilt intertwined with the very nature on which man has laboured.

The landscape in *A Man and His Dog* acts, however, as another counterpoint to the life of Bauschan, which presents in a still more dramatic and explicit manner the contrast between human civilization and that which truly remains 'good': Bauschan, the dog who cannot follow his master among the terrors of the city, and whose affections for his master are frequently and painfully frustrated by the propriety and habits of men. One can say, indeed, that Bauschan is not merely a dog—or at least that his story also reflects a human destiny. When he falls ill and isolated in the veterinary clinic, Bauschan endures an adventure which will later also be that of the protagonist of *The Magic Mountain*, the great novel which Thomas Mann left unfinished at the beginning of the First World War and began again only after the conclusion of *A Man and His Dog*. It would nevertheless be an error to recognize the symbol of a kind of man in Bauschan: Bauschan is a dog, an animal, a lump of living material within which joy and pain are reduced to their primordial realities. For as much as such passions can be recognized as human, or at least archetypical of human passions, the evocation of the figure of Bauschan is a return to origins: an *eternal return* related to the primordial character of myth, equal to that theorized by Nietzsche and his more or less legitimate heirs.[22]

In this sense, *A Man and His Dog* bears witness to a 'return' manifested in a descent into the biological: into those structures of existence which are indeed those of man, but are not only subjected to a level of human consciousness. A 'return'—or at least an apologia of a 'return'—is, however, any doctrine which evokes the primordial forms of being as depositories of innocence and of a lost value of the good.

Thomas Mann's parodical attitude, by his own confession, nevertheless determines the mode of this 'return'. Bauschan is not a 'noble savage' in which one recognizes the fundamental human goodness supposed by Expressionists but a genuine dog in whom we recognize form and colour with a rich zoological precision. Mann thus maintains an ironic distance from the humanitarianism of some of his contemporaries while not failing to reveal that the recognition of an authentic goodness in a dog is a symptom of an unhappy situation, even a dramatic one, a

---

22 See, above all, the works of Mircea Eliade: *Traité d'histoire des religions* (Paris: Payot, 1949); as well as *Le mythe de l'éternel retour*.

bearer of torments; the situation, that is, of bourgeois culture on the edge of its own failure, at its very end.

* * *

In his autobiographical writings and in the correspondence with Károly Kerényi, Thomas Mann claims that his
interest in mythology came from his childhood, when he
gained a passion for reading a particular book on mythology—a volume that one can recognize in the red-bound
tome with a golden Athena on the cover given to Hanno
Buddenbrook for Christmas. But this interest—he writes
—then passed over the years to another level, up until it
re-emerged in his great mythological narrative of Joseph.

This autobiographical claim, however, should not be
taken literally, as it is quite conceivable that Mann would
not have denied a 'mythological reading' of his other
writings preceding the Joseph stories. An involuntary
mythology? Genuine mythology is, on the contrary, a
supremely spontaneous deed, and such spontaneity can
oppose itself, in Mann's work, to the deliberate evocation
of myths enacted by their technifiers: by those who
enslave myth for their own ends, mutating it, shedding
its original reality.

These considerations allow us to see *A Man and His
Dog* as a mythological work in the original and genuine
meaning of such an expression. For while employing
the structures of parody, Mann manages to return to
primordial realities in this work—not the archetypes then
theorized by Jung but, rather, the archetypes of human
passions: joy and pain, desire and loss. In placing these
archetypes in the figure of a dog—while also frequently
emphasizing its human aspects—Mann carried out an
authentic descent into a biological realm which is not
quite human but which nonetheless is that of man. It is
'beneath' man, in the underworld: a *katábasis*, therefore,

the historical basis of which is revealed with clarity and the character of drama. Man has tried to impose over nature—over the pre-human reality—laws and forms which he is neither strong enough nor 'good' enough to endure. In this effort, he has created an imbalance, one which derives through positioning himself on the same level of values that he cannot embrace; it is in this that the observation and denunciation of bourgeois society exists in *A Man and His Dog*, emphasized by the parody of the idyll. The pedagogic value of the narrative is therefore inherent to the demonstration of the impossibility of bourgeois society to enter into a calm and productive relation with nature, if it does not draw on the pure sources and the healing quality of myth. The absence of a mythic precedent, that is, of a healing reality of the relations between man and the extra-human, leads only to discord and disaster.

It thus also shines a light of humanistic warning on the relationship of twentieth-century German culture with nature, and allows us to understand the love that Mann always confessed for the 'old Fontane', whose wondrous evocations of landscapes—the desolate and solitary nature of *Effi Briest*—constitute an unbroken counterpoint to the pathos of his human stories.

We use the word 'counterpoint' in order to underline the musical nature of the relation between nature and human passion in Fontane's novel, and so as to repeat Kerényi's idea contained within the following questions: 'What is music? What is poetry? What is mythology?'[23] As in *A Man and His Dog*, in which vegetative life is musically interwoven into the 'passionate' experiences of Bauschan, reducing human passions to their primordial

---

23 These are the first words of the introduction to *Science of Mythology* [p. 1].

substrate, so too in *Effi Briest* the narrative of the protagonist's plot draws its structure from the evocations of
nature, conferring a mythic dimension on Effi's story.
Gardens and countryside cradle Effi Briest's adolescence;
desolate dunes along the sea are the theatre of Effi's long
walks with Captain Krampas, walks that precede and
foreshadow the adultery; 'Krampas' is the name of the
lover but also of a village; and finally Effi will be buried
in the middle of her childhood garden. Within these evocations of nature, the image of Effi reveals its profound
mythic nature, that of *kore*, mirrored—and altered—in
the narrative events: the 'abduction' of the young woman
by a bourgeois who grotesquely personifies the ancient
abducting god, and who 'abducts' Effi while she plays in
a garden with her friends; Effi's sepulchre in her childhood
garden equates to the Kore venerated in the place of
burial. But Effi's tomb is also an almost profane place, the
source of mourning and remorse rather than of healing
and serenity, as with the tombs of ancient Korai. The frac-
turing with genuine myth, announced through Fontane's
novel about the greatest decadence of bourgeois society,
is then openly indicated in Mann's novel *Tristan* which
repeats some of the moments of *Effi Briest*, placing them
in the harsh light of parody. Herr Klöterjahn, the husband of the female protagonist of *Tristan*, represents the
young woman's grotesque kidnapper, suddenly appearing
in the garden where she spends time with her friends.
Both in *Effi Briest* and in *Tristan*, the adultery—whether
actually carried out, or on a level of desire and guilty
surrender—has fatal consequences. In *Tristan*, this comes
as a consequence of an 'intimacy' with life which, by dramatic and parodical means, shines a light on the negative
aspects of, or inherent dangers in, the artistic condition.
But *Tristan* is also an act of accusation against those bourgeois institutions that regulate sexual relations, already

clearly denounced in both *Effi Briest* and in *Buddenbrooks*—in the marriages of Tony Buddenbrook and her daughter Erika, the triple failure of which is included among the symptoms of the great bourgeois family. The theme of adultery, furthermore, is also included in *Buddenbrooks* in the life of Thomas and his wife Gerda, whose love of music unites her with Lieutenant von Trotha. As in *Tristan*, here music acts as a determinant of adultery, a witness to how the institution of bourgeois marriage cannot withstand the emergence of obscure forces containing the firm, profound and mysterious basis of sexual union.

In *Effi Briest*, there are already some allusions to the myth of Tristan, destined to loom over nineteenth- and twentieth-century German culture as an emblem of tragedy born from the inability of bourgeois institutions to accept the reality of the obscure bond between love and death. Effi Briest uses a cup, together with her lover, which Captain Krampas conserves 'like the King of Thule': this is the reappearance of the cup which, in Goethe's *Elective Affinities*, is engraved with the interwoven initials of Eduard and Ottilie, and also the cup which in *Così fan tutte* seals the fake wedding. This cup has an evident mythic archetype in the glass of Tristan's potion, which for Olga Freidenberg is 'the ritual drink of fertility' but which Vladimir Propp has recognized more accurately as a symbol of the blood union practised in primordial wedding rituals.[24]

In *Elective Affinities*, the chalice is *accidentally* incised with two interwoven initials which just so happen to

---

24 Vladimir Yakovlevich Propp, *Istoriceskie Korni Volsebnoi Skazki* (Moscow: Labirint, 1998[1946]); available in Italian as: *Le radici storiche dei racconti di fate* (Clara Coïsson trans.) (Turin: Einaudi, 1949).

coincide with those of Eduard and Ottilie; thus, in Schiller's *Wallenstein*, the stars form themselves into a crown of love in the moment of Max and Tekla's birth: fate, therefore, determines the lovers' union above and beyond the events of human lives, just as the potion is *fatal* only due to the guilty bond of Tristan and Isolt in the most ancient version of the myth (Béroul and Eilhart von Oberge).[25] In Wagner's *Tristan und Isolde*, the fatal element undergoes a significant alteration: Isolt is meant to drink a death potion with Tristan but instead— fatally—drinks a love potion with him. But in Wagner the *Liebestrank* is always also a *Todestrank*, for Tristan and Isolt's love is conjoined to the desire for death, and death becomes its final conclusion:[26]

> When for the first time
> a loving affection,
> is born in the heart's depths
> at once the breast, languid and tired,
> a desire for death doth feel:
> how come, I know not: but such
> is the first effect of true and potent love.

Leopardi's verses are a genuine document of that religion of death which, made into a theology in Schopenhauer's thought, would become the basis of Wagner's drama, stirring up profound disturbances within

---

25 See Gertrude Schoepperle, *Tristan and Isolt: A Study of the Sources of the Romance*, 2nd EDN (New York: Franklin, 1960).

26 Giacomo Leopardi, *Amore e morte*, ll. 27–33:

> Quando novellamente
> nasce nel cor profondo
> un amoroso affetto,
> languido e stanco insiem con esso il petto
> un desiderio di morir si sente:
> come, non so: ma tale
> d'amor vero e possente è il primo effetto.

German culture after him. The parody of the artist developed by Mann in his narrative of *Tristan* does not, however, entail a resolution to such disturbances. In *Tristan*, Wagner's music is the harbinger of death, corresponding to the enmity with life to which Detlev Spinelli is led, but this does not in any way entail a radical refusal by Mann of the poetic reality created by Wagner in *Tristan und Isolde*. Mann knew very well that Wagner had drawn on the shadowy depths of myth and human experience, in which lies the ultimate justification for man's behaviour. In *Tristan*, he points to the risks of an artistic experience which annihilates any awareness of humanism as well as to those bourgeois institutions that ignore such abysses or attempt to exorcize them by merely turning their gaze the other way. Thus the myth of Tristan—which Wagner's music had evoked in a direct relation to the reality of nineteenth-century German culture and society—re-emerged both in the devotion to death and within the fate of bourgeois institutions unable to embrace or normalize the bond between love and death in a humanly lived experience.

Mann, furthermore, did not limit himself only to this accusation but directed his gaze into the very depths of myth, in the search for the healing forces which lie within its genuine essence. We owe this deepening of the myth of Tristan to the evocation of the images of the incestuous siblings which constitute, in the writer's spiritual life, the primordial archetype of Tristan and Isolt. In this sense, we could say that Mann 'explained' *Tristan und Isolde* through *Die Walküre*, because the incestuous love between Siegmund and Sieglinde represents a symbolic identity between the masculine and the feminine that counterpose the nuptial relation between Isolt and King Mark: the relation between the Kore and her abductor.

Classical mythology presents two fundamental, interlinked forms of sexual union: one exemplified through the great divine couples of wedded siblings; the other based on the rape of the virgin by the god of the underworld. The simultaneous occurrence of these two antithetical forms is one of the paradoxes of myth which draws on the depths of human being, by which sexual union demonstrates the concurrent presence of a rape, and the recognition of an identity. In the medieval versions of the Tristan myth, and in Wagner's drama, the mythic paradox is nevertheless substituted by the tragic contrast of the two primary components of the sexual relation—alienation and fraternity, rape and identification. In referring to these later evocations of the myth, Mann pedagogically utilized exactly those emblems of such a contrast, reflecting within them the crisis of bourgeois marriage, incapable of realizing the paradoxical and living unity of myth.

We might say, in other words, that Mann employed the image of adultery in order to show how the bond between love and death might acquire a destructive force, overturning the sexual relation, when this bond—in bourgeois marriage—is no longer controlled by the mythic paradox determining the union of fraternity and rape between man and woman. If marriage—as in bourgeois society—becomes no more than 'rape', it exposes itself to the destruction wreaked through the bond of love and death, which flows into the space left open by the absence of 'fraternity', of the profound identity between the betrothed. The 'raped' woman is without any defence before those forces sanctioned by law, forces that push the woman towards a 'brother' necessarily different from the 'rapist'. Alien from and in conflict with the 'rape', this force becomes a harbinger of destruction inherent in the lover–death relation: the union of the adulterous bride with her 'brother', or the incestuous union of brother and sister, are harbingers of death for they represent a limit point in the mutation of the 'humanistic' form of the sexual relation, containing within it fraternity and identity as much as rape. By analogy, sexual rape alone is of course a mutation and limitation, and therefore it too leads to anti-humanism and death.

* * *

In his autobiography *The Turn* [*Die Wendepunkt*], Klaus Mann writes: 'Whoever lives long enough and has a sensitive heart can feel tenderness for more than one face. But one can love only one face. And it is always the same face, which one recognizes among thousands.'[27] With these words, Thomas Mann's son takes up a fundamental aspect of his father's experience: the intrinsic and mysterious identity and unity of those images which, under different masks, fatally exercise a strong force of seduction over man. Such identity is already that which, in *Tonio Kröger*, unites the two people with whom the protagonist is in love—Hans Hansen and Ingeborg Holm—two 'blonde creatures with blue eyes' for whom his love becomes 'deep and secret'. But in *Tonio Kröger*, Tonio's erotic problem is thus intimately bound to the problem of the artistic condition and its relation to the bourgeois world, through intermixing the element of identity between Hans and Ingeborg who *also* symbolize 'those of a light life, the happy, lovable and communal'.[28] We

27 Klaus Mann, *Die Wendepunkt* (Frankfurt: Fischer, 1952), p. 128. 'Man mag für mancherlei Gesichter Zärtlichkeit empfinden, wenn man lange genug lebt und ein empfindendes Herz hat. Aber es gibt nur ein Gesicht, das man liebt. Es ist immer dasselbe, man erkennt es unter Tausenden.'

28 Thomas Mann, 'Tonio Kröger' in *Erzählungen* (Frankfurt: Fischer, 1958), p. 174: 'Aber mein tiefste und verstohlenste Liebe

emphasize this *also* because we have no doubt that, in *Tonio Kröger*, Mann refers to an erotic problem within which Hans and Ingeborg are not only creatures that are 'different' from the artist but also represent the final point of homosexual and heterosexual love. The same theme, furthermore, was taken up by Mann in *The Magic Mountain*, beyond the problematic of the bourgeois artist and in a way that makes the identity between the seductive images entirely explicit. Hippe, the school friend with whom the adolescent Hans Castorp falls in love, has blond hair and grey-blue eyes just like Hans Hansen, and both the colour of his eyes—'a vague and uncertain colour, comparable to that of far away mountains'[29]—and his Slavic name (Pribslav) reveals a particular identity with the young Tadzio of *Death in Venice*. The latter, on the other hand, was an instrument of the same seductive force by which Madame Chauchat touches Hans Castorp on the 'mountain'. In Castorp's meetings with Madame Chauchat, the exact events which have already come to pass in the love story of Castorp and Hippe are repeated—one thinks of the 'pencil episode'[30]—and Madame Chauchat, at the moment of her first appearance in the novel, does not show her face, because hers is the same as the 'Kyrgyz' face of Pribislav Hippe. What seems noteworthy to us, beyond the oriental reference, is the mysterious repetition by which two people with the same face but of different sexes seduce Hans Castorp in two different moments, and both at the same time coincidentally

---

gehört den Blonden und Blauäugigen, den hellen Lebendigen, den Glücklichen Liebenswürdigen und Gewöhnlichen.'

29 Mann, *Die Zauberberg*, p. 111: 'es war eine etwas unbestimmteund mehrdeutige Farbe, die Farbe etwa eines fernen Gebirges.'

30 This is an example of the use of psychoanalysis by an otherwise 'suspicious' Mann.

so; love's seduction therefore has a double face, masculine and feminine, under which is concealed a primordial identity, the mysterious reality of which is that which in *Death in Venice* Mann calls 'passion'. It is juxtaposed to 'form', being that which leads the artist to 'become a beast', and seems in the end to be that which ferments destruction. Love and death: here again we find Tristan's motif.

Whether masculine or feminine, the identity between the lovers is united in the seducer's identity— masculine and feminine, brother and sister, a being led by the passions to recognize a part of reality which includes both of the sexes, like the first living being in Platonic thought. At this primordial level, love is not susceptible to the limitations of heterosexuality and homosexuality but is merely the force which drives the loss of personality itself within a stream of destruction in which the unification of the primordial is enacted. Driving the artistic experience itself into the abyss means enacting a descent into the biological depths of being: a fall into the underworld identical to that in which he had searched for the archetypes of human passions through the passions of the canine Bauschan.

* * *

In 1906, Thomas Mann sent a story entitled *Wälsungen-blut* ['Völsung Blood'] to the *Neue Rundschau* for publication, but some scruple or other led him not to republish it in the successive collections of his writings.[31] *Wälsungenblut* is the story of a pair of incestuous twins, whose names and fate literally mirror those of the protagonists of *Die Walküre*, Siegmund and Sieglinde. Their incestuous union is, however, preceded by a performance

---

31 The novella had been previously published, as a separate edition, in 1921, after which Mann sent it to the *Neue Rundschau*.

of Wagner's work which the two of them attend on the eve of Sieglinde's wedding to a third party. In the story, the existence of a mythic precedence to the protagonists' passionate act is thus firmly emphasized, imbuing it with a primordial depth. It is a 'repetition' analogous to that of Hans Castorp's love for Hippe and Madame Chauchat; but the repetitive precedent is, in this case, explicitly mythical. In one and the other case, the repetition attests to the perennial character of the action of the primordial forces manifest in erotic passion, running through the structures of human existence like a river of destruction.

In *Tonio Kröger*, the identity between the two instruments of seduction, Hans and Ingeborg, is framed within the environment of the relations between artist and bourgeois society. In *Wälsungenblut*, however, the incest unfolds within the heart of the bourgeois world, almost as if to demonstrate the ability for the forces of destruction which lie in the depths of its being to permeate a world on the limits of its decay, forces that bourgeois society is no longer capable of exorcizing. The incestuous twins are members of an extremely rich bourgeois family in Munich, living in a house filled with precious and antique heirlooms, objects which thus take on the character of the rubble of a past, the vital relation with which bourgeois society can no longer hold on to. The wondrous antiques conserved in Siegmund and Sieglinde's home are the equivalent of the survivals of the past which furnish Patera's kingdom in Kubin's *The Other Side*. And Siegmund reveals the utmost care for his grooming and routine, behaviour that coincides with the analogous preoccupations of Thomas Buddenbrook on the edge of death: this formal impeccability is thus bourgeois society's final vain defence against the destruction represented by Thomas Buddenbrook's 'horrid' death and Siegmund and Sieglinde's incest. It is, in other words, an

extreme recourse to form against passion by men who
have also lost contact with those genuine forces of form
that might have rescued them.

The moment of healing, in which the pedagogue of
bourgeois culture opposes the healing purity of myth
(which is a force of passion and the primordial matrix of
form) to the illness and guilt of an unravelling world, is
found in another story which develops from the events
of two other incestuous twins: *The Elect* [*Der Erwählte*].
The story, in a certain sense, represents a new *Tristan*: the
world here is that of the medieval fable which, in a modern consciousness, symbolizes more than any other the
identity between myth and history. But it is also a *Tristan*
in which the greatest guilt is guaranteed salvation: an
epiphany of myth which heals the guilt and evil born
from the deformations of myth.

In *The Elect*, the 'golden' parody reveals itself through
accessing myth, in juxtaposition to the tarnished or guilty
mythology in the self-styled mythologies of the bourgeoisie. Such innovation takes on, furthermore, an explicitly linguistic character: the language in which Mann
penned *The Elect* is no longer the German of his great
novels, pure even if stylistically tuned for the necessities
of parody, but a hybrid language, a mixture of romance
and archaic German vocabularies, and set in the metric
structures appropriate to poetry (as had already been the
case in *A Man and His Dog*, according to the author's own
remarks).

The Elect tells the story of a pair of incestuous twins,
Wiligis and Sibylla, and of their son Gregorious, who
commits incest with his mother. The psychoanalytical
references in this story—amply developed by scholars—
only have any meaning if one considers the specific position of the work in the context of Mann's creative life. One
already finds a reference to the life of Pope Gregory in

Doktor Faustus; in *The Elect*, Mann deals with the theme more fully, seeing in it the possibility to resolve that looming ancient drive which the figure of Tristan represented for even him since the days of his youth. With *The Elect*, the 'descent into the biological' seems to find its deepest limit. Male and female are identified in the very instant in which the abyss of guilt is opened up by their incestuous love. The moment of their embrace, the famous nocturnal moment in which Wiligis is united with Sibylla, is preceded by a few words which we will need to cite in the original German to understand them in all their mysterious linguistic value. After Wiligis has killed the dog Hanegiff—who had been disturbed by his caressing of his sister—Wiligis reminds Sibylla that their father is dead and thus there is no one who could dare ask them to explain themselves: it is as if King Mark had died, and the embrace of Tristan and Isolte can no longer be guilty: 'No one can dare ask anything of us, now that Grimaldo has died, no one, sister-Duchess, *my sweet next-to-me myself*, my love.'[32]

To which Sibylla responds: 'Consider that he died but today and lies down there in his rigid state. Let him stay there, the night belongs to the dead.'[33]

'The night belongs to the dead': there could be no more explicit denunciation of the mutated, guilt-ridden survivals of the Romantics' Germany. In the chaos of the

32 Thomas Mann, *Der Erwählte* (Frankfurt: Fischer, 1951), p. 44: 'Uns darf niemand fragen. Seit Grimald tot ist, niemand, Schwester-Heryogin, mein süsses Neben-Ich, Geliebte.' [English translation: *The Holy Sinner* (H. T. Lowe-Porter trans.) (New York: Alfred A. Knopf, 1951), p. 40, modified. Henceforth, Lowe-Porter translation.]

33 Mann, *Der Erwählte*, p. 44: 'Bedenke, dass er erst starb und drunten starr liegt in Parade. Lass, die Nacht gehört dem Tode!' Lowe-Porter translation, p. 40.

night, Mann points to the site of horror borne out of the bourgeois evocations of myth. Thus Sibylla announces the deepest aspect of her coming guilt, the act of incest which is also proof of the horror inherent in the inter-mixing of myth with those structures of bourgeois society unable to receive it.

Wiligis responds: 'Out of death are we born, and are his children. Abandon yourself to him, oh sweet bride, to the Death-brother and grant what courtly love craves as its fulfilment.'—'*In ihm, du süsse Braut, ergib dich dem Todesbruder und gewähre, was Minne als Minnenziel begehrt!*'[34] With the Old German word *Minne* (romantic, courtly love), he begins a descent into the past which opens the road to that which the two siblings now mur-mur: 'that which is not understood and does not need to be understood.'

Death stands at the beginning of the incestuous embrace. In particular, it is the death of the mother, her act of giving life to the twins made defunct, but it is also the death implicit in the access to deformed myth and in the deformation of myth itself, and above all the notion of the mortal and destructive element at the root of every myth, that which can become the annihilation of man if man does not experience myth with the serenity of an alert, awake conscience. It is the death by which the twins are born: the identification of male and female. It is the substrate of organic being, the putrefied reality from which life is born. It is up to man to exercise that life either as an element of a dialectic with death (and thus

---

34 Mann, *Der Erwählte*, p. 44: 'Aus dem Tode sind wir geboren und sine seine Kinder. *In ihm, du süsse Braut, ergib dich dem Todesbruder und gewähre, was Minne als Minnenziel begehrt!*'. [Lowe-Porter maintains the Old German word, rendering the sentence in a faux Middle English: 'and grant what minne covets as minne-boon'. The Italian translator opts for a simpler 'amore'.]

to access morality) or as a consequence of death (and thus throw themselves into illness or guilt).

In *The Elect*, the twins' embrace is brought through Germanism and into a sphere of mythic purity of the self, independent from any moral qualifications, even if susceptible to them, via a use of language which is more romantic than Germanic, entailing the 'not understood':[35]

> *Nen frais pas. J'en duit.*
>
> *Fai le! Manjue, ne sez que est. Pernum ço bien que nus est prest!*
>
> *Est il tant bon?*
>
> *Tu le saveras. Nel poez saver sin gusteras.*
>
> *O Willo, welch Gewaffen! Ouwê, mais tu me tues! O, schäme dich! Ganz wie ein Hengst, ein Bock, ein Hahn! O fort! O, fort und fort! O engelsbub! O himmlischer Gesell!*
>
> [I shan't. I am unsure.
>
> Do it! Eat, you know not what it's like. Let us take what is there waiting for us!
>
> Is it truly so good?
>
> You cannot know unless without the tasting of 't.
>
> O Willo! O how you wound me! O shame on you! You are as a stallion, a buck, a cockerel! Oh away, away! Oh angel boy! Oh heavenly wayfarer!]

Away from the romantic 'tone' which accompanies the very moment of the embrace and guilt, language itself gradually returns to its Germanic notes just as, in *The Magic Mountain*, French dominates the intimate and revealing meeting of Hans Castorp and Madame Chauchat, then transforming into the narrator's own

---

35 Mann, *Der Erwählte*, p. 44. Lowe-Porter translation, pp. 40–1, modified. [Mann employs a mixture of French and Old German.]

German. This mutation of language[36] has a meaning which lies deep within the reality of myth and repetition (residing in the narrator), of a mythic archetype who heralds the introduction of the standard events of another reality. In *The Elect*, however, when the old romance language gives way to German, it resounds with an exclamation—*O himmlischer Gesell*! [oh heavenly wayfarer]—which also draws on the genuine character of myth. *Gesell, wüster Gesell* is the wayward one, the rogue, leading us to the 'divine trickster' [*der göttliche Schelm*], the eponymous protagonist of the study by Paul Radin, Carl Gustav Jung and Karl Kerényi on the ithyphallic protagonist of a series of stories from the Winnebago Indians.[37] In a mythological commentary on such stories, Kerényi correctly observes that the 'divine rogue' of the Winnebago recalls Herakles more than Hermes. *Schelm*, on the other hand, is not equivalent to *Gesell*, for the latter also bears the meaning 'companion', appropriate for the twins' incestuous union. The *Schelm* is the protagonist of picaresque novels (*Schelm-roman*) and the appearance of a *Gesell* in *The Elect*, seems almost 'consumed' by literary over-use. And indeed Herakles is not really so different from Hermes (in both religion as well as literature) in this 'consummation' through over-use: we have already written on his aspect as a god of the underworld and psychopomp, standing on the edge of the great beyond and who, in Euripides' *Alcestis*, reacquires his original function as intermediary between the realms.[38] That is, this

---

36 Also see p. 93 above.

37 Paul Radin, Karl Kerényi and Carl Gustav Jung, *Der göttliche Schelm. Ein indianischer Mythen-Zyklus* (Zurich: Rhein Verlag, 1954). [English translation: *The Trickster: A Study in American Indian Mythology* (London: Routledge, 1956).]

38 Jesi, 'The Thracian Herakles'.

aspect refers above all to the 'tone' of the Thracian Herakles, which probably provided the reason for the presence of his cult in the sanctuary of Dodona, next to the most ancient oracular temple. The exchange between Mann and Kerényi demonstrates a further occasion in which Hermes, in all the mythic purity of his character, keeps vigil over Mann's work. The incestuous embrace of Wiligis and Sibylla is permeated precisely by the deep, 'hermetic' value which dominates the entire story, and which confers a particularly mythic dimension on the relation of *great guilt* and *great punishment*, suggesting furthermore the Faustian 'dark gallery'.

The name of Hermes will also be attributed to another '*himmlischer Gesell*', Felix Krull (who could even be a '*göttlicher Schelm*') in the very moment in which he, like Wiligis, provides proof of his heroic virtue, granting his act of theft with a sexual overtone which, through Hermes, takes on an ancient, mythic character. The ageing author Diana Philibert, in her meeting with the adolescent Felix Krull, assumes the part of Potiphar's wife; unlike Joseph, however, Felix Krull does not hesitate to satisfy the *madame* but, rather, on his own initiative, steals from her just like the young Hermes, a god with a phallic emblem, 'god of thieves'.

The concept of the *great guilt/great punishment* seems entirely foreign to the memoirs of Felix Krull, a concept which after *Doktor Faustus* had re-emerged in *The Elect*. On the other hand, *The Confessions of Felix Krull* represents a kind of perennial 'memento' in the works of Mann, the presence of which is exactly the limit of moral reference; Krull's lack of any scruples, and the constant identification which is suggested between a captain of industry and the artist, stands as an evocation of the 'guilt' the poet can incur, as Mann had already so tragically claimed in *Death in Venice*. But the accusation, in its very statement, contains the limits of the process of healing: Felix Krull is not only a villainous human being, but even a '*himmlischer* Gesell', or a '*göttlicher* Schelm', a genuine figure of myth who heals and calms. The pure flow of myth had already engulfed the guilty embrace of Wiligis and Sibylla under the light of salvation: now it redeems the artist's own guilt, casting it out from the demonic sphere.

* * *

The particular phenomenon by which, through her epiphanies, the virgin of myth demonstrates the tendency to reveal herself as also a mother while maintaining, at the margins of her own sphere, the figure of a 'hidden' bride, has been profoundly understood by Leo Frobenius who cited in *The Head as Destiny* [*Der Kopf als Schicksal*] the words of an Abyssinian woman: 'only a woman can understand and talk about this . . .' These very words have been transcribed by Kerényi as the epigraph to his essay on Kore, as evidence and partial resolution of an analogous, not entirely rational perception. Neither Frobenius nor Kerényi, however, stopped at this point, and their intuitions on the organic reality of this paradox have provided the basis for admirable investigations. The German material which we are working on here leads us now to repropose the problem and, indeed, it seems to be provide us with the elements for an alternative response.

We would like, nevertheless, to begin at a point in the distance ('Is not the pastness of the past all the more profound, complete and fairytale-like the more immediately "before" before the present it takes place?'),* with

---

* [From the foreword to *Der Zauberberg*, p. 1: 'Aber ist der Vergangenheitscharakter einer Geschichte nicht desto tiefer,

four lines by Parmenides (Fragment 12, 3–6): 'And in the middle of these a goddess, who steers all things; For she rules over hateful birth and mixing of all things, sending female to mix with male and again the opposite, male with female.' The character of the goddess of whom Parmenides speaks is a kind of *Ananke*, a 'necessity'; and that which justifies the 'necessity' of the virgin (in which the fullness of femininity is manifested) to be both mother and bride. We have observed, however, that the virgin is 'necessarily' a mother, but that her 'necessity' to be a bride seems much weaker: the virgin's groom is 'obscure' and disappears from her sphere early on, at which point, in fact, he is not missed at all. Kore's solitary virginity, while she is also a mother, thus seems to stand in contrast with a cosmogonic, mythological structure relating to the everyday intermixing of the sexes in coitus. With the virgin mother, however, there is the possibility for much broader mythological visions, such as those observed by the Frobenius Institut's mission to Indonesia,[39] which are not truly cosmogonic but refer to the primary forms of human life, to the origins of provision and sustenance. In other words, the necessity represented by Parmenides' goddess manifests itself when the origin of human existence are in play, while the mythic virgin who runs to this necessity appears at the origins of the *continuation* of life. Kore's epiphany thus coincides with the birth of historic time, different from the time of origins, and with the participation of human beings in a continuation, rather than in the motionless instance of birth.

One might say, even if in a hypothetically, that Kore's virginity and solitude, inasmuch as it is a prerogative of

---

vollkommener und märchenhafter, je dichter 'vorher' sie spielt?' Lowe-Porter translation, p. 1, modified.]

39 See p. 67n5.

a mythic epiphany typical to historical time, contains within it the guarantee of the permanently sacral character of eroticism, *despite* the process of deconsecration implicit in the historic character of continuation. Kore's perennially virginal sexuality participates in death, and thus perennially draws on the only sacral element not susceptible to deconsecration: death. The very maternity of the virgin does not look towards the future as does the union of the sexes, for Kore's son is not the boy who becomes a man but an eternal youth: the divine youth.

If we now return to the scene of *The Elect* in which the two twins carry out their own wedding night, we can note that the scene contains symbolic elements which refer back to the image of the virgin and her 'improvised', 'obscure' groom. Before conjoining with his sister, Wiligis bathes himself in the blood of the dog Hanegiff: this is almost a substitution for the ritual blood[40] poured over the virgin before the wedding night (which in ancient wedding rituals had the value of a sacral proof of the consumation of the marriage). And when Sibylla realizes that she is pregnant, she blames the brother-groom for not having warned her of the possibility of impregnation: a possibility she thought impossible through coitus between brother and sister. All of which leads to the perception, in the union between the two twins, of an embrace which in reality is not consummated, but from which a child will be born; these are the transient relations between the virgin and her 'obscure' groom, relations that nonetheless give birth to a child. And the twins' son, Gregory, will perennially remain the divine youth: he will have sexual relations only with his mother (and therefore is essentially limited to the sphere of infancy). For as much as the

---

40 Similar to the blood recognized in Tristan's potion.

nominal protagonist of *The Elect* is Gregory, in reality the novel is a celebration of eternal femininity, in the guise of daughter, sister, bride, mother and once again wife and daughter. It is, therefore, a profound recognition of the erotic sacredness inherent to femininity, and of the contrast extant between that sacredness and the course of historical time.

All that which a man loves in the different moments of his existence and under different guises is here united in the image of the virgin who, paradoxically, is without a groom. The moment of first love thus becomes the sign of entrance into the historicity of time: the birth which leads into continuation, beyond the primordial river bed. In this context, the following words of Goethe take on very particular meaning: 'Better never to love in that time in which one still believes in being the only one who loves, and that no one else has ever loved, no one else will love as we do.' The virgin has taken the youth for her self—the divine youth—in a mythic vision which—and this is the 'necessity'—brings together the two poles of human experience: historical continuation and the motionless time of the primordial.

* * *

Again you show yourselves, oh flickering phantasms, revealed to my vision as in youth, still engulfed in clouds. Shall I attempt this time to hold you fast? Can this graceful madness still make my heart palpitate? You crowd so near! Very well: from out of your mists and clouds, you overpower my thought! The magic breath breathes within, shaking my breast with a thrill of youth.

> You bring with you the images of halcyon
> days, and more than one beloved rises up. First
> love returns.[41]

This is the dedication to *Faust*; a dedication that bridges the distance between Goethe and his protagonist, so that Goethe's past becomes eternal, contained in the instant in which it becomes Faust's present. The great descent into the Underworld begins with a song which echoes with the sound of the past, embroiling the drama in his own experience of rebirth, a drama which is otherwise characterized by the pathos for the multiplicity of people (if not of faces) who Goethe has loved.

Goethe wrote the dedication to *Faust* in his advanced old age, in a moment in which his knowledge had reached a lucidity capable of opening up deeper secrets for us. For that moment, one refers back to the finale of *Lotte in Weimar*, when Mann cited the final words of *Elective Affinities*: 'and it will be a happy moment when one day we awake once more together!' Some scholars have recognized the problem of divorce in *Elective Affinities*; but the esoteric elements of the novel must be

---

41 Goethe, *Faust*, Dedication:

> Ihr naht euch wieder, schwankende Gestalten,
> Die früh sich einst dem trüben Blick gezeigt.
> Versuch ich wohl, euch diesmal festzuhalten?
> Fühl ich mein Herz noch jenem Wahn geneigt?
> Ihr drängt euch zu! nun gut, so mögt ihr walten,
> Wie ihr aus Dunst und Nebel um mich steigt;
> Mein Busen fühlt sich jugendlich erschüttert
> Vom Zauberhauch, der euren Zug umwittert.
>
> Ihr bringt mit euch die Bilder froher Tage,
> Und manche liebe Schatten steigen auf;
> Gleich einer alten, halbverklungnen Sage
> Kommt erste Lieb.

smoothly followed along the way signposted by *Stella*—not the divorce but, rather, the multiplicity of images of love. Such multiplicity is problematic not so much from the point of view of the social institution of marriage but from the point of view of the secret forces which move in every image of love and which cannot be exorcized by the structure of a social institution. It is only in this context that one can understand a work such as *Lotte in Weimar*, and the contemplation of those forces remains the most mysterious aspect of the novel. The suggested identification between Lotte and Christiane Vulpius (one thinks to the meeting of Lotte and August) opens a small window onto the genuine revelation, and thus onto the poetic material of the novel. Thus citing Klaus Mann's autobiography,[42] in which he speaks of a single face which one truly loves (and which can reflect itself in so many human faces), it is not enough to resolve the problem. The solution lies rather in the hellish component, that of death, which determines the metamorphosis of the lover and the beloved, or those who are loved. '*Alles Vergängliche*': this is the reality of the metamorphosis, in which the stationary figure of myth opens itself up to a mysterious mutation that transcends the figure, bringing together destinies that draw on the sphere of the divine rather than that of myth. A hidden god dominates the events of the beloved, allowing them to find a common denominator in the person of the lover, who is both divine messenger, guide of the soul, 'thief' and 'man of torments'. Thus the figure of Hermes binds his spectral features and his divine paradox to the drama suffered by a mortal creature. Thus the 'thieving' lover, through many women, hands his genuine passion over to the divine psychopomp. Solitude and silence or fear and trembling signal the final stage of these

---

42 See above, p. 147.

events in the moment in which the 'first love' returns and promises a final experience. The power of life and death which the lover had over the beloved becomes the faculty to confer immortality; looking across the plains opening out before the sea, Anadyomene returns to be born again.

CHAPTER 4

Among all the works produced by German painters at the end of nineteenth century, Arnold Böcklin's painting entitled *Isle of the Dead* (*c*.1880), enjoyed exceptional notoriety, a fame that has not entirely faded away today.[1] Reproduced in countless engravings, it exercised a profound influence over all those who, throughout the final years of the nineteenth century, believed that they recognized the sign of a new era in a deliberate descent into the abyssal depths of the human soul and being: into Nietzsche's darkness, prophecies and suffering. We can recall the words of Rilke's friend 'Benvenuta'—Magda von Hattingberg—whose thought is symptomatic of those who are fascinated by such obscure depths. One day she took a Venetian gondola to the island cemetery:

> The gondola glided silently across the calm water, the evening sun already setting on the tops of the cyprus trees peeping over the cemetery walls. At home I used to have an aquatint of Böcklin's *Isle of the Dead*, and one day I wrote this fragment from *Zarathustra* along the lower border: 'This is the silent island of the sepulchres, on which stand the tombs of my youth. There I carried the evergreen crown of life.' It

---

1 *Die Toteninsel*, five versions: two in Berlin and one each in Basel, New York and Leipzig, painted between 1880 and 1886.

seemed to me that this painting was becoming a living reality . . . [2]

Madga von Hattingberg was in good spiritual company: her thought was the same as all those who, by the 1950s, had become the old men of Europe; in adorning their homes with signed canvases, they fantasized with a calm consistency not of a Cézanne and Picasso but of a Lenbach and Böcklin. In this they respected their own spiritual needs, even if these were in contrast with those imposed on them by newer customs.

Spellbound by Böcklin's mysterious evocation, they nevertheless attempted to become aware of the deep roots which bound them to the *Isle of the Dead*, immersing themselves in the dark emotions roused by the painting, rightly convinced that such emotions might guarantee a more profound spiritual bond than that determined, in the end, by a rational analysis.

In a certain 'unfortunate' sense, today we are encouraged to justify such emotions through a scientific apparatus, one whose value surely lies only in satisfying our cognitive needs, without providing us—in the best of cases—anything beyond experience itself. But so be it: thus the moment of our culture can seem either good or bad, and it is in this particular mode that we stand before the sources of such emotions. From such a point of view it is not futile to observe that the *Isle of the Dead* conserves a genuine charm for us as well, in the moment in which—maintaining our belief in the science of myth—we recognize therein a particular and dark image of the mythical floating island of Leto's labour pains and the

---

2 Magda von Hattingberg, *Rilke und Benvenuta. Ein Buch des Dankes* (Vienna: Wilhelm Andermann, 1947), p. 241.

panhellenic miracle of Apollo's birth. That is, when we recognize the *Isle of the Dead* as the mythic Delos.

The interpretation of the image of the 'island' as a symbol and place of birth is not new, but simply an original re-evaluation within the modern study of myth; in terms of German culture, Oken had already noted this interpretation in his vision of the birth of the first human being. Kerényi recalls that in Jena, at the end of 1819, Oken had lectured on the involuntary aspect of myth, according to which the first being must have 'developed in a uterus much larger than that of a human. This uterus is the sea . . . .'[3] In the sea-origin myths, the island is almost equivalent to the 'fish' or the 'ship' which Usener and Dölger recognized as perhaps the very first symbols of birth, floating on the waves of being and non-being.[4] We say 'almost' equivalent, because the island—Delos— is also a wandering *piece of land*, and therefore introduces the element of the Grandmother Earth onto the watery horizon of primordial birth.

In the history of Greek religion, the appearance of such an element within the narrative of Apollo's birth anticipates the second coming of the god to Delphi, 'womb of the earth'. And as such the bond between the god—both healer and harbinger of death—and the earth expresses a deep reality in which birth and death accumulate and intermix. Thus the *Isle of the Dead* draws on the mysteries of genuine mythology while offering to

---

3 The text of Oken's doctrine can be found in the encyclopedic journal *Isis* 4 (1819), cols 1117ff: cited by Kerényi in *Science of Mythology*, p. 56.

4 Hermann Usener, *Die Sintflutsagen* (Bonn: F. Cohen, 1899), p. 233ff; Franz Joseph Dölger, *ΙΧΘΥΣ: Das Fischsymbol in frühchristlicher Zeit*, 2nd EDN (Munich: Mohr Siebeck, 1928).

those who look upon it the fascination of a night like that in the second act of *Tristan und Isolde*, in the depth of the cypresses contained between two stony walls, as if they were the two Delphic peaks of Parnassus.

The religion of the earth—of the Grandmother—and the religion of death are both demonstrated in Böcklin's vision. The earth, the Greeks said, is the mother of dreams; and such dreams—nocturnal epiphanies of myth—overpowered Rilke: 'In Florence, Bologna, Venice and Rome, wherever, I stopped before the stones like a scholar of death, and allowed myself to learn.'[5]

Kore perhaps dominated Rilke's thought more than Demeter; but we know the mysterious identity which unites the maiden to the mother, and parthenic femininity to the earthly healer.[6] The paradox of myth, according to which virgin and mother are identified as birth and death, is the same that unites Gretchen and the Mater Gloriosa in *Faust*, resulting in the final chorus:

Eternal Feminine
Appears from on high.

The same experience of myth led Herman Broch to impose a dramatic and shameful return to the mother on his Virgil,[7] before grasping the cosmic vision of the Virgin and Son shining down on the metamorphosis of man: he wills himself to be entirely susceptible to divine intervention.

Furthermore, fate appears 'in the course' of that German culture which penetrated the reality of the mystic nights in Novalis; with Thomas Mann it even reaches

5 Magd von Hattingberg, *Rilke und Benvenuta*, p. 61.

6 See Kerényi, 'Kore' in *Science of Mythology*.

7 Broch, *Der Tod des Vergil,* p. 42ff.

the claims of a humanism founded on a 'nocturnal' experience. Such a 'course' can be understood only as a series of stages in devotion to the Grandmother:[8]

> So that your prayers disperse on his behalf
> all clouds of his mortality and let
> the highest beauty be displayed to him.

* * *

To be abandoned is the primordial experience of the foetus expelled from the mother's womb, the experience which opens the void within the human soul and its future longing for the night. On the basis of the 'maternal religion', an experience of this abandonment remains forever within the soul of the devotees, an experience which coincides with the epiphany of consciousness and the pains provoked by it in the first departure. A typical form of agony which this consciousness suffers is the dread of history which Mircea Eliade examined in her essay on the myth of the eternal return, claiming the impossibility of escaping this agony without attributing history with a transcendent form of justification—without, that is, revolting against that historical time in which the historical event of the mythic night is immersed.[9]

The birth of consciousness, on the other hand, determines the human condition in order to bind its moral sphere to the activity of consciousness itself, so that the night appears before it as painful and desolate: a place in

---

8 Dante, *Paradiso*, 33, ll. 31–3:

> perché tu ogni nube li disleghi
> di sua mortalità co' prieghi tuoi,
> sì che 'l sommo piacer li si dispieghi.

[English translation: Dante, *Paradiso* (Robert and Jean Hollander trans) (New York: Doubleday, 2000).]

9 See p. 139n22.

which man loses consciousness of himself and lies down in sleep.

In his elegy *Bread and Wine* [*Brot und Wein*], Hölderlin attempts a cosmic synthesis of this double attitude towards the night, recognizing the mediating activity between night and day in the mission of the poet who travels from land to land like the priests of Dionysus 'in the sacred night': he who, that is, keeps consciousness itself alive in the very moment of participation in the sacred reality of the darkness. Giorgio Vigolo has rightly observed that, for Hölderlin, the night is 'the period of the absence of the divine, the time of privation, in which the gods are far away, are fading and the nocturnal era of the Christian night passes over the world, something similarly to that which, in the *Phenomenology of Spirit*, Hegel will herald the era of "unhappy consciousness".[10] This observation refers us back to 'being abandoned', cosmically transferring the abandonment by the Mother into the historical abandonment of men by the gods. And the reference to Hegel seems to us to acquire still greater meaning once we recognize that, at the roots of this 'unhappy consciousness', lies the basic myth of original sin, reconfigured as the involuntary guilt of those abandoned by the Mother.

In *The Death of Virgil*, Broch unites this with the idea of guilt and shame as inherent in the return to the Mother. Virgil's humiliating experience of being carried in his sedan chair through the streets, subjected to the insults of the plebeians and especially women reminds him of his shameful childish condition of being 'carried'. These feelings of shame represent a 'pathetic' return to the Mother, revealing the hidden, shadowy guilt inherent

10 Giorgio Vigolo, 'Saggio introduttivo' to Friedrich Hölderlin, *Poesie* (Turin: Einaudi, 1958), pp. 44–5.

in the return to the womb. Both abandonment by the mother and the return to her are tied up with guilt; one cannot say that this depends only on the reaction of consciousness with the darkness because, from the point of view of consciousness, while the return to the night is imbued with guilt, it is not a return to guilt itself. There is, therefore, something which casts a value of guilt over the dynamic relations of expulsion and the return between man and Mother. The relations of man and Mother are, furthermore, always dynamic—they always consist in an expulsion or in a return—so long as man no longer remains within the maternal womb. It is in fact impossible for man, already departed form the womb, to stand before his Mother without being subject to an attraction to her, a desire to return and renew the darkness. Every epiphany of the Mother represents the manifestation of an attraction towards the night. And that—as we have seen—carries with it a secret guilt, analogous to that which coincides with primordial abandonment.

The nature of such guilt and the modality according to which it impacts human events remains in darkness. Broch's novel provides only some suggestions in these terms, when it narrates how, in the moment of his death, Virgil falls into a passivity analogous to that of a newborn child, and how the newborn is 'carried' and 'being turned'.[11] Becoming an object in the cosmos, Virgil discovers the infantile condition of the cessation of consciousness on the edge of death, of his consciousness as rendered inactive through the immense projection of the cosmic reality that participates in it, until making it an objective part of itself.

---

11 Broch, *Der Tod des Vergil*, p. 538: 'Da durfte er sich umwenden, da kam ihm der Befehl zur Umwendung, da wendete es ihm um.'

Broch says that Virgil 'is allowed to turn': this singular image is easily comprehensible inasmuch as it alludes to the *object-becoming* of man participating in death, but it would be incomprehensible in its specific meaning— why exactly to be *turned*?—if one does not also take into account the importance in the writer's language of the symbolism of Jewish esotericism.[12] Broch, in fact, was particularly sensitive to the heterodox Judaic doctrine according to which God possess two faces, and the 'demon' is truly 'the other face of God'. To be turned means—from this point of view—to be faced with 'the other face of God', that of darkness and the abyss. Attributing this second face of God with a demonic character thus leads to a misunderstanding, for this means that the *demonic face* of God is only demonic inasmuch as contemplation coincides with the annihilation of human consciousness. Jewish esoteric thought thus resembles Gnostic teachings without nonetheless accepting the Gnostic paradox of a God who sees good and evil in a transcendent synthesis. 'The other face of God' is not that of evil: Virgil is not turned towards the face of evil, but towards the abyss of divinity.

Broch, however, provides us with some suggestions concerning the problem of guilt inherent in the departure from the Mother and the return to her as acknowledged in German culture. His experience of Jewish esotericism is not common to a German culture which instead contained forms of Gnostic and Manichean thought—as denounced by Buber and were present in the works of Jung. Not even this Manichean dualism was enough, however, to exhaustively reform the relations between German artists on the one hand, and the night and the

---

12 See Ladislao Mittner, *La letteratura tedesca del Novecento* (Turin: Einaudi, 1960), p. 334ff.

Mother on the other. Hölderlin, as we have said, had already seen the absence of the divine in the night, the experience of abandonment which represents something more than mere contact with the demonic. And Novalis would recognize a reality estranged from demonism in the nocturnal darkness—as an element characterized by theological guilt—in the same moment in which he attributed the darkness with a primordial motherhood.

Novalis' 'nocturnal' lyrics, however, possess an erotic value of exceptional depth, which seems to be confirmed in Thomas Mann's work through the presence of erotic bonds between humans and the night. The erotic is the basis of *The Betrothed* [*Die Betrogene*], which Károly Kerényi's copy was inscribed with a dedication describing it as: 'A little myth about Mother Nature'.[13] The erotic stands beyond every religious relation with the Mother in the sphere of Hellenic tradition: and scholars have rightly commented on the specific dominance of the female deity over the masculine *paredroi* always pointed towards *death* and rebirth. Such an erotic element can take us very close to a resolution of the problem. The dynamic relation with the Mother—the departure and return to the maternal womb—is, as we have said, imbued with a form of guilt. This mysterious guilt can be better understood when one sees it as an erotic guilt: the 'return' represents the guilt of the sexual violator who, as with Oedipus, reacquires the fetal condition in the moment in which he re-enters the Mother; in the departure, when man repeats the expulsion of the fetus 'abandoned' by woman, as noted in genuinely mythic terms by D. H. Lawrence: 'The man lay in a mysterious stillness

---

13 See Kerényi's preface to Karl Kerényi and Thomas Mann, *Felicità difficile: un carteggio* (Ervino Pocar trans.) (Milan: Il Saggiatore, 1963), p. 40.

. . . His very stillness was peaceful. She knew that, when at last he roused and drew away from her. It was like an abandonment.'[14] And still further:

> She could only wait, wait, and moan in spirit as she felt him withdrawing, withdrawing and contracting, coming to the terrible moment in which he would slip out of her, and be gone. Whilst all her womb remained open and soft, and softly clamouring, like a sea-anemone under the tide, clamouring for him to come in again and make a fulfilment for her.[15]

For Lawrence, the anemone alludes to Kore: recall the poem 'Purple Anemones' in which the anemones are 'hell-hounds' that fascinate Kore; she pauses to pick them in the moment before her abduction by Hades.[16] The fragment cited above from *Lady Chatterley's Lover* refers to a single anemone, a marine flower-animal, immersed in the waters which rest on the borders of the Underworld.

The guilt in the relation to the Mother is perhaps the same which one finds in every erotic act, and which is 'the other face' of love: death. As we have already said in relation to God's 'other face', the dark 'other face' of love is not intrinsically demonic but coincides with the darkness of the annihilation of consciousness and the destruction of man within that flow, which, in some times and places, has been explicitly recognized as divine.

In a study of adultery myths in Greece and Egypt, we have shown that, in Western culture, the figures of the

---

14 D. H. Lawrence, *Lady Chatterley's Lover* (Cambridge: Cambridge University Press, 2002[1928]), p. 117.

15 Lawrence, *Lady Chatterley's Lover,* p. 133.

16 D. H. Lawrence, 'Purple Anemones' (1921) in *The Complete Poems* (Ware: Wordsworth Editions, 1994), pp. 244–6.

abandoned and the *evil woman* can be traced back to the same primordial image of an infernal Kore, one who also harbours some aspects of the Original Grandmother and which only later was subjected to those alterations that made her take on negative characteristics.[17] Her virginity —aside from a deep, continuous relation to a masculine figure—provided a place for the image of the *abandoned* and *rejected*; her infernal nature, now misunderstood, gave rise to the image of the *evil woman*, harbinger of death (unlike the original Kore, this figure is not a guar- antor of salvation and rebirth). And along with her, the *rejected woman*, vainly offering her embrace, seen as a form of *evil* inasmuch as she leads whoever rejects her to evil or even death: Phaedrus and Hippolytus, Stheneboea and Bellerophon, Potiphar's wife and Joseph.

The memory of the 'dangerous' bride of the first wed- ding night thus survives in the altered figure of the most ancient version of Kore as studied by ethnologists and placed by them in a relation to the ancient religious notion of the *jus primae noctis* exercised by a God. The man who attempts to substitute himself for god and deflower the bride is forced to meet such horrific obsta- cles as the 'toothed vagina' of folk tales.

However, while all of this enriches our understanding of the 'guilt' inherent in the erotic relationship (on which the 'guilt' in the relation with the Mother depends), it fails to pose any solution to the problem itself. Here we merely see that the notion of the erotic 'guilt' is extremely ancient, corresponding to the mythic and cultural formations of a certain religious experience. We remain unable to explain the profound origins of the idea of guilt which,

---

17 Furio Jesi, 'Il tentato adulterio mitico in Grecia e in Egitto', *Aegyptus* (1962): 275–96.

in Germanic culture, coincide with the relations between man and Mother.

The study of myth has nonetheless shown that to be abandoned is an experience inherently analogous to abandonment itself: the foundation of this experience is the dramatic idea of the identity and solitude of the individual with sex, the basis of the sexual union understood as violation and rape. We can say therefore that the 'guilt' of the violator and of the woman who offers herself consists in the tragic act of the man throwing himself into the void that surrounds his solitude. And because it is an erotic impulse which determines this will to overcome the limits of the Ego—and thus, implicitly, of opening oneself up to the nothingness that surrounds the Ego—it is natural that is is recognized as the 'other face' to love: that of destruction and death.

The experience of the nothingness which surrounds the Ego, made by the 'primitive' in the instant in which it passes from the stage 'thought is within me' to the stage 'I think',[18] is not intrinsically demonic; the nothingness becomes, in fact, the obscure matrix of the Other which emerged before the Ego: not only the enemy but also the member of the community, the brother. Nevertheless, in evoking the experience of the primordial, and attributing nothing but the function of limiting the Ego to the night, therefore removing from it the value the notion of collectivity, it becomes demonic. Thomas Mann warned against the dangers of this aberration when he denounced the guilt-ridden aspects of the night which pervade the second act of *Tristan und Isolde*. The night is not demonic when, as with Novalis, one intends that fertile uterus with powers that, faced with the Ego, can determine the birth

18 These are concepts from Jung. See *Science of Mythology*, pp. 86–7.

of the mysterious figure of the Other, the brother. But it becomes profoundly demonic if one establishes within it a solitude hostile to every form of Other, an experience of life which is solitary because it carries with it the rejection of every fraternal Other.

Gottfried Benn represents a truly emblematic figure of this demonic access to the Night—excluding every Other, recognizing only the Ego and substituting it with the impersonal '*Es*'.* His name is relevant here, now that we have referred to prehistory and the origins of the solitude of the Ego, in order to recall the Jungian concept of the passage from 'thought is within me' to 'I think.' Benn, in fact, frequently referred to his teachings on solitude, recalling not only Jung but also, apologetically, the prelogical, 'mystically involved' theories of Lévy-Bruhl, which for him became a condition of a paradise lost, surviving in the experience of the pcet.[19] As such, the poet is thus disposed to submerging their own Ego in the '*Es*' ('it becomes experienced'), repeating in reverse the course of human spirit's metamorphosis. Ronne, the medical protagonist of the novellas written by Benn in 1915–16, 'only knew the rhythmic self-opening and self-closing of the Ego and of the personality, the eternal voyage of the inner being which, faced with the sentiments of a profound, unconfined and mythically bound estrangement of people from the world, believed unconditionally in myths and their imagery.'[20] Benn, however,

---

* It is worth nothing that Jesi uses the Italian 'Io' for I/Ego, whereas he employs the German 'Es' for It/Id.

19 Gottfried Benn, 'Zur Problematik des Dichterischen' [1930] in *Sämtliche Werke. Band III* (Stuttgart: Klett-Cotta, 1987), pp. 232–47.

20 Gottfried Benn, 'Epilog und lyrisches Ich' [1921] in *Sämtliche Werke. Band III*, pp. 127–33: 'der nur das rythmische Sichöffen und

attempted an extreme moral exorcism, leading again to the concept of the 'laws of the form-imposing force of nothingness.' The fertility from which form is born is intrinsic to this nothingness. But this approach must not be confused with that which we have described as the non-demonic access to the Night; for Gottfried Benn, *form* is born from the nothingness: not the brother, and not even his negative—the *form*, rather, is that which Benn would recognize as Stefan George's greatest virtue in *Algabal*, and it is this that remains estranged from every possibility of brotherhood in the poem.[21]

Limiting ourselves to recognizing the demonism of Benn's approach and his moral guilt is not enough to penetrate to the very depths of the poet's experience, essentially a religious experience. And it is the religion of death: for Benn the devotee, death becomes a matrix of forms, one which does not redeem man but allows him the only possible remaining option—self-expression.[22]

Every religious experience brings a peculiar mode of being with it for the devotee. Benn's 'lifestyle' was that of those 'for whom all of life is a call from the depths, from

---

Sichverschliessen des Ichs und der Persönlichkeit kannte, das fortwährend Gebrochene des inneren Seins und der vor das Erlebnis von der tiefen, schrankenlosen mythenalten Fremdheit zwischen dem Menschen und der Welt gestellt, unbedingt den Mythen und ihren Bildern glaubt.'

21 (i) 'Gesetz, der formfordernden Gewalt des Nichts': Gottfried Benn, 'Akademie-Rede' [1932] in *Sämtliche Werke. Band III*, pp. 386–93. (ii) See Gottfeied Benn, 'Rede auf Stefan George' in *Sämtliche Werke. Band IV* (Stuttgart: Klett-Cotta, 2001), pp. 377–82.

22 Gottfried Benn, *Doppelleben* [1950] in *Sämtliche Werke. Band V* (Stuttgart: Klett-Cotta, 1991). Also see Mario Pensa, *Stefan George: Saggio critico* (Bologna: Zanichelli, 1961), pp. 27–8, and p. 28n1.

ancient and early depth, and every moment is equivalent to an unknown experience, a search for memories from within him.'[23] To grasp a religious experiences implies, however, a necessary moral evaluation in the same instant in which one participates intellectually in the 'lifestyle' of the devotee. Faced with Benn's religious experience, such moral evaluation once again proposes the problem of the foundation of a humanistic access to myth—the problem which we have already confronted in Chapter 1; the formulation of Benn's thought seems to harmonize with that which we had defined as 'access to genuine myth' while also implying an approach by which anti-humanity is revealed through the adhesion of the poet to Nazism.

It is very difficult to place Benn among the technifiers of myth: the genuineness of his hearing the 'call from the depths' is beyond doubt, and his biography never attests to any deliberate alteration of myth for contingent ends. At the same time, the majority of scholars who have investigated his creative activities have agreed in recognizing in him, long before the events of Nazism, an acceptance of the presuppositions on which Hitler's ideology would be founded. This is—we believe—a misinterpretation entirely to Nazism's advantage: that is, it is a misinterpretation which leads to attributing Nazism with profound— even if culpable—ideological foundations and structures, rather than recognizing in it a criminal phenomenon alien from every ideology, deprived of spiritual form. It is, in the end, the misinterpretation into which some defenders of humanism have fallen, attributing their adversaries

---

23 Benn, 'Zur Problematik des Dichterischen', p. 247: 'Für den alles Leben nur ein Rufen aus der Tiefe ist, einer und frühen Tiefe, und alles Vergängliche nur ein Gleichnis eines unbekannten Erlebnisses, das sich in ihm Erinnerungen sucht.'

(even if in all good faith) with a non-existent spiritual dignity, and recognizing in Nazism an extreme and monstrous offshoot of the anti-humanist irrationalism latent within Germanic culture.

Given the importance of this theme, we will take the opportunity to dedicate the following chapter to it. At this point, however, it seems necessary to make the argument that Nazi-Fascism was entirely a phenomenon of base criminality, and that intellectuals' adherence to it represented simply the participation of educated but sick souls under the guidance of a group of delinquents alienated from any intellectual experience.

* * *

In the framework of the metamorphoses undergone by the Mother, Gottfried Benn's thought, focusing on the 'laws of the form-imposing force of nothingness', represents an alternative intellectual event generated from the experience of 'being abandoned', that is, the religion of the Mother. In order for this to become clearer, it is useful to recall the poem 'Menon's Lament for Diotima' ['Menons Klagen um Diotima'] in which Hölderlin constructed a creative, poetic act on the basis of abandonment as a religious experience. The course of this poem demonstrates, in fact, the passage from the desperation determined by the abandonment to the return of calmness through finding mysterious healing forces within the abandoned being once more. Such healing forces are not accessible through a revolt against the abandonment:[24]

---

24 Friedrich Hölderlin, 'Meinos Klagen um Diotima' in *Sämtliche Werke. Band II* (Stuttgart: Kohlhammer, 1953), pp. 78–83 [Original translation; for a full version, see *Hyperion and Selected Poems* (Eric Santner ed., Michael Hamburger trans.) (New York: Continuum, 2002), pp. 169–177, verse 2]:

It will not do, you gods of death! When once
You have taken and caught the wounded man,
When, you evils, you have taken him into the
    horrific night,
Then either he tries to flee and rage against you,
Or patiently live with you in that terrifying
    captivity,
And smiling, hear your austere song.
If it thus, you forget your well-being in soundless
    slumber!
But nonetheless a song of hope arises in your
    breast,
You cannot but—oh my soul!—still you cannot
Accustom yourself to this, dreaming in an iron
    sleep!

To dream 'in an iron sleep' of being abandoned—for
the night is the abandonment, and the absence of gods—
meaning exactly to fulfil the mission of the poet who
awakes and wanders in the night. The poet's waking is a
'dream' inasmuch as it is a 'trance' (as Benn wrote), being
a priori knowledge: the dream is thus a form of waking
more lucid than that usually granted to normal mortals.
For the poet who awakes—or 'dreams'—the mysterious

Ja! Es frommet auch nicht, ihr Todesgötter! wenn einmal
Ihr ihn haltet und fest habt den bezwungenen Mann,
Wenn ihr Bösen hinab in die schaurige Nacht ihn genommen,
Dann zu suchen, zu flehn, oder zu zürnen mit euch,
Oder geduldig auch wohl im furchtsamen Banne zu wohnen,
Und mit Lächeln von euch hören das nürchterne Lied.
Soll es sein, so vergiss dein Heil, und schlummere klanglos!
Aber doch quillt ein Laut hoffend im Busen die auf,
Immer kannst du noch nicht, o meine Selle! Noch kannst du's
Nicht gewohnen, und träumst mitten im eisernen Schlaf!]

paradox of the nothingness is unveiled, out of which forms emerge. He is alone, abandoned:[25]

> I want to celebrate, but what? And to sing with others,
> But, thus alone, I lack anything divine within me.
> This, this is my wrong-doing, I know, an anathema lames me
> And thus my tendons, and I begin to prostrate myself . . .

But 'more immortal still than care and anger, is joy.'[26] A secret force calms Hölderlin at the peak of his solitude:[27]

> and finally
> From the light breast the singer's prayer returns and expires.
> And how, when I was with her, standing on the sunlit peaks
> A god from within the temple spoke and vitalized me.

For this, Hölderlin thanks Diotima, who he lost when he began his experience of being abandoned but who he indicates as 'singing with more joy than the gods,

---

25 Hölderlin, 'Meinos Klagen um Diotima', verse 5:

Feiern möcht' ihr: aber wofür? Und singen mit andern,
Aber so einsam fehlt jegliches Göttliche mir.
Dies ists, dies mein Gebrechen, ich weiss, es lähmet ein Fluch mir
Darum die Sehnen, und wirft, wo ich beginne, mich hin . . .

26 Hölderlin, 'Meinos Klagen um Diotima', verse 8: 'dass unsterbilcher doch, denn Sorg und Zürnen, die Freude.'

27 Hölderlin, 'Meinos Klagen um Diotima', verse 9:

. . . und endlich
Atmet aus leichter Brust wieder des Sängers Gebet.
Und wie, wenn ich mit ihr, aus sonniger Höhe mit ihr stand,
Spricht belebend ein Gott innen vom Tempel mich an.

and silent as them.'[28] This is the fundamental concept which approaches the poet's 'mode of being', the religious 'lifestyle': he sings of gods yet is also silent like them. The silence of the gods is the night, the nothingness, that which stands before the solitary Ego. But when the poet is sympathetic to this nothingness and silent 'like the gods', he 'sings of the gods', and the forms emerging from the nothingness are welcomed in his silent voice.

The fecundity of the nothingness, in Hölderlin's poem, is personified through Diotima, and the bond which unites the poet to such fecundity is his love for her; thus, it is the ancient bond which unites him to the woman, the Mother by whom they have been abandoned. And thus Gundolf quite rightly recognizes that, at the basis of Hölderlin's Hellenic sentiment, stands Lessing's notion of Hellenicity as the 'site' of exemplary forms.[29] Goethe's monologue in *Lotte in Weimar* emphasizes the presence of a religion of death in Winckelmann's neo-classicism, and therefore of a particularly profound experience of devotion to Hellenism, that experienced by Lessing. The 'exemplary forms' thus become overcast by a mysterious matrix of death, the night and the nothingness, and it is in these that the poet participates in the event, by means of the 'exemplary forms' of consciousness prior to being.

---

28 Hölderlin, 'Meinos Klagen um Diotima', verse 7:

froher die Götter zu singen,
Schweigend, wie Sie.

29 Friedrich Gundolf, *Hölderlins Archipelagus* (Heidelberg: Weiss'sche Universitäts-Buchhandlung, 1916). Gundolf emphasizes the originality of Hölderlin's 'a priori' Hellenism while also searching for precedents to his desire for a Hellenic rebirth.

The Mother's uterus is thus the seat of nothing, and the religion of the Mother entails this experience as a sea in which destruction is the prerequisite for the consciousness of form. Herder had already spoken of a historical relation between nature and destiny. The Mother is Nature, and the recognition of such an identity transfers the relation between nature and destiny onto a metaphysical level, becoming an obligatory rule for the life of the poet, situating the bond between landscape and human drama in a revelatory light, to which we have already referred in Chapter 3 in relation to *Effi Briest*.

Destruction as a condition of access to form: here we find ourselves in the camp of the dialectics on which *Death in Venice* is based. In that narrative, Thomas Mann had shown destruction and form as alternating stages of an inevitable rhythm marking out the poet's life. If one recognizes that the form is born from the nothingness via a law inherent to its very nature, the life of Gustav von Aschenbach becomes paradigmatic of the suffering imposed on the artist by being as such.

In his essay on Chekhov, some decades after *Death in Venice*, Mann expressed his faith in form with dramatic clarity as the extreme inheritance of bourgeois humanism; a disenchanted faith, deprived of certainty in the redemptive faculties of form: 'It is like this: one delights in a lost world with such story-telling, without offering even a shadow of salvational truth. Poor Katya's question—'What ought I do?'—receives no other response but:

> On my honour and conscience, I do not know.
> And yet one works, one tells stories, one shapes
> the truth and thus one changes a miserable
> world, in the obscure hope, almost in the faith,
> that truth and serenity to form might have an

emancipatory power over the soul and the ability to prepare the world for a better existence, a more beautiful one, lighter on the spirit.[30]

Even when faith is not a certainty, for Mann, it represented the only guide available. This uncertainty is due to the terrifying mystery of the religious experience—in terms of the religion of the Mother—which allows form to arise from destruction. This is no longer faith in the 'material' of myth, but in that mythic force that determines form. It is thus again the drama of music—the drama of *Doktor Faustus*—for it is in music that this myth of 'formal laws' takes place, rather than in the material, in 'people', neither created nor primary. The laws of form are mythical, something primordial surviving in magic, like a sacred relation of numbers. Just like humanist thought and language: a sacred relation of numbers, not unlike the magic square which Adrian Leverkühn puts up on the walls of his room. This too pretends to be universal, founded on the inevitable, like a numeric relation.

But humanistic faith in the moral goodness of form is inherently ambiguous, even if in Mann's case it is founded on a unilateral and wilful choice. One can wilfully hope in form as a guarantor of the good, and act in a mode which becomes as such; but form is in itself able to contain everything that is evil as well as good. Through this objective acceptance, it functions as the locus of Abraxas' epiphany, the God-Demon evoked in Hesse's *Demian*. Abraxas' access to devotion in *Demian* is conditioned by the love for a Mother in whose uterus lies the sea of nothingness: the primordial egg floats upon that sea, from which the mythic bird will emerge, a form generated from the nothingness, a form in which man

---

30 Thomas Mann, 'Versuch über Tschechow' [1954] in *Essays VI. Meine Zeit, 1945–1955* (Hermann Kurzke and Stephan Stachorski eds) (Frankfurt: S. Fischer, 1997), pp. 260–79.

recognizes himself in the same instant in which he destroys his Ego; as such that which is born from nothing, from the Mother's nocturnal womb, is that which we fundamentally are, which Broch's dying Virgil saw in the arms of the Virgin: 'the undetermined eternal: the young boy'.[31]

The consciousness of the religious experience of the nothingness as the matrix of form cannot be exhausted in the evocation of the religion of the Mother; or, at least, the religion of the Mother seems frequently to allow the devotees the perception of an extra-human abyss which opens up beyond the images of its mysteries. Having recalled Holderlin's notion of the Night as the absence of the gods, we do well to look towards Benn's *Ptolemy's Disciple* [*Der Ptolemäer*]:

> One morning he got up, the rooster sang, it sang three times, it clearly cried of treachery—but there was no one to betray or be betrayed. Everyone was asleep, the prophet and the prophesised; dew lay on the Mount of Olives, the palms whispered with an imperceptible breeze —then a dove took flight, the Holy Spirit, its wings beating, disappearing into the cloud, never to return—the dogma was dead. I thought I saw something similar before me. Another such moment, a moment in which something pulls back from the earth: spirit or God or that which once had been human being.[32]

---

31 Jung and Kerényi, *Science of Mythology*. p. 82.

32 Gottfried Benn, *Der Ptolemäer: Berline Novelle* [1947] in *Sämtliche Werke. Band V* (Stuttgart: Klett-Cotta, 1991), p. 20: 'Ein Morgen erhob sich, der Hahn krähte dreimal, er schrie geradezu nach Verrat—aber niemand war mehr da, der verraten werden konnte oder der verriet. Alles schlief, der Prophet und die

It is very likely that Benn refers here directly to Hölderlin; unlike Hölderlin, however, he has excluded the possibility of a return of the gods and the ceasing of the Night. This does not mean, however, that his thought negates the possibility of contemplating the divine; in the poem 'The Voice Behind the Curtain' [*Die Stimme hinter dem Vorhang*], God replies to those who have questioned him, saying to his children: 'You say that I have made you? This is a far too personal and mechanical way of seeing things, I certainly didn't think about you . . . Children are an alien people, you will have to go back to something older than me if you want to speak about creation.'[33] It has been said that this 'something' older than God is Being, the eternal father and mother of man's existence. But God too, the Darkness ('der Dunkle') possesses the attribute of Being itself for Benn:[34]

and only the Darkness remains in his place.

The task is thus, in Benn's thought, to divide the *deus absconditus* from Being; Benn, nonetheless, was a fervent pupil of Nietzsche, and it seems unlikely that in invoking

---

Prophezeiten; auf dem Oelberg lag Tau, die Palmen reuschten in einem unfühlbaren Wind—da flog eine Taube empor, Spiritus Sanctus, ihre Flügel schwirrten und die Wolken nahmen sie auf, sie kehrte nicht mehr zuück—das Dogma war zu Ende. Etwas ähnliches sah ich vor mir. Wieder war eine solche Stunde da, eine Stunde in der sich etwas abzog von der Erde: der Geist oder die Götter, oder das, was menschliches Wesen gewesen war.' [Original translation].

33 Gottfried Benn, 'Die Stimme hinter dem Vorhang' in *Sämtliche Werke. Band VII/1* (Stuttgart: Klett-Cotta, 2003), p. 154 [Original translation].

34 Gottfried Benn, 'Der Dunkle' [1950] in *Sämtliche Werke. Band I* (Stuttgart: Klett-Cotta, 1986), p. 270: 'Und nur der Dunkle harrt auf seiner Stelle' [Original translation].

the 'dark God' he would not have thought of the 'unknown God' to whom Nietzsche himself dedicated a poem:[35]

> Deeply engraved upon [these altars]
> Are the glowing words: 'To the unknown God'.
> I am his, even if till now
> I have stood in the ranks of the wicked:
> I am his and feel the ties,
> Which bring me down in struggle
> And, if I want to flee,
> Force me to yield and serve him.
> I want to know you, Unknown one,
> You, who penetrate deep into my soul
> Blowing through my life like a storm
> You, oh ungraspable kindred!
> I want to know and serve you!

Certainly, the claim 'I want to know you, Unknown one' might seem to openly run against Benn's 'dark God';

---

35 Friedrich Nietzsche, 'Dem Unbekannten Gott' [1863–64] in *Sämtliche Gedichte* (Zurich: Manesse, 1999), p. 61.

> Darauf erglüht tief eingeschrieben
> Das Wort: Dem unbekannten Gotte.
> Sein bin ich, ob ich in der Frevler Rotte
> Auch bis zur Stunde bin geblieben:
> Sein bin ich—und ich fühl' die Schlingen,
> Die mich im Kampf darniederziehen
> Und, mag ich fliehn,
> Mich doch zu seinem Dienste zwingen.
> Ich will dich kennen, Unbekannter,
> Du tief in meine Seele Greifender,
> [Mein Leben] wie ein Sturn Durchschweifender,
> Du Unfassbarer mir Verwandter!
> Ich will dich kennen, selbst die dienen!

[Note that in the Rodolfo Paoli's Italian translation, used by Jesi, the words 'Mein Leben' are omitted, which I have rendered in the English.]

but, on second glance, such a contrast depends above all on the consequences of the assumed substitution of God with Being at the peak of physical and metaphysical reality, a substitution which Benn never explicitly made. If at this peak there is truly Being and not the 'dark God', it would make no sense in Benn to want to know this 'darkness'. But Benn only claimed that 'if one speaks of creation', then one would need to go back 'to something older' than God. The misunderstanding is born from this. 'Something older' does not necessarily mean something *closer*. Thus Benn wrote in his essay 'The Construction of Personality' ['Der Aufbau der Persönlichkeit'] that the 'geological' strata of the human being—that which conserves 'the remains and traces of past stages of evolution'[36]—is strictly limited to man, alien to every divine sphere. Even when Benn claims in the *Essays* that 'there is [. . .] only *Ananke*: only an attempt at breaking through bodies: swelling, whether phallic or central, only a transcendence: the transcendence of sphinx-like desire',[37] he speaks of man and of that which enters into man's surroundings. This could mean, by elimination, that which is defined as a symptom of victory or of frustration, but it also includes the recognition of any discourse relating to the divine. Such a discourse is found in a poem by Benn in which he speaks explicitly of God:[38]

---

36 Benn, 'Der Aufbau der Persönlichkeit' in *Sämtliche Werke. Band III*, p. 267: 'die Reste und Spuren früherer Entiwcklungsstufen'.

37 Benn, 'Zur Problematik des Dichterischen', p. 237: 'Es gibt [. . .] nur eine Ananke: den Körper, nur einen Durchbruchsversuch: die Schwellungen, die phallischen und die zentralen, nur eine Transzendenz: die Transzendenz der sphingoiden Lust.'

38 Benn, 'Der Dunkle', pp. 268–70:

> Hier spricht der Dunkle, dem wir nie begegnen,
> erst hebt er uns, indem er uns verführt,

The Darkness speaks here, that which we never
    encounter
until it rouses us by seducing us,
regardless of whether it is dream, blessing or
    curse,
by which it leaves everything human
    undisturbed.
   . . .

Myths by Incas and Zanzibarians,
the saga of the flood surrounds and stays
    peoples—
indeed, no one has ever truly experienced
something which does not pass before the
    Darkness.
   . . .

And now it has begun the tightly closed cycle
trudging, tragic, quickening,
perceiving the great return
and only the Darkness remains in its place.

This poem is a 'discourse on the divine' precisely
because it provides no response, other than in a negative

---

doch ob es Träume sind, ob Fluch, ob Segen,
das lässt er alles menschlich unberührt.
   . . .
Mythen bei Inkas und bei Sansibaren,
die Sintflutsage rings und völkerstet—
doch keiner hat noch etwas je erfahren,
das vor dem Dunkeln nicht vorübergeht.
   . . .
Und nun beginnt der enggezogene Kreis,
der trächtige, der tragische, der schnelle,
der von der grossen Wiederholung weiss—
und nur der Dunkle harrt auf seiner Stelle.
[Original translation]

form, to the question 'Who is God?' In his essay on Heinrich Mann, Benn had already written:

> In my village, everything had been bound up with either God or death and never with anything worldly. Every thing had its place and was rooted there in the heart of the earth. Until the plague of knowledge struck me: it didn't happen in any particular place, everything occurred merely in my brain. There, things began to vacillate, becoming despicable, unworthy of any consideration. And even the big things: who is God? what is death? Little things. Heraldic beasts. Words from my mother's mouth.[39]

Benn thus warns us: it is a profanation for man to attempt a positive discourse regarding God, that is, if one attempts to respond to the question 'who is God?' with any words other than a general admission of obscurity.

> This distance from God, as I envision it, is pure reverence for the Great Being. Remaining continually fixed with our look and lips upon him is, to my eyes, a serious profanation, for it presupposes that we mean something to him, while my own reverence accepts that he passes through us,

---

39 Gottfried Benn, 'H. Mann. Ein Untergang' [1913] in *Sämtliche Werke. Band III*, p. 26: 'Früher in meinem Dorf wurde jedes Ding nur mit Gott oder dem Tod verknüpft und nie mit einer Irdischkeit. Da standen die Dinge fest auf ihrem Platze und reichten bis in das Herz der Erde. Bis mich die Seuche der Erkenntnis schlug; es geht mirgends vor; es geschieht alles nur in meinem Gehirn. Da fingen die Dinge an zu schwanken, wurden verächtlich und kaum Ansehens wert. Und selber die grossen Dinge: wer ist Gott? und wer ist der Tod? Kleinigkeiten. Wappentiere. Worte aus meiner Mutter Mund.' [Orginal translation.]

in the slightest of ways, and then he passes through to something different.[40]

Here, therefore, we find the limit point of the religious experience of the nothingness, an intuition of the abyss which remains 'beyond the nothing'. In his book *The Religion of the Greeks and Romans* [*Die Antike Religion*], Kerényi emphasizes the fact that, in the figure of Hades, the Greeks gave form also to non-being, interpreting this as a kind of being.[41] An analogous phenomenon was experienced by those who saw in the nothingness an eternal matrix of forms, and thus being itself in power. In his conception of the divine, Benn goes beyond this, glimpsing a nothingness beyond the nothing: the *true* divine nothingness, beyond that image of nothing of which men can conceive. Attributing God's name to such a human concept of nothingness is blasphemy: it is 'God covering over shame like a glass dome over a cheese.'[42]

* * *

Everything passes before the Darkness, it only remains eternal, unmoving. 'Der grosse Wiederholung', the great return, passing in front of its unmoving character. This juxtaposition between the unmoving Darkness and human

---

40 Benn, *Doppelleben*, pp. 190–1: 'Diese Distanz zu Gott, wie sie mit vorschwebt, ist eine reine Ehrfucht vor dem grossen Wesen. Ihn fortgesetzt mit Blicken und Lippen anzustarren, ist in meinen Augen ein grosser Frevel, es setzt ja voraus, dass wir überhaupt etwas für ihn sind, während meine Ehrfurcht annimmt, er geht nur mit etwas, einem geringen etwas, durch uns hindurch, und dann geht er auch zu etwas anderem.' [Orginal translation.]

41 Kerényi, *The Religion of the Greeks and Romans*, p. 124.

42 Gottfried Benn, 'Der Arzt III' in *Sämtliche Werke. Band I*, p. 88: 'Gott als Käseglocke auf die Scham gestülpt.'

events conceived as a 'great return' or 'eternal return' is extremely revealing, for it allows us to understand the religious meaning of *repetition*, which scholars have usually examined only from the standpoint of the aesthetic and creative technique, for example, in Wagner or in Mann.

It is by now hackneyed to note that the technique of *Leitmotiv* and repetition coincides with a reference to myth whose value has been amply demonstrated by religious studies in the mythic-cultural disciplines. It can almost be taken for granted that myth manifests itself in human experience under the form of repetition, of rhythmic and always renewed epiphanies. All of Thomas Mann's work, with its recurrent motifs, already demonstrated by scholars, provide the richest document of the access to myth via repetition in an artistic creation.

It has still not been noticed, however, that the repetition in mythic epiphanies presupposes, in modern German culture,[43] the concept of a divine 'Darkness'. Only if one believes that God is 'Darkness' and forever unmoving beyond the limits of nothingness is one able to interpret human experience as essentially a series of repetitive mythic epiphanies. Attributing an 'eternal return' to the epiphanies of myth, implies God's immobile, static character, distanced from men; for, if matters were not as such, if God were in some way accessible, he would be situated in myth's intrinsic reality.

Thomas Mann's religion is an obscure part of his spirit's adventure, on which he was never disposed to shed any light. Without doubt he always escaped from that form of guilt that Benn denounced, that of 'remaining continually fixed with our gaze and lips upon God'. God

---

43 We want to limit ourselves here for this is not the place to confront a more general problem.

is rarely included by name or image in Mann's works, save perhaps in the Joseph novels, in which God is nevertheless not spoken of as such but, rather, 'the Biblical God' who, in the framework of the narratives, evidently pertains to myth as much as the ancient Greek and Egyptian gods, and as such is included within a 'golden' parody. Similarly in *Doktor Faustus*—a novel which Kerényi described as 'Christian'[44]—God is cited only once; *Doktor Faustus* is indeed a religious work, of pain and confession in the Christian sense, but God remains as Darkness in the novel, unnamed, and religion is above all a human experience in the face of the unknown.

Such darkness, applied to the divine, is thus so deep—and even, for the human gaze, a nothing beyond the nothing—that it stops us from understanding the boundary of Mann's religious experience as anything other than 'the dark God'. Identifying this attitude in the writer allows us, however, to interpret the religious meaning of mythological repetition, that is, a constant in artistic creation: from this point of view, for the artist, creation is the essential 'religious' part of the ritual on which he establishes his human life.

The gods of myth who emerge in this ritual are precisely 'gods of myth', perennial structures of a dark flow that pours forth from the sources of myth: Hermes and Kore, the Grandmother, Apollo—not only God but also the experience of the divine, contained within the sphere of myth. These are 'the gods', not God. It seems as such that history, through the event of monotheism, selected the Jewish religious experience from out of Western culture, that of a single and unknown god as the paradigm for a notion of the divine, alien to myth, and therefore

44 See Kerényi's preface to Kerényi and Mann, *Felicità difficile*, pp. 38–9.

opposed to that of the Greeks. Men such as Mann, Rilke and Broch, who felt themselves to be heirs both to such monotheism and to Greek survivals, resolved this conflict in different ways. But for as different as the solutions which these artists found, it seems that all sides held onto the highest point of the ancient, Jewish notion of divinity. Like Mann, Rilke in the *Duino Elegies* did not name God even though previously he had often confronted the problem of the Christian God with 'sympathetic' turmoil, in the Greek sense of the word. Rilke's utmost creative experience was overshadowed by the 'dark God' who he never named: instead, he evoked the angels—not Christian angels, just as the angels who speak in the prelude to *Joseph and His Brothers* are not Christian. These angels are precisely the result of the difficult relation between myth and divinity: hybrid creatures 'similar to God' who, at the same time, can be conceived by man (as terrifying), and who thus do not in essence reflect God. In the final elegy, Rilke attempts to overcome the conflict between myth and divinity, carrying out a process of 'healing' through the image of the angels and situating the human story, in life and death, under the dark and unknowable sky of an unnamed and 'dark God'.

Herman Broch, having recognized myth as Virgil's divine experience on the edge of death in *The Death of Virgil*, turned to the Hasidic image of 'the magician of active love' in his subsequent novels, juxtaposing the Virgilian 'demiurgic magician' with the possibility of accessing the divine through the mythic, 'dark' imagery of God:[45]

---

45 Herbert Broch, *Der Schuldlosen* (Frankfurt: Suhrkamp, 1976 [1950]), p. 243: 'Mir jedoch gelte kein Gebet; Ich höre es nicht: sei fromm um Meinetwillen, selbst ohne Zugang zu Mir; das sei dein Anstand, die stolze Demut, die dich zum Menschen macht . . . Und

... But no one turns to Me to pray; I do not hear it. Be pious, for my sake, even without a way into Me; this would be your decorum, that proud humility, which makes you human. [. . .] And see: that is enough.

* * *

If the 'dark God' stands at the peaks of divinity, the space of existence consigned to men is thus the place of an eternal return of the figure of myth, which allows man to draw on the depths of being. God remains distant from being and non-being: it is the nothing beyond the nothing.

In the introduction to *The Magic Mountain*, Thomas Mann claims that the story which existed from the start was that of Hans Castorp; it is *his* story: 'not every story happens to everyone'.[46] Thus, with the observation of the mysterious personal value assumed in the confrontation of man with mythic epiphany, Mann recognizes the importance of the 'coincidence' of being's consciousness of itself, and the objective reality of myth inherent in history. Such an objective reality necessarily coincides with each personal life event, for it derives from the intrinsic nature of mythic epiphany, from within which man draws on its being, that which is 'community' in the same instance that it is also 'individual'. Jung's great intuitive idea—the collective unconscious—has rightly been exorcized by Buber[47] through reference to Heraclitus' thought,

---

siehe, das genügt' [Original translation]. See Ladislao Mittner, *La letteratura tedesca del Novecento* (Turin: Einaudi, 1960), p. 336.

46 Mann, *Die Zauberberg*, p. 3: 'nicht jedem jede Geschichte passiert.'

47 Martin Buber, 'Dem Gemeinschaftlichen folgen' in *Werkausgabe. Band VI* (Asher Biemann ed.) (Gütersloh: Gütersloher Verlaghaus, 2003), pp. 103–123 [English translation: 'What Is Common to All' in *The Knowledge of Man: Selected Essays* (Maurice

according to which men in a state of waking have a cosmos in common: *the* cosmos. Even in this instance, we are in the arena of myth and its faculty to determine a collective experience of being. Mann wrote, again, in the introduction to *The Magic Mountain*, 'Is not the pastness of the past all the more profound, complete and fairytale-like the more immediately it falls before the present? Furthermore, it might be that our own story, by its very nature, has here and there been formed along with fairy tales.'[48]

The reality of the 'dark God', casting its shadow from an unmeasurable distance over the mythic epiphany, reveals its continually unmoving character in the moment in which myth manifests itself as eternal return. Beyond human experience, far from the most distant borders of humanity, the God lasts forever, unnamed. Through the law of contrasts, *raison d'etre* derives from this mobility— the perennial dynamic of myth, which is not divine. Thus myth can open up an experience of horror as in *Wälsungenblut*, in which Wagner's music becomes the intrinsically fertile prototype of the leitmotifs, the seeds of repetition. In *Wälsungenblut*, the guilt of myth is not denounced—for here myth is susceptible neither to good nor evil. Instead, it is the guilt of men that transforms the divine darkness into a faculty that allows good and evil to enter myth. In Hesse's *Demian*, such a faculty becomes a divine norm, and as such the dark God hides behind the gnostic paradox of the Demon-God.

Friedman and Ronald Gregor Smith trans) (New York: Harper and Row, 1965), pp. 79–99.]

48 Mann, *Die Zauberberg*, p. 3: 'Aber ist der Vergangen-heits-charakter einer Geschichte nicht desto tiefer, vollkommener und märchenhafter, je dichter 'vorher' sie spielt? Zudem könnte es sein, dass die unsrige mit dem Märchen auch sonst, ihrer Natur nach, das eine oder andere zu schaffen hat.'

Through its incorporation of Judaism (for the family of the incestuous twins is Jewish, as was that of Thomas Mann's wife), *Wälsungenblut* takes the radical conflict of the reality of myth and that of the dark God to an extreme, recognizing horror in the mythic repetition of forms of vengeance wreaked against whoever does not partake in the religious experience of the dark God, before whom the perennial repetitions pass by.[49]

Many years later, in *Doktor Faustus*, Mann gave form to the image of a repetition of the sites of childhood which coincide with the Faustian experience. In Adrian's repeated infancy, the possibilities in Mann's work of the repetition of myth as a healing force in itself finds a tragic conclusion. *The Elect* stands beyond this point, comprising both the absence of man as well as the human vegetation determined by myth. Wiligis and Sibylla are semblances of human beings, just as in *Doktor Faustus* the dead, osmotic vegetation kept by Adrian's father are counterfeits of organic reality. The dark God stands before this. Thus great guilt and suffering can be compensated for through the weakness of myth when confronted by the absolute transcendence of the dark God; it is thus that the religious experience of the Mother can overwhelm man within the nothingness, if he abandons the category of human activity so as to allow reality itself to enter into confrontation with the category of the divine.

* * *

When, in 1933, Franz Werfel finished *The Forty Days of Musa Dagh* [*Die vierzig Tage des Musa Dagh*], he could only have seen in a quite general way the future correspondence between the events of his novel and the horrors of Nazi-Fascism. Nevertheless, it is significant

---

49 Fourrier, *Thomas Mann*, p. 134.

that in the same year in which Hitler came to power, a story was published in the German language of an atrociously persecuted people—the story of the massacred Armenians—and the resistance of a small group of them against the Turks, demonstrating the writer's fear of matters which were already coming to a head. The Turkish political-military elite who Werfel accused as responsible for the Armenian genocide was born out of a self-styled revolution—as the Nazi-Fascists would themselves claim—and those 'new men' possessed all the cynicism, ambition and criminality of Hitler and his accomplices. With tragic irony, Werfel entitled the chapter of the novel in which the Turkish characters appear, on whom the fate of the Armenians hangs 'the intermezzo of the gods' [*Zwischenspiel der Götter*]: gods, because the salvation or extermination of a people ensues from their one quick decision. But are they truly gods? The response given by Enver Pascia in order to justify the Turkish policies against the Armenians to the pastor Lepsius is the same by which the Nazi-Fascists would justify their own persecution of the Jews: a lack of patriotism on the behalf of an ethnic minority, betrayal of the nation-state, allying with foreign enemies, etc. Pascia's clear hypocrisy is equal to the criminal hypocrisy of Nazi-Fascism, and whoever reaches such depths is clearly not only not a god but indeed very far from any relationship with the divine.

The prologue to the 'intermezzo of the gods' reads: 'The Homeric heroes struggle before the Scaean Gates and each of them believes that victory and defeat is due to his weapons. But the battle of the heroes is none other than a reflection of the battle waged over their heads by the noisy gods who decide human fate. The gods themselves, however, know not that their struggle does nothing other than reflect that which has already been decided in the breast of the Almighty, from which flows both peace and war.'[50]

These words are the paradigm of a typical human defence against history, one which lies in attributing to painful occurrences a meta-historical justification: the will of God; a similar attitude, of a Judeo-Christian influence, is juxtaposed to that of the novel's protagonist, Gabriel Bagradian, who believes one can find healing in the 'return to origins' i.e. in the renewed submersion in the primordiality of ethnicity, always equivalent to the primordiality of childhood. It is no accident that Gabriel Bagradian is a classics scholar: 'He is allowed to live as an intellectual and scholar, dedicating himself to archaeology, the history of art, philosophy . . . '.[51] He finds peace and a fullness through being in the past, but in a past studied at the Sorbonne; and thus he ends up being stuck within a tragic misunderstanding: finding the past once again, not the sterilized past of archaeology but, rather, that dormant in his blood. A 'circumstance' which leads him to return to the land of his persecuted forefathers, and which transforms his momentary return to the

---

50 Franz Werfel, *Die vierzig Tage des Musa Dagh* (Berlin: Aufbau, 1955), p. 118: 'Die homerischen Helden kämpfen um das skäische Tor, und jeglicher von ihnen wähnt, dass Sieg oder Niederlage seinen Waffen anheimgegeben sei. Der Kampf der Helden aber ist nur ein Spiegelung des Kampfes, den über ihren Häuptern die rufenden Götter führen, um das menschliche Los zu entscheiden. Doch selbst die Götter wissen nicht, dass auch ihr Streit nur den Kampf spiegelt, der längst ausgetragen ist in der Brust des Höchsten, aus dem die Ruhe und Unruhe quillt.' [English translation: *The Forty Days of Musa Dagh* (Geoffrey Dunlop and James Reidel trans) (New York: Viking, 2012). p. 129, modified.]

51 Werfel, *Die vierzig Tage des Musa Dagh*, p. 9: 'Er darf als Gelehrter und Schöngeist leben, als Archäologe, Kunsthistoriker, Philosoph . . .'

ancestral past into a mortal experience: his ancestors' painful suffering.

Reaching Armenia, Gabriel asks his son (whose mother is French) to draw a picture of Musa Dagh, that is, the place bound to his childhood and the life of his ancestors. Not without some irony, Gabriel Bagradian feels reborn through the Armenian child, and 'accidentally' begins to speak with his son in Armenian rather than French.

But the return to the past entails not only the full restitution of the present but death itself. The ancestral and personal childhood no longer represents a form of salvation: now it is the will of God that looms over man, 'from which flows both peace and war.' History—as Werfel implicitly claims—is no eternal return of the ancestral realities, justifying a continual pain within a transcendent healing, but a new divine epiphany, offering both life and death. There is no salvation in the mythical return because God does not mean Darkness, distant from human beings, but a sovereign looming over existence.

We cite Werfel's novel because the religious experience which it documents provides a useful introduction to the thought of another great writer from Prague, Franz Kafka. Kafka's religious thought has often been considered as a contribution to the theology of the dark God. We are personally grateful to Max Brod, however, for having taught us to consider Kafka's 'dark God' from a slightly different perspective. Such a perspective can be synthesized through the words of Brod himself, responding to a letter in which we noted that Kafka could never reach 'Castle': the Castle, Brod replied 'is only *very difficult to reach* or *almost* impossible to reach' ['ist nur *sehr schwer zu erreichen* oder *beinahe* unmöglich zu erreichen'].[52]

---

52 Max Brod, letter to the author, 21 December 1964.

We are inclined to agree with Brod. *The Castle* is not the story of a man eternally distanced from God and his own salvation but, rather, that of a man who labours and suffers in the difficult—but not necessarily impossible—path towards God and towards salvation. The final fragments of *The Castle* recount that K. on his deathbed manages to recognize a final outcome to his search. Even if in agony, he may finally reach the castle. *The Castle* is thus not a nihilistic message, not a declaration of the inaccessibility of God and grace. Rather, it is a document of the terrible and inevitable suffering of whoever attempts to reach God. It is thus an eminently religious document of the human condition, of human limitations and pain. As such, *The Trial* is not an acknowledgement of the injustice directed at a man but a witness to the guilt inherent in *a man*—not *in man* as such: it is a feeling of guilt, a culpability that prevents this particular man from finding salvation.

We see it fit to emphasize here that Kafka also never spoke *of man* as such, but of himself, while recognizing the religious character of his evocation of the human condition. Here, in fact, we are interested in considering those elements that point to the relation between man and myth in Kafka's observations, when man recognizes a particular culpability within the nucleus of his own existence. Such guilt, in Kafka's case, is characteristic of the self-aware depth of the Ego, and therefore also the relation between the Ego and the collective reality of myth.

What is most surprising, however, is the profundity and power of the mythic evocations in the work of a man such as Kafka, who always denounced his painful difficulties in inserting himself into a collective. In this sense, he represents the solitary figure, a man isolated from everyone due to his culpability, formed into an instrument of exceptional sensitivity in respect to the lonely character of the mythic substrata, and a master of the pure and genuine evocations of myth which emerged from within him. On the other hand, he is not divisible even for a moment from the guilty figure with whom his self-portrait coincides: he is inseparable from him in the very moment in which he acts as one who invoked myths and, with an extraordinary purity, participated in the emergence of collective forces. We have to ask, therefore, whether his guilt—a fundamental component of his personality—remains in a mysterious relation with his ability to expose himself to myth—as well as being intimately rooted in his own being.

The first confirmation of the accuracy of this supposition is shown through Kafka's attitude towards his Jewish origins, the bond with an ancestral collective reality but in which, nevertheless, he does not find salvation. For Kafka, Jewishness is a mysterious heritage of mythic imagery which he does not draw upon as a guarantor of salvation but horrific symbols and harbingers of death. Mittner's research on this point has highlighted some very important aspects:[53] 'Kafka's work teems with strange esoteric figures' and 'the exotic—which is always oriental—clearly conceals the Jew.' The Jew, moreover, always takes on a Christian mask. This interchange—Oriental/Jewish/Christian—is probably founded on the collective relation with the divine which acts as the common element among the different masks with which Kafka covers over threats and the dangers that lurk on the margins.

He knows the guilty lie behind such masks all too well: that God knows that man is guilty. One can be guilty without desiring guilt, but one cannot be guilty without

---

53 Mittner, *La letteratura tedesca del Novecento*, p. 249ff.

being aware of it. Throughout Kafka's work, this is the author's, not the character's, consciousness; through the character, Kafka assumes God's attitude towards man: K. does not understand his guilt simply because Kafka maintains him as such. The dark God has arrived at the highest level, subjecting the characters—the figure of myth—to a moral norm which resides in the nature of his attitude towards them. In confronting God, Kafka is the character; in confronting the characters of his work, he is the author, in turn similar to God. And the God is an obscure one, to be searched for. Faced with this God, Kafka becomes part of a series of *characters*, mythic men and images that have now become indivisible and inter-mixed, in search of an author, in search of *the* hidden author.

Our explicit reference to Luigi Pirandello seems to us to be particularly apt and revealing, if we consider the double notion of time—mythic and historical time—in a quite particular way, i.e. as it is presented in *Six Characters in Search of an Author*. Alessandro Pellegrini recalls that, the day before the first performance, Pirandello spoke to him about 'the contrast between real time, paradoxically represented by comic authors and the-atre scenes, and the time of fantastic reality, the time in which everything has already happened and in which the tragedy of the six characters is constantly repeated. This contrast is the fundamental axis of the drama, and its painful, bitter humour originates from this very point.'[54] The time in which the events of the six characters occurs is that which remains in the perennially 'returning' archetypical figures. We insist on *that which remains*, because Pirandello's vision yet again shows a fading trace

---

54 Alessandro Pellegrini, *Incontri in Europa* (Milan: Garzanti, 1947), p. 13.

of the healing aspect of myth and, indeed, Pirandello draws on the observation of this fading away as a document of its pessimism, with exceptional profundity. In the words of Mircea Eliade, the Pirandellian man has been irreparably exiled from the paradise of archetypes, the perennial return of which healed the pain imposed by history, offering them a meta-historical justification. But, Pirandello adds, the man who no longer has the potential to be healed by these archetypes continues to be assailed by their emergent traces. Mythic time continues to intersect with historical time: instead of a justification and healing, it implies a perennial exhortation of pessimism, one that does not spare even the most desperate escapism of the unconscious.

And here we must again open the pages of *The Castle*:

> It was late evening when K. Arrived. The village lay under deep snow. There was no sign of the Castle Hill, fog and darkness surrounded it, not even the faintest gleam of light suggested the large Castle. K. Stood a long time on the wooden bridge that leads from the main road to the village, gazing upward into the seeming emptiness.

The end of a first group of propositions. Then a climax, and the second group:

> Then he went looking for a night's lodging; at the inn they were still awake; the landlord had no room available, but, extremely surprised and confused by the latecomer, he was willing to let K. Sleep on a straw mattress in the taproom, K. Agreed to this. A few peasants were still sitting over beer, but he did not want to talk to anyone, got himself a straw mattress from the attic and lay down by the stove. It was warm, the peasants

were quiet, he examined them for a moment with tired eyes, then fell asleep.[55]

These two groups of propositions constitute a kind of prologue, isolated from the rest of the novel. Historical time exists only in this prologue. After it, when the novel truly begins with K.'s reawakening ('But a little later they woke him. A young man in farmer's clothes . . . ' etc.), historical time and mythic time are intimately interwoven in a painful, uncomfortable material: K. immediately fails to locate himself in the new ambiguity and mysterious temporal conditions, asking: 'What village have I wandered into? So there is a Castle here?'[56] The image of the Castle stands at the intersection of historical and mythic time, seemingly symbolic in that moment of the presence of the dark God. In the 'prologue' of historical time, K. attempts to glimpse the Castle: 'there was no longer any

---

55 Franz Kafka, *Das Schloss* (Frankfurt: Fischer, 1951), p. 5: 'Es war späatabends, als K. Ankam. Das Dorf lag in tiefem Schnee. Vom Schlossberg war nichts zu sehen, Nebel und Finsternis umgaben ihn, auch nicht der schwächste Lichtschein deutete das grosse Schloss an. Lange stand K. auf der Holzbrücke, die von der Landstrasse zum Dorf führte, und blickte in die scheinbare Leere empor. Dann ging er, ein Nachtlager suchen; im Wirtshaus war man noch wach, der Wirt hatte zwar kein Zimmer zu vermieten, aber er wollte, von dem späten Gast äusserst überrascht und verwirrt, K. in der Wirtsstube auf einem Strohsack schlafen lassen. K. war damit einverstanden. Einige Bauern waren noch beim Bier, aber er wollte sich mit niemanden unterhalten, holte selbst den Strohsack vom Dachboden und legte sich in der Nähe des Ofens hin. Warm war es, die Bauern waren still, ein wenig prüfte er sie noch mit den müden Augen, dann schlief er ein.' [English translation: *The Castle* (Mark Harman trans.) (New York: Schocken Books, 1998), pp. 1–2.]

56 Kafka, *Das Schloss*, p. 6: 'In welches Dorf habe ich mich verrirt? Ist denn hier ein Schloss?' Harman translation, p. 2.

firelight to point towards the great Castle.' But quite soon, after the intermixing of historic and mythic time has begun, K. fully takes on the very nature of the character in that particular conjuncture:

> 'Enough of this comedy,' said K. In a remarkably soft voice as he lay down and pulled up the blanket: 'You are going a little too far, young man, and I shall deal with your conduct tomorrow [. . .] Besides, be advised that I am the land surveyor sent for by the Count [. . .]. I didn't want to deprive myself of a long walk through the snow, but unfortunately lost my way a few times, which is why I arrived so late. That it was too late to report to the Castle is something that was already apparent to me without the benefit of your instructions.'[57]

In Pirandello's play, the six characters, having been introduced into exclusively historical time (as announced from the doors of the theatre), fall back into the mixture between mythic and historical time, living out their lives of the eternal return on the stage of the 'theatre within the theatre'.

In the play, the author stands before the six characters as the Castle stands before K.: before both Pirandello

---

57 Kafka, *Das Schloss*, p. 7: ' "Genug der Komödie", sagte K. auffallend leise, legte sich nieder und zog die Decke über sich. 'Sie gehen, junger Mann, ein wenig zu weit, und ich werde morgen noch auf Ihr Benehmen zurückkommen [. . .] Sonst aber lassen Sie es sich gesagt sein, dass ich der Landvermesser bin, den der Graf hat kommen lassen. [. . .] Ich wollte mir den Marsch dirch den Schnee nicht entgehen lassen, bin aber leider einigenal vom abgeirrt und deshalb erst so spät angekommen. Dass es jetzt zu spät war, im Schloss mich zu melden, wusste ich schon aus eigenem, noch vor Ihrer Belehrung.' Harman translation, p. 3.

and Kafka stands the evidence of the impossibility of finding healing and salvation in archetypes, and while they continue to be assailed by the tormenting presence of these archetypes, of the characters, who come at them from every angle, emerging out of the shadows, they are transformed into mere phantoms through the presence of the dark God who has destroyed their ability to save mankind.

It is known that Pirandello outright refused George Pitoëff's decision to make the six characters appear descending from hoists (a refusal made in vain however). And without doubt such an invention was outside the moment of exclusively historical time—corresponding to the 'prologue' of *The Castle*—that Pirandello had imagined as the moment of the six characters' entrance into the theatre as normal people, *historical* people, announced by an usher. Notwithstanding the author's opposition, in the first performance on 10 April 1923, 'first their feet appeared, then their clothed bodies and heads—these "marionettes", as still as mannequins, descending onto the stage on hoists [. . . illuminated by a green light . . .], abruptly announcing to the master of comedies that they be granted the right to represent the drama of their lives.'[58] Pitoëff as such made the intermixing of historic and mythic time coincide with the characters' appearance. But with greater profundity, Pirandello had wanted the characters to appear during exclusively historical time, in order to show, with the utmost theatricality, the wasting away of the figures of myth, 'announced by an usher': remnants, traces of the great healing archetypes. Analogously, Kafka precedes *The Castle* with a 'historical prologue', deigned to show, within the surveyor K., the wreckage of the mythic hero

58 Gaspare Giudice, *Luigi Pirandello* (Turin: UTET, 1963), p. 370.

who moves wearily, despairingly through the novel. As such, on the other hand, in *Doktor Faustus*, Mann puts the (historic) time of present, that of the narrator, Zeitblom, side by side with the (mythic) time of the past, *despite* (or better still, *because of*) the detailed references to reality—thus showing Adrian to be man who gains access not to myth as such, but only its traces: to the demon.

At the end of the first chapter of *Doktor Faustus*, Zeitblom regrets that he does not possess the artistic mastery of his musical friend in too obviously anticipating themes that he will develop later on: 'Here I interrupt myself, with the shameful feeling of having committed an artistic error and lack of self-control. In a symphony, Adrian himself would not, I believe, have included such a theme so prematurely—he would have, at most, distantly signalled it, delicately, not quite tangibly.'[59] On the other hand, Mann's desire to emphasize the intersection between the 'mythic' and 'historical' events is quite evident here: he is clearly referencing Wagner and his preludes that notoriously anticipate every theme of the work. This reference to Wagner acquires extra significance if one recalls that Mann's novel shows the nature of mythic wreckages—and therefore of demonic reality; of the survivals of myth in the 'mythological' German culture that had found its greatest interpreter in Wagner. To exclude the 'historical prologue', that is, to evoke mythic imagery directly within mythic time or in the intermixed temporal

---

59 Mann, *Doktor Faustus*, p. 11: 'Hier breche ich ab, mit dem beschämenden Gefühl artistischer Verfehlung und Underherrschtheit. Adrian selbst hätte wohl kaum, nehmen wir an: in einer Symphonie, ein solches Thema so vorzeitig auftreten—hätte es höchstens auf eine fein versteckte und kaum schon greifbare Art von ferne sich anmelden lassen.' Woods translation, p. 9.

conjuncture of myth and history, means to hold to (or imitate) belief in the vitality of myth as it emerges from the psyche itself. Mann opposed this conviction—as Kafka and Pirandello before him—through the anticipation of the figures of myth in an exclusively historic moment, making evident the state of demonic alteration, of traces, within it.

Analogously, in Mann's work, citation and precise historical referencing assumes the function of unmasking the deformations of mythic imagery surviving in the traces of a German culture destined to come to a conclusion. And as such, one can interpret even an aspect of parody—which Mann, at a certain point in his life, considered to be indivisible from language itself. Parody is the return of love across hatred but it is also the certainty of an end, of love condemned to sterility.

We have already said that the manifestation of the dark God at the very highest level brings with it the subjection and death of mythic imagery, rendering it unable to heal mankind. The finale of *Doktor Faustus*, the prayer to that God, is thus the novel's tragic and firmest seal, representing the horrific sunset of myth—myth that has been ruined by men. Mann's final hope, that which is 'like a light in the night', is an act of devotion to man, to his soul, twisted and tormented by myth and history: it is not a prayer to the dark God, but the words of Frau Schweigestill: 'A good human understanding, believe you me, that is enough for everything!'

* * *

'One can speak with God, but not of God'. These are the words of one of the greatest religious spirits of our times, Martin Buber; they could stand as an epigraph to this chapter, not only because they relate to the 'dark God' (a

Hasidic expression) but also because they have a direct relation to 'maternal religion'. When the image of the 'Germanic night' is evoked, it seems almost necessary to cite the 'night' of *Tristan und Isolde* and Novalis' 'night'; it is also important, nonetheless, to recall another intimately Germanic night: that of Mozart's Queen of the Night. In the juxtaposition between the soprano of the celebrated 'nocturnal' arias and the basses evoking the solar light (Sarastro and the *Sprecher*), the profoundly maternal character of that night is revealed, excluding the pathetic, ringing out not as a supreme evil but as the seduction of terror and—literally—of darkness (aside from the ethical symbolism).

The observation of the lack of pathos in *The Magic Flute* is by now obvious and perhaps hackneyed. It nevertheless acquires a particular depth when referring to the Queen of the Night, the figure of an inaccessible, eternal femininity, from whom flows forth a darkness that does not oppose salvation but represents the genuine survival of an essentially religious quality in the Greek experience. One might say that the Queen of the Night, in her lunar features (emphasized by the traditional scenography as envisioned by Karl Friedrich Schinkel in 1816) is a version of Isis, transformed in a negative sense—like a Kore turned into a witch. But this would concede too much to a schematic approach demonstrated by a certain kind of science of religion. Such schematics can be corrected through phenomenological method. Thus Mozart appears to us as holding a spiritual attitude not dissimilar from that of Apuleius, who, at the end of his *Metamorphoses*, having parodied magic, evoked the rescuing image of Isis the sorcerer. This lack of pathos is thus a symptom of a religious experience that transcends Gnostic dualism and is inserted harmonically into

Mozart's experience at the same moment as his initiation into Masonry. 'At the same moment' or rather 'as a consequence of': for as much as the Masonic thought of Mozart's era actually deviated from its usual tradition of embracing religious experiences of different origins, it seems important to us to note that Mozart's 'Masonic' years appear under the sign of a religion of the dark God, for whom the adjective 'Masonic' could beneficially be substituted by that of 'Hasidic'. Beyond the theological structures and rituals of Catholicism and Masonic esotericism, the events of Mozart's spiritual life seem to converge around the discourse of a 'dark God' with whom one can speak—within the secrecy of organic being itself—but *of whom* it is impossible to speak. Before the dark God, images such as the Queen of the Night become secondary, inasmuch as they are alien from an ethical symbolism; they are merely the passive components of a cosmos whose highest peaks stand in darkness. This is the destiny of the figures of myth, when the 'dark God' appears before them. It is significant that such a destiny manifests itself so evidently in the most 'German' of Mozart's works, drawing more heavily on popular material ('deconsecrated' myths) than Brentano's work will. That is not to prejudge the genuine character of the evocation of mythic imagery—to which *The Magic Flute* bears witness—but it means that such an evocation possesses the intimate value of a human *ludus*, carried out in the illuminated zone which corresponds to the realm of humanity. For his reason, a work such as *The Magic Flute* does not represent a break in relation to Mozart's other comic works. Quite rightly, in *Steppenwolf*, Herman Hesse evokes Mozart as the genius of 'justness' and the 'necessity' of creation: Mozart's work represents an epiphany of genuine myth in the realm of man's existential consciousness, in which *ludus*, thanks to its mythic elements, becomes a 'necessary' activity, alien to metaphysics. And according to Thomas Mann, the manifestations of healing and salvational form are to be found within this genre of *ludus*.

CHAPTER 5

In the essay 'Frederick and the Great Coalition' ['Friedrich und die grose Koalition'], written during the First World War, Thomas Mann presents a character acutely different from those of his previous narratives; as Fourrier observed, 'Hamlet's formula cannot be applied' to Mann's Frederick II.[1] In this essay, one cannot find, as with so many other of Mann's figures, a man tragically forced by destiny to live out events not made by himself. Frederick was born to be that which he was, and the vocation imposed upon him by superior will, of whom he is an instrument, turns out to be entirely compliant with his own nature. With Adrian Leverkühn, his destiny—quite clear through the particular nature of his father—harmonizes with the most intimate structure of his personality, from which it draws its power. Both Frederick II and Adrian are thus particularly close to each other: over a gap of more than 30 years, Mann's version of the King of Prussia ('made to be as such') stands beside that of an artist who is entirely different from the figure of Tonio Kröger, for he is no longer tormented by an inherent discord between a bourgeois soul and the attraction towards the ambiguous charm of art. In *Doktor Faustus*, this antimony is resolved through the division of the central character into Adrian Leverkühn and Serenus Zeitblom: a division which is not absolute, inasmuch as the two

---

1 Fourrier, *Thomas Mann*, p. 249.

characters possess a secret identity,[2] but, rather, revelatory, through the moment in which such an identity exists only as 'the anthropomorphosis of Germanism' or, in confessional terms, 'Thomas Mann'.

The determining factor in this splitting of German man into Adrian and his humanist biographer is certainly not merely of a literary nature, and can be properly interpreted only if one considers the great novel from a religious perspective (Mann spoke of 'confession' and approved of Kerényi's observation that *Doktor Faustus* could be seen as a Christian novel). The same religious perspective allows us to understand the more or less secret bond which unites Adrian Leverkühn to Mann's Frederick II, which—we believe—was established by Mann's desire to never truly realize an authentic solution to the continuity between his own thought in 1914 and 1940.

Frederick II is the instrument of a superior 'dark' will. And this darkness—which nearly attains to the Gnostic notion of a God comprising everything good and evil—is heavily emphasized by Mann when he cites the Prussian king's 'evilness', the king who Maria Teresa described as above all 'an evil man'. The fact that he represents a harmonious instrument of will, without pangs of conscience, attests to a relation between predestination and the particular nature of a human persona who, in German culture, frequently became paradigmatic of a spiritual and historical composition of Germanism. This is the philosophical basis of Leo Frobenius' own histories, who theorized that man's historic mission is to realize his own destiny in 'reciting the part that was written for him'.

It is a dangerous error to identify Frobenius' appeal directly with the propositions of Nazism (which never

---

2 See Mayer, *Thomas Mann*, pp. 251–2.

looked upon Frobenius with great pleasure). For anyone familiar with Frobenius' work and who recognize, without prejudice, its extraordinary richness and spiritual nobility—the error is all too clear once one integrates the words of the great German ethnologist into Rilke's thought. Rilke claims that everyone must die their own death, meaning that everyone must gain access to the invisible in a way characteristic of their own individual personality.

Rilke's thought leads us directly into the arena of religious phenomenology, evoking the image of the dark God in the presence of each person's death, subjecting an individual's character to his presence—and it is from that that their unique death derives. Personal individuality, for which everyone is predestined to recite their own proper part in life and above all in death, is a mysterious reality set cosmologically within an existential dependence on the dark God. Accessing the invisible world, over which the God looms more closely still, is conditioned by the personal death: by the kind of death appropriate to each person. Everyone, therefore, is alone in the presence of the invisible (one recalls the warning of being alone that Rilke gives to the 'young poet'). Both Frederick II and Adrian Leverkühn are extremely solitary; their solitude nonetheless bears an aspect of guilt, for they are guilty in the same way as Alberich in *Das Rheingold*, having sacrificed love for power. But that very same power is, in both of them, fundamentally the form of mastery for which both are predestined. If for Rilke solitude is resolved through dedication to humanity, for Frederick II and Adrian it is the dark lightning by which the unknown God intervenes in human events.

Mann and Rilke did not share the same attitude. In his desire to fully participate in the human experience,

Mann wanted to accommodate good and evil, horror and love, within his capacity to evoke and order form, convinced that man's function consists both in the classical *nihil humani a me alienum puto* as well as in the exercise of a formal mastery through which one *might* be able to reach a form of pedagogic serenity. Thus he counterposed his Frederick II with whomever might be able to exclude the 'dark lightning' from human experience politically; and as such, faced with the horrors of Nazism, he again proposed the image of man formed in harmony with his true destiny as a harbinger of lightning without nevertheless remaining silent in relation to the atrocity and suffering implicit in such destiny.

Thomas Mann was always an overt enemy of Nazism. Nonetheless, he opposed it as the political systemization of horror, of that which he acknowledged as existing within the human experience. His moralistic activity never made any claim to the goodness of man, but, rather, of faith in the likelihood that form in itself has a healing function, a proposition that might win out over history's co-mixture of good and evil.

Like anyone, Mann's thought is an unfathomable abyss. We cannot attempt here to provide the key to it, but, rather, merely some indications of its accessible constants by studying its external manifestations. It is impossible to provide a full interpretation and describe all of that which he experienced in the extraordinary life of the spirit. The fact that he made recourse to irony and parody seems to bear witness to the presence, within his experiences and visions, of horrific and dangerous elements— for irony in the hands of an artist and a humanist is, from the very start, a weapon against death, while parody represents the love for a reality which one has recognized as outdated and in decline: a love which can eliminate the sterility of such a decline and, for one last time, allow one to draw on the purity and healing vitality of myth.

Irony towards death in *The Magic Mountain*; irony too towards death in the narrating of Frederick II's life. After death, Frederick's body appears strangely small, hollowed out, like the dry remains of a gnome or a child; the final words of Mann's essay thus possess an extraordinary effect and synthesis, not without a painful parody. But death comes to Adrian too as a kind of deformed residue of himself, a shell dessicated by the force which he had instrumentalized. Analogously, the years of Frederick's old age are narrated by Mann in a way which demonstrates all the misery and defects resultant from a strong will, just as the last years of Adrian's life in *Doktor Faustus* make for a painful chronicle of man's most extreme impoverishment.

Frederick's strange and monstrous return to infancy via death, the quasi-magical shrinking of the body of the great king, demonstrates a reference already made, in the fate of Gregorius (the protagonist of *The Elect*) to the redemption of predestined guilt—for he becomes small like the young man on a solitary rock surrounded by waters, a rock to which he has been chained. The fabulous events of Gregorius, the great sinner, cast a mysterious and tranquillizing light over the lives of Frederick and Adrian. Both of them, after the resolution of their guilt, return to the mother: the one becomes, in his body, small like a boy; the other is swept up by the mother, deprived now and forever of consciousness. While in his 1914 essay and in *Doktor Faustus* Mann made no attempt to surpass the limit of that return to the mother, and thereby nor to nourish real hope, in *The Elect* he made his universal vision of the great cycle of guilt and redemption, death and resurrection entirely explicit, providing the moment of salvation with a form that is both solemn and joyous.

But it is mythic reality itself—the theme of *The Elect*—that must lead the reader back to the notion of an eternal present, and thus allow them to overcome the semblance of the temporal successions of good and evil, guilt and redemption. This is in accordance with the two Faustian characters' destinies—Adrian and Frederick— destined for evil and, therefore, also good. Good and evil never appear in the works of Mann as stages of a meta-morphosis but emerge instead as fixed points of the human condition in which one perennially participates. Nonetheless, he never abandoned himself to those gnos-tic ideas that render Hesse's *Demian* so ambiguous,i.e. he never implied that the divine is simultaneously good and evil. Mann's discourse is religious exactly inasmuch as it refers only to the condition of man: it is not that God par-ticipates in both good and evil but, rather, that both are elements intrinsic to humanity.

Mann's greatness consists not only in the depth of this vision but also in the desire to affirm the most pedagogic of messages when faced with this vision: the necessity of accomplishing goodness while closing one's eyes to the possibility of any redemption inherent to sin. Frederick and Adrian are emblems of the human condition in all its fullness but both are also symbols of a society destined for death: a death welcomed with a fatal acceptance in his *Reflections of a Non-political Man* [*Betrachtungen eines Unpolitischen*] and with a stark confessional desire in *Doktor Faustus*. Frederick and Adrian's destiny is not the inevitable fate of man in general, but that of a society and a world standing in the shadow of its final moment. Such a destiny is juxtaposed to the 'nobility of spirit' that Mann—even if without any absolute certainty—entrusted with the salvation of humanism.

Form as salvation: this is the message of *The Elect*, in which an event of predestined horror and healing is exorcized through form, through the 'spirit of narration'. Thus the function of the narrator becomes moralizing and pedagogic in the deepest sense.

* * *

On 3 October 1914, around a hundred German intellectuals sent a message to the 'civilized world', the 'Appeal to the World of Culture' ['Aufruf an die Kulturwelt'] in which they defended the German cause from the accusations of barbarity elicited by the political and military actions of Germany at war. The signatories of the message included scientists such as Roentgen, Haeckel and Wundt, poets like Dehmel and Hauptmann, artists such as Klinger and Liebermann. It was a real collective front formed by people who the whole civilized world considered to be of undisputed intellectual merit. The signatories laid their authoritative names on the scales of history, trusting in their moral weight and in the morally healing action that ought to derive from it. How could the German cause be that of barbarians, of contempt for humanity, if it was also represented by these exponents of human thought?

There is no doubt that any criticism of such an initiative lies within its very premises. It is clear, in fact, that the value of the message did not consist in its text—rhetorical and, at the same time, blunted by the assertion of the goodness of the German cause—but in the international prestige of the signatories. And to attribute the guarantee of the moral good of a political cause to the intellectual prestige of a name is evidently no more than demagogy played out on the level of an elite.

One can compare this message from these German intellectuals to the protests made by others, among whom

Einstein's name stands out. These figures were frustrated in appearing through the refraction of the prestige of others, and instead formed their own parade of the greats, a painful conclusion to the morality of German culture. Romain Rolland's reply to this German self-justification is well known.

What interests us here however is to note that, in some cases, the polemic became one of anti-Germanism, directly attacking the very foundations of the glory on which the prestige of the message from the German intellectuals had been founded; and, from the point of view of our research, it is particularly important to examine the approach taken towards the principal German exponents of the study of antiquity by their opponents. Such an attitude was radically summarized—not without some fictions, errors and misunderstandings—in the articles published by Ettore Romagnoli in the journal *Gli avvenimenti* in 1915–16, and later collected in the volume *Minerva and the Ape* [*Minerva e lo scimmione*].[3] Romagnoli was also a nationalist, whose being did not live long enough to see the spiritual lowliness of Fascism. We cite him here merely as an exponent of a line of thought within European culture in the first decades of the twentieth century, in the same moment in which the symptoms of an imminent Fascism began to appear.

Romagnoli proposed the dismantling of Germanic glory in the study of antiquity, directly attacking the methods of classical philology as established by the Germans. He recognized the merits of philology in the restoration of ancient texts, but found the capacity of interpreting the *meaning* of classical culture lacking in German scholars of his generation. For him, German philologists were

---

3 Ettore Romagnoli, *Minerva e lo scimmione* (Bologna: Zanichelli, 1917).

artisanal pedants who unduly appointed themselves as spiritual interpreters of ancient civilization. He wrote that German-influenced philology had had its golden age—the nineteenth century—but was now reduced to the pedantic activity of erudite true believers, devotees to the 'esoteric' goodness of algorithms devised for publishing classical works, and constitutionally, *ethnically* incapable of emotional insight into the texts themselves. While Romagnoli's book denounces the foolishness of a certain P. Richter, supervisor at the Breslau Gymnasium, who had the courage to write that Aeschylus' *Oresteia* 'uses a monotonous and superficial tone to deal with such powerful material',[4] it does not say anything substantially new. The incipience of the teaching at the Gymnasiums—of the 'Gymasium professor'—had already received much more serious criticism on German soil from Heinrich and Mann, as well as from Wedekind, even becoming a kind of constant in certain forms of German literature that blamed matriculation with suicides and runaways. Romagnoli's discourse becomes much more significant, however, when he calls into question not an obscure supervisor like Herr Richter but the solemn and celebrated Ulrich von Wilamowitz-Moellendorff himself.

This illustrious name, venerated by generations of scholars of antiquity, had also been at the centre of a polemic whose events are identified with that of German philology at the turn of the twentieth century. From the day that the young Wilamowitz took on the heavy burden of excavating an abyss between academic philology and Nietzsche's work, he became the barricade and banner for the study of antiquity as professed in German universities: a discipline which without doubt took a position against 'irrationalism' and the corresponding emotional

---

4 Romagnoli, *Minerva e lo scimmione*, p. 93.

participation of scholars in the phenomena under examination. The accusations formed by Romagnoli against the German philologist lie entirely in his 'neglect or ignorance of those irrational elements that gloss every artwork'.[5] The question is nonetheless complicated by the fact that the same Wilamowitz, in the preface to his volume on Aeschylus' interpretations, wrote: 'The interpretor of an artwork must do much more than merely explain words and propositions: he must feel sympathy with the poet, must understand the work and poet as something living, and show others how to feel as such.'[6]

These words, penned by a critic of Nietzsche—'the goat who nibbled at the crown of roses'—are specific enough: Wilamowitz did not criticize the 'sympathetic' participation of the scholar in the artwork but actually proposed it as a necessary element. Yet he said as such with a particular mental reservation: 'The interpretor of an artwork must feel sympathy with the poet': here there is only one path of access to poet's sentiment, that of the philological methodology professed by Wilamowitz himself. In order to really understand this attitude, it is useful to turn to a page of Leo Frobenius, who knew the procedures of the German universities well enough:

> The most learned and ingenious philologist has the talent of a Year Ten school boy. One night the pupil is fascinated by an argument, which seems huge, important, strange. The next day he runs to the teacher and explains the thought with enthusiasm. Foregoing meanness and pedantry, the teacher is surprised and lets him continue. The voice comes from another world. This might

5 Romagnoli, *Minerva e lo scimmione*, p. 29.

6 Romagnoli, *Minerva e lo scimmione*, p. 16.

be something important. Go ahead! But with the greatest care. I advise you to leave nothing unturned. Re-examine everything that has been said by this or that scholar; inform yourself regarding one or the other interpretation available, naturally, from the hundred, two hundred dissertations published on a similar argument. The pupil gets to work. First he studies the great masters, work that cheers him along in the originality of his idea; when he immerses himself in the works penned by authors of a secondary order, he is dismayed by the number of possible opinions; his spirit is exhausted. But once he reads all the dissertations, then the activity of his thought itself is exhausted; he has lost the acumen; the clear-cut crystal has become no more than a round pebble, indiscernible among all the other identical pebbles in the river bed.[7]

---

7 Leo Frobenius, *Kulturgeschichte Afrikas: Prolegomena zu einer historischen Gestaltlehre* (Zurich: Phaidon, 1933), p. 28: 'Ein außerordentlich gut beschlagener und auch geistvoller Philologe hat einen sehr tüchtigen Schüler, sagen wir: etwa zehntes Semester. Dieser Schüler wird eines Nachts von einem Stoff so ergriffen, daß er ihn groß, bedeutend, eigenartig sieht. Andern Tags eilt er zu seinem Lehrer und trägt seinen "Gedanken" in schwung voller Weise vor. Der—wie gesagt als weitherzig und großzügig gedachte —Lehrer stutzt, läßt sich hinreißen. Wahrlich, das ist die Stimme aus einer anderen Welt; dies könnte etwas Großes bedeuten. Also angepackt! Ja, aber nur mit der allergrößten Sorgfalt. Also bitte kein Versäumnis. Da muß natürlich nachgeprüft werden, was dieser große Gelehrte gesagt und jener; da muß diese und jene Interpretation herangezogen werden und natürlich die 100 oder 200 Dissertationen, die über ein verwandtes Thema gedruckt wurden.—Der Schüler geht an die Arbeit. Studiert er die ersten großen Meister, so bleibt ihm noch die Freude an der Erstmaligkeit seiner eigenen Auffassung; vertieft er sich in die Schriften der

The image of the schoolboy who 'one night' is fascinated by an argument so much as to become the mouth-
piece of a 'voice from another world' recalls certain lines
from the young Goethe:[8]

> At midnight thus I truly begin
> Leaping from the bed like a madman:
> Never was my breast more full
> With the song of journeying man . . .

It is right that the name of Goethe, 'the great dilettante', appear here next to that of Nietzsche, treated by
Wilamowitz as a dilettante in the study of antiquity.

Returning to our initial discussion, we would now
like to propose that Wilamowitz's guilt and that of academic German philology has exactly that mental lack that
accompanies the feelings of a university 'caste' prevented
from any sympathetic reaction with the emotions of
poets, and thus of revealing the *meaning* of the artistic
experience of antiquity. This mental lack is characterized
by the utmost respect for a method that became an end
in itself, and the cause of sterility and misunderstanding.

Zweitklassigen, so erschrickt er über die vielen Möglichkeiten der
Auffassungen; sein Geist ist ermüdet. Hat er dann aber all die
Dissertationen gelesen, so—ist die Aktivität seines Gedankens
verbraucht; er hat seine Schärfe verloren; aus dem gestaltklaren
Kristall wurde ein runder Kieselstein—der sich als gleichartiges
Gebilde im Bachbett nicht unterscheidet von der Form der
anderen.'

8 Cited by Thomas Mann in the essay 'Über Goethe's "Faust" ' in
Adel des Geistes. Sechzehn Versuche zum Problem der Humanität
(Stockholm: Berman-Fischer, 1945), p. 573.

> Um Mitternacht wohl fang ich an,
> Spring aus dem Bette wie ein Toller:
> Nie war mein Busen seelvoller,
> Zu singen den gereisten Mann . . .

The crisis of German academic philology, and therefore of that discipline officially charged with opening up access to myth, does not lack its political features, one which we will do well to focus on.

At the beginning of the First World War, during a session of the Academy of Sciences in Berlin, and after some fiery nationalist speeches by illustrious persons, Wilamowitz 'solemnly stood up, in the white majesty of his flowing beard. Religious silence. And while everyone waited for god knows what flow of Demosthenian eloquence, he vigorously intoned the *Deutschland über alles*.'[9] This demonstrates many things, further clarified through a recollection from Barbara Allason who visited the Berlin university in 1928:

> a classroom sprung open; a river of young people burst through three doorways. At the head, encircled by a group of assistants, was a man with a white head of hair and a lordly posture. It was Wilamowitz. I watched him avidly, as one watched men one has venerated since youth, in whom we have seen the teachers of our life and thought . . . Achille Vogliano said to me: 'Yes, Wilamowitz. Great admirer of Mussolini.' I have never forgotten it.[10]

Wilamowitz took the opportunity to sing nationalist hymns in a solemn hall of science over which the memory of Leibniz still hung; Wilamowitz, the great admirer of Mussolini. If these were the authoritative figures qualified to open the path towards myth, we ought not be surprised by the monstrous fortune enjoyed by Nazi pseudomythology.

---

9 Romaglioni, *Minerva e lo scimmione,* p. 16.

10 Barbara Allason, *Memorie di un'antifascista* (Milan: Edizioni Avanti!, 1961), p. 72.

It is no accident that Wilamowitz is one of the main figures denounced in the correspondence between Mann and Kerényi. But to bring up Mann once again induces the problem of posing that which we have already cited; Mann and Wilamowitz, in the First World War, were in fact 'on the same side', that is, on that of *Culture* against *Civilization*. Was Mann thus at that point a genuine battle companion of Wilamowitz—even if he later 'repented'— or was there perhaps already at that point a dramatic misunderstanding which had induced the two men to fight side by side?

The crisis of academic German philology cannot be separated from the general crisis of bourgeois culture, a culture that became sterile from the moment in which it gained confidence in a dominating elite granted with the ability to draw on truth. The German nationalists of 1914 often spoke with enthusiasm about the German *people*, but without doubt the word *Volk*, was for them equivalent, on an ethnic level, to the spiritual elite of which they believed themselves to be a part. It is significant, and revealing, that at the apex of its crisis, bourgeois culture searched for a great escape in extending the very notion of an elite to an entire people which thus became 'elect'— and such an extension included the transformation on an ethnic, racial level, of a superior quality which the intellectual elite claimed for themselves: from the specific intellectual faculties possessed by the elite, it passed thus to the notion of predestined and pure blood, naturally predisposed to power.

These are the ideological bases of racism; and it is natural that these were already repugnant to a great spirit like Thomas Mann. A spirit that gave expression to far nobler convictions, even if adhering to the same political activity recognized and sustained by racists. Conscious heir to bourgeois culture, Man was radically and painfully faithful to the ideology of the social class of his ancestors; without wanting to concede anything to the lowliness of racism, he nonetheless affirmed the dark reality of a human experience based on the adhesion of rational man to those looming metaphysical forces recognized by him as dominating existential events.

Without doubt, it is nobler to accept and finally recognize guilt than to transform it. But independently of the individual moral situation of the more and less noble, the active consequences of the two attitudes are the same: acceptance of violence (through suffering or enthusiasm) in defence of the destiny of a people claimed as worthy of particular respect, and the denouncing (whether painfully or with monstrous pride) of whoever is opposed to the completion of that people's 'marked destiny'.

To attribute the conscience of myth to a closed caste of academics—sterilely closed within a dogmatic method —is the first step towards the political and terrifying exploitation of pseudo-myth by the manipulators and propagandistic criminals 'à la Sorel'. Here lies Wilamowitz's guilt. But to remain faithful to bourgeois thought when it represents death and devotion to death, and to excavate from one's own intellectual greatness the weapons to defend that basis of death, is humanism's own guilt: and this is Thomas Mann's guilt in *Reflections of a Non-political Man*.

* * *

By now there have been many studies on the origins and nature of Nazi ideology, often of significant depth. It seems to us, however, that in these there is too much reference to a misunderstanding on the meaning of the word *myth*, which—independently of the goodwill or honesty or the researchers—determines some inaccuracies concerning the attitude of the theorists of Nazism and those thinkers, writers and artists who adhered to Nazism, in the framework of the Germanic world. To provide just one example, we can cite Franz Schonauer's *German Literature in the Third Reich* [*Deutsche Literatur im Dritten Reich*],[11] a work carried out with intelligence and appropriate severity, in which almost every page speaks of Nazi *myths* (of blood, race, nation, Germanism, etc.).

The Nazis, starting with Rosenberg, spoke continually of 'myths' and certainly proposed giving life to a mythology which constituted a metaphysical 'precedent' and justification of their crimes. But this proposition, this intention to evoke myths in order to justify a political action and drag along the masses, would already be enough to exclude the idea that the Nazis ever understood, evoked or propagandized authentic myths. The self-appointed Nazi mythology was none other than the terrifying result of a political will that conformed to the teachings of Georges Sorel, whose doctrine on the technification of myth is condemned by Mann in Chapter 35 of *Doktor Faustus*. In relation to Mann's works, it is worth noting the admonishing words of Kerényi in 'From Genuine to Technified Myth' ['Dal mito genuino al mito tecnicizzato']—to which we referred in Chapter 1—which recalls how genuine myth, the only kind worthy of the name, is born spontaneously from the depths of human being and has a fundamental ability to heal humankind from the sicknesses of the human spirit.

That the self-appointed Nazi myth was not in any way spontaneous and that Nazi pseudo-mythology had nothing to do with the spirit is by now evident to

---

11 Franz Schonauer, *Deutsche Literatur im Dritten Reich* (Freiburg: Walter Verlag, 1961).

whoever studies the activity of the principal manipulators of the Nazi 'myths', from Rosenberg to Goebbels and Himmler. There are innumerable witnesses to the Nazi initiatives to technify myth. Here we can cite, if only as an example, the case of the 'Oera Linda Book', the celebrated forgery by which Professor Wirth attempted to 'document' the oldest origins of the Teutons, in deference to directions from his superiors. When falsifications gave way to polemic, Himmler cut through the question, claiming: 'In all this troublesome business we are only interested in one thing—to project into the dim and distant past the picture of our nation as we envisage it for the future.'[12]

The histories of Nazism drafted after its fall usually include an opening chapter entitled 'precursors', referring to the paladins of German irrationalism, almost as if Nazism were a spiritual phenomenon with 'precursors' in cultural and spiritual spheres. This attitude on the part of historians is unhelpful, however, in as much as it favours the misunderstanding of attributing Nazism with a spiritual dimension that it did not in fact possess. Nazism and Fascism, in all of their forms, were phenomena of a simple and vulgar delinquency, favoured by economic and social causes and sustained through the participation of intellectuals who made the cause of the criminals their own. It grants too much honour to Nazism and Fascism to recognize within them the results of a certain intellectual attitude of the European bourgeoisie that became Nazi and Fascist. One could say, instead, that a part of the European bourgeoisie was sick

---

12 Hermann Rauschning, *Hitler Speaks: A Series of Political Conversations with Adolf Hitler on His Real Aims* (Ernest Walter Dickes trans.) (London: Thomas Butterworth, 1939), p. 225.

to such an extent that it identified the manifestations of its own sickness with the initiatives of a group of criminals aiming at the conquest of power. That is what happened in Italy, in Germany, in Spain, in Portugal and recently in Greece, and in every nation where Nazi-Fascist delinquency gains power or has attempted to gain it.

To call on Nietzsche and Wagner as precursors to Nazism, or even on figures of much more modest intelligence, such as the proponents of the 'Germanic renaissance' from Langbehn to Lagarde and Bartels, is inaccurate. What is true is that the work of such thinkers and artists—to different extents—had already manifested the symptoms of the sickness which led intellectuals to indulge Nazi-Fascism. This does not mean, however, that an authentic guilt affected those intellectuals who adhered to Nazi-Fascism, those who endorsed the activity of the delinquents.

For the rest, as far as the attitude of those who developed an irrationalism before Nazi-Fascism are concerned, coinciding with racism and the annihilation of humanism, returning back into the sphere of spiritual sickness: this passage from illness to guilt seems determined by practical activity, that is, through the decision to contribute to the realization of a criminal political operation, resulting in spiritual sickness itself. This sickness is the sin of idolatry, contained within the spirit of some intellectuals; their guilt is the participation of the sick intellectual in the political activity of delinquents.

Nietzsche was above all a sick man; Gottfried Benn was above all a guilt-ridden one. Within the boundaries of his own personal experience, Nietzsche lived through the tragedy of a sickness that transformed his thought and imposed terrible suffering upon him. Gottfried Benn was a sick intellectual who decided to aid criminals in their crimes in the very moment in which these crimes were carried out. In the end, he deliberately enslaved his sickness for the activity of delinquents.

One might object that sickness clouds reason and therefore excludes the responsibility of the sick even when they commit such crimes. In order to sustain such a point of view, we would, at most, have to speak of a criminal sickness, but we will insist on speaking of *criminals* because it designates an attitude within the sick themselves which is concretely dangerous to them as well as others, to be denounced without reservation as a baseness that took hold of the crisis of bourgeois culture.

It was world of the sick that embraced the squalid genesis of Nazi-Fascism: in Germany, in Italy, in Spain, a great number of intellectuals revealed their own illness in the moment in which they became active or passive accomplices in the groups of criminals who based their own victories on violence, assassination, fraud and moral baseness. Through these intellectuals, the delinquents gained confirmation of the supposed spiritual dignity of their ravings, claims otherwise entirely alien to the different spheres of thought concerned. Nazi-Fascism did not have intellectual precursors: it simply had intellectual accomplices in its delinquency. The so-called precursors to Nazism are in reality precursors to the illness and guilt which led certain intellectuals to become accomplices to criminals.

Those intellectuals guilty of complicity in Nazi-Fascist delinquency can only boast in vain of Nietzsche's great spirit as their precursor. The purity and nobility of his suffering, united with the depth of his genius, excludes any relation between him and his self-appointed heirs who include him alongside their forgeries and murders. Nietzsche was a sick man, but to simply single out the signs of his sickness and carry them to extreme concrete consequences entails a guilt-ridden act of which he cannot be named as an accomplice.

Every intellectual who did not openly rebel against Nazi-Fascism was therefore guilty, as such enslaving their own sickness to the criminal will of the gangsters. In talking of the German intellectuals in whom one can then recognize so-called internal resistance or internal emigration, one is forced to recognize that even they— Carossa and Wiechert, to cite the main examples—were sick enough to not take part in an open and indispensable condemnation of Nazi criminals. They were sick enough to believe that the moral battle against assassins could be carried out within the constrained borders of their own solitary soul, rather than publicly in an open fight against the forces of evil.

* * *

It would be gross to unite the name of Wagner with those of Germans whose morality and intellectual level are clearly so base: thus Franz Schonauer writes that 'the incoherent pan-Germanism of people like Langbehn and Lagarde had received an artistic-cultural blessing through Richard Wagner, via his interests in "the most German of all German arts", the musical drama conceived within the spirit of Germanic mythology.'[13] At the same time, within the figure of Wagner, anti-Semitism and nationalism sat side by side with the greatness of the artists in a way which has caused unease and turmoil. A figure entirely separate from the most minor authors and falsifiers of

---

13 Schonauer, *Deutsche Literatur im Dritten Reich*, p. 27.

history, Wagner was without doubt a great evoker of myths: genuine myths, emerging spontaneously from his soul and flowing into his creative work. Above all, he provides an illustrious example of that 'sickness' of the artist which we spoke about in Chapter 1: that is, he did not always bring himself close to the flow of myth with a purity of the soul, influenced by moral law and discriminating between 'health' and 'sickness', between honesty and delinquency. It would be wrong, however, to trick ourselves into dividing the 'sick' Wagner from the 'healthy' one by separating the theoretical writings from the man's musical creations. Wagner 'the man' is entirely organic, in whom one finds an inextricable interweaving of good and evil, moral 'sickness' and moral 'health'. Nor can one resolve the 'Wagner case' by limiting it to a merely individual problem, that of Wagner 'the man', characterized by a health and sickness which was exclusively his own. Wagner's thought cannot be explained independently of the conditions of nineteenth-century German society and culture. Wagner's work, in fact, bears witness to that phase of the crisis in bourgeois culture in which the experience of evil had not yet transformed into a pedagogic warning and humanistic defence of the good, as would come to pass with Mann. We do not want, through these words, to associate ourselves with a unilateral course of history and especially not in terms of the history of bourgeois culture; we mean rather that Wagner was affected by the evils which characterized the crisis of bourgeois culture while for Mann the experience of these evils impelled him into a pedagogic activity of healing. We argue, furthermore, that it would not be right to overvalue the influence of 'sickness' in Wagner's work, and that above all it would not be right to mix the traces of such 'sickness' with the fruits of *genuine* mythological activity. When Wagner recognized genuine myth and respected its genuine character within his own artistic creations, he was very far from the 'sickness' which otherwise overcast him, indeed he acted against such 'sickness' through celebrating the healing faculties within the deep reality of myth, those that myth possesses and exercises over the human mind. We maintain that it is necessary to emphasize that Wagner distanced himself from the evils of bourgeois culture which were leading to nationalism and racism exactly in that moment in which he acceded to genuine myth, the rescuing of humanism.

One might object that Wagner based his nationalist and anti-Semitic doctrines on his mythological experiences, constructing the foundations of pseudo-mythical justification on which Nazism rested. In response to such an objection we note that while 'sickness' undermined the artistic mind and deformed the results of the artist's healing, there was still 'healthy' activity within his conscience. In Wagner's music, there are forces of destruction and death which oppose the humanistic access to myth, forces which lead to the annihilation of reason through irrationalism. These forces are shown, however, when the myth disappears and the Gorgon's grin appears in its place, like that which Odysseus was afraid of seeing emerging from the depths of the Underworld. It would be enough to illustrate this through what we have said in Chapter 3 in relation to *Tristan und Isolde*.

The name of Houston Stewart Chamberlain is associated with the tragic connecting bridge by which Wagner's work adjoined the ideals of Wilhelm II and then of Hitler. Chamberlain's *The Foundations of the Nineteenth Century* [*Die Grundlagen des XIX. Jahrhundert*] solicited the enthusiasm of the Kaiser and led Rosenberg to recognize Chamberlain as the 'professor of the Third Reich'.[14] Such horrific exploitation of the 'sick' aspects of Wagner's personality is the true symptom of the crisis of bourgeois society, while the entire Wagnerian corpus, within which there are pure and genuine evocations of myth, actually contains those elements of healing and salvation whose discriminate use by Thomas Mann received such brutal reactions from the Nazis. Nazism, however, could not admit that within the work of Wagner—Hitler's favourite musical artist—lay the weapons to combat delinquency and criminal ignorance. By this point, Nazi propaganda had included the identification of genuine myth as evoked by Wager with the crazed, self-appointed mythologies of the paladins of the Germanic race.

* * *

We have just mentioned Thomas Mann as a pedagogue of bourgeois society, and we are presented with his initial adhesion to Germanism, laid witnessed to by the *Reflections*. Before confronting such a problem it will be useful to refer back to Klaus Mann's memoir, in which he recalls the severe face of his father who, the day before the First World War, amazed his children by saying: 'Now a flaming sword will appear on the horizon.' And we also recall those years of war, which remain etched into Klaus' memoir, in which Thomas Mann presented himself to his children, stern and silent, descending fom the study in which he had put his writing on hold so as to dedicate himself painfully to the book on his Germanism, a dramatically chosen work in which he believed he pushed loyalty to the world crisis in which he was rooted to its extreme. Thomas Mann's moral and artistic greatness allows us to overcome

14 Schonauer, *Deutsche Literatur im Dritten Reich*, p. 32.

the dismay with which we read the pages of the *Reflections*, just as Rilke's greatness allows us to win over in the turmoil enacted through his celebrated songs to the 'god of war'. This was a moment in which the artists' conscience became overwhelmed by the sickness that presented itself as a necessary force of honesty. And it is undoubtedly painful to recognize in Thomas Mann's voice an appeal to Germans, urging them to realize themselves against the rest of the world, just as one can only hear Rilke's voice with fear and sadness, in the apologetic verses to Mars' dark epiphany.

The proximity between the mysterious forces of art and demonic horror was never as close and as revealing of tragedy as when experienced by the greatest artists in the depths of their being. But the history of the spirit often brings renewal and redemption: the tenth Dunio elegy and *The Magic Mountain*, while demonstrating the painful results of catharsis, are enough to calm those who see Rilke and Mann as masters of humanism. The renewal was carried out in the secret space of the artists' hearts, where every analysis stays firm. For Rilke, it was solitude which was renewed, through the aesthetic consumption of human destiny; for Mann, it was the new occupation as a pedagogue, the master of an exhausted bourgeois culture but also of every free spirit. The freedom of the spirit, the supreme good which is the singular basis of every good human action, stood on the other hand as a negative, sterile declaration through whoever defended crime. On 27 May 1933, Martin Heidegger opened the academic year of Freiburg University thus: 'The German university rejected the lauded "academic freedom"; this is not real freedom [. . .]. The concept of freedom of the German student has now been brought back to its real basis. From now on, it is from this that the bonds and service of the German student body will emerge.'[15] It is difficult to remember that these words were not pronounced by some obtuse hierarchical functionary devoted to the Führer but by one of the most ingenious philosophers of modern Germany. Here, 'service to the state' (but which state!) has substituted 'service to humankind'.* Whoever accepted and promulgated such a situation has no faith in humankind. Heidegger's guilt-ridden error did not, however, consist so much in a mistrust in people (which can be born of a painful moment in any spirit) but in having proposed this mistrust as the very basis of life; he proposed the foundations of crime as those of life. Whoever may be sure in themselves of the failure of every form of humanism, ought at the very least not make a political programme of such a certainty.

* * *

We have mentioned Heidegger as an accomplice in the Nazi abolition of myth and its capacity to heal. We ought say the same of Gottfried Benn and with an equally heavy heart. Just as Martin Heidegger was a great philosopher, so too Gottfried Benn was a great poet: is that which we have said of them the same as we ought say of Wagner? Not entirely. For, notwithstanding his wrongdoings, that seem to coincide with the Nazi disease, Wagner would

---

15 Schonauer, *Deutsche Literatur im Dritten Reich*, p. 160. 'Die vielbesungene "akademische Freiheit" wird aus der deutschen Universität verstossen [. . .] Der Begriff der Freiheit des deutschen Studenten wird jetzt zu seiner Wahrheit zurückgebracht. Aus ihr entfalten sich kuenfitg Bindung und Dienst der deutschen Studentenschaft.'

* [The reference to the state derives from the Italian translation of Heidegger's speech. Further on in the German text, Heidegger does speak, however, of service to the 'fate of the nation'.]

not see the horrors which the Nazis carried out every day of their squalid rule, and in his work the forces of love stand opposed to the Nazis' baseness. Gottfried Benn, like every one of Hitler's subjects, recognized Nazism's monstrosity; at the same time he believed it necessary to involve his own creative strength in the actions of murderers who destiny pressed 'irrevocably, indisputably' upon Germany. Horror and death are the darkness which enchant the spirit like the Gorgon's mask. But the Gorgon was, for the Greeks, a symbol of the most remote and ancient terror: Gottfried Benn believed that a truth hid in such terror, one that could not be accessed through the face of a god, and never wanted to admit that this was not only not a god, but a murderer—not a mystery, but a crime.

Benn's poetry was that of man's final moment: the sometimes frozen, sometimes pathetic lyrics of the Apocalypse. But even when he believed he had evoked the genuine imagery of myth, he charged into the horrors of an infernal kingdom, different from that of the Greeks, no longer recognizing the gods. The pact with Hitler must remain in European history not as evidence of a religion of the dead—which could even be noble—but as that of a shameful baseness of the human being. The religion of the dead demands a level of respect, to the extent that those—such as Leopardi—accept in it a tragic distortion of the spirit. Yet it becomes mere guilty devotion to a monster when it implies any absence of rebellion against those who created Auschwitz and Buchenwald.

In 1965, the Federal Republic of Germany authorized a rally of SS veterans, treating it almost as any other assembly of free persons allowed to meet and discuss their own ideals. Thus arose a further confirmation of Brecht's line:

'The womb from which it crept is fertile still.'*

This confirms that the horror of Nazi-Fascism was ingrained in the survival of the bourgeois social structures which today dominate a part of the world and which are entirely refracted through Thomas Mann's admonishment, the great pedagogue of the bourgeoisie. But despite the vitality and depth of his instruction, this admonishment sounds hollow to those politicians who rule over the majority of the hemisphere. The total absence of genuine myth—healing and calming in its humanism—from the structures of Nazi-Fascism is entirely confirmed in the current state of affairs.

That genuine myth was absent in Nazi Germany is clear. That it continues to be absent from post-Nazi German bourgeois culture is confirmed by our thesis, but also frighteningly witnessed by the survival of those forces which we hoped had been destroyed. During his electoral campaign of 1965, Ludwig Erhard emphasized time and again the 'degeneration' of German culture, and, thanks to this approach, even achieved an electoral victory. The front lines remain active. Bourgeois society, after its crisis of war, reasserts itself in Germany without having learnt anything from the terrifying experience of the past. Thomas Mann thus actuallu continues for many to be a 'traitor', even if no one—or almost no one—dares to really strike out against a writer whose glory has officially been restored.

* * *

* Bertold Brecht, *Der aufhaltsame Aufstieg des Arturo Ui* (*The Resistable Rise of Arturo Ui*) [1958], Epilogue: 'Der Schoß ist fruchtbar noch aus dem das kroch.' *Gesammelte Werke. Band IV* (Frankfurt: Suhrkamp, 1967), p. 1835.

Whoever wants to uncover the documents of genuine mythology of late-eighteenth- and early-nineteenth-century Germany ought not overlook the beautiful designs by Philipp Otto Runge which contain an authentic renewed epiphany of Hellenic *Erotes* and Roman cupids, those that Francesco Albani had already evoked with wondrous vitality and purity. Runge's four depictions—morning, midday, evening and night—used to hang in Goethe's music room in Weimar. The master of the house described them as 'beautiful and crazy at the same time'. For him they connected the clear—we might even say almost 'archetypal'—images of the vegetable world. Runge's divine youths appear in a cosmic perspective that represent the realm of myth, while the fertility of the seed is recognizable in their mysterious dignity; they grasp the event in an eternally present moment, that of perennial infancy.

While German culture at the end of the nineteenth century and in the first decades of the twentieth is rich with images of youths, they are on the whole quite distant from the mythic genuineness of Runge's depictions. Kerényi rightly notes in his essay that mythology is not—or is not merely—the biography of the gods, and that the imagery of the young god is not connected with that of the same god as an adult through a genetic phenomenology or even a chronological historical succession.[16] In the flow of myth, the image of the youth and that of the adult are autonomous, parallel realities. In the German culture we are discussing, the youth more often appears as the adult's past: Runge's eternal youth, whose epiphany entails a perennial, cosmic and non-specific childhood, is usually substituted with one from whom will develop the

---

16 Jung and Kerényi, *Science of Mythology*, p. 29.

man, a particular man: Knulp, Emil Sinclair, Tonio Kröger, Adrian Leverkühn or Felix Krull. At the same time, even in these figures there survive altered images of myth; we ought to say, rather, that in them bourgeois culture opens itself up to the evocation of the divine youth, within its own limits. Such limits, on which depend a transformation in the genuine character of mythic reality, are shown quite precisely through the biographical structure within which the image of the youth is systematically inserted. And it is precisely in the violence committed against the mythic nature of the divine youth that one perceives the fracture or alteration suffered by the mythic time of origins, now a biographically structured personal past.

To absorb the transformed image of the divine youth into a biographical (and frequently autobiographical) life attests to a sympathy for remembrance as sympathy for the past, even when masked by parody. To open up one's past or that of one's people to the images of myth—while transforming them in a way that subjects them strictly to a personal characterization—is a way to 'valorize' the past, or, better yet, of recognizing a particular value and charm within it, without transforming it into an eternal present. It is a symptom of the desire for past which is truly gone, and at the same time imbued with a value that seems to be lacking from the present: a symptom, that is, of the attitude of those who, after the confrontation of the past and present, doubt that they have lived through unrepeatable experiences, and above all who believe that they are witnessing a decline.

Various remedies are juxtaposed to this decline: for Knulp, after the moment of his regrets for his childhood, death is the soothing communion with God; for Emil Sinclair, it is the knowledge of the divine invoked within himself and within the cosmos; for Tonio Kröger, it is the exercise of art as an evocative and healing force. For Adrian Leverkühn, this fall is felt when he is projected back into his 'predestined' childhood, with all its warning signs. Thomas Mann never finished narrating the life of Felix Krull.

On the other hand, it is necessary to recall that Hanno Buddenbrook dies young, and that with his death Thomas Mann dramatically recognized the impossibility of opening up the bourgeois biography to genuine, soothing myth, instead implicitly denouncing the transformation suffered by the mythic imagery of the divine youth, forced into a structure of personal biography. In Mann's work, the regenerative moment comes, in fact, in *The Elect* when the youth returns to being a pure image of myth, freed from biographical reference.

Genuine myth excludes remembrance, because it implies an eternal present. Late-German-bourgeois culture's sympathy for remembrance—and the discussion could also be widened beyond the limits of German culture—is fundamentally a tendency for the transformation of myth which might allow the bourgeoisie to acquire that form of noble inactivity already sacrificed to the preoccupation with 'Calvinist' activity, as described by Max Weber. It seems to us, however, that in ceding to the charms of a memory open to myth—even if a transformed one—the bourgeoisie was able to satisfy their own urge 'to be an artist', and therefore to observe their own decay, a satisfaction which clearly could not be achieved through a attitude turned towards the present and the future.

This turning to the past does not include, however, a radical and self-destructive nihilism because—and this is perhaps the force of survival which moves it—it offers up new values of a 'contemplative' character in the very moment in which the values of activity are chipped away by reasons independent from the spiritual metamorphosis of the bourgeoisie.

In *Buddebrook*, Consul Jean Buddenbrook rereads and expands the family history book year after year, but the past which he has turned towards is deprived of myths. Instead, it is the past which Thomas Mann tends towards in narrating the events of a family pregnant with mythic imagery; only incitement to the activity and sustenance of the present can arise from Jean's remembrance of the past, while Mann's remembrance of the past—far more enchantingly—gives birth to images of decay and death. These, however, allow the son of the grand Lübeck bourgeoisie to 'become an artist', i.e. to substitute those values of practical activity that have fallen into the void with new values of a noble inactivity. In the place of those conversations with God to which Jean dedicates so many pages of his family history book on the occasion of every new event, Mann's turning towards the past sets up past acts of devotion to a dark God who arises from behind the mythic imagery—acts that become all the more apparent as the mythic imagery loses its genuine character.

* * *

In their book *The Morning of the Magicians* [*Le matin des magiciens*], Louis Pauwels and Jacques Bergier observe that 'the climate of Nazi terror, which no one could have predicted, was forewarned in the terrifying stories by the German writer Hans Heinz Ewers, *The Mandragore* [*Alraune*] and *In Terror* [*Das Grauen*], who was destined to become the official poet of the regime, and to write the *Horst Wessel Lied*.'[17] This is undeniably true; yet from the

---

17 Louis Pauwels and Jacques Bergier, *Le matin des magiciens*

beginning of the century there was another work in the German language that seems to be more profoundly revealing: Alfred Kubin's novel *The Other Side*, to which we have already referred in preceding chapters as a typical example of the technification of myth and the vitiated relation with the past which derives from this.

Kubin wrote his only novel in 1908, at the apex of a psychic crisis culminating in the death of his father and marked by a painful spiritual sterility. The context is similar to that of the novel *Demian*, written by Hesse at the end of the crisis that led him to subject himself to a psychoanalytic cure administered by a follower of Jung—with the difference, however, that Kubin never seems to have imparted his knowledge of psychoanalytic techniques on his work—techniques towards which he shows a certain irony instead ('Whoever tries to explain things nowadays draws on the work of our quite ingenious psychologists')—while drawing on esoterica to explain the same matters on which psychoanalysis usually focuses.

The Other Side is told in first person, from the point of view of a distanced observer. It is the story of Claus Patera, a man granted with unique powers and immense riches, through which he establishes the 'Kingdom of Dreams' in a remote part of central Asia. He has old and ancient buildings brought in from every part of the globe, and moves them to his distant Asian land, through which he constructs a city, adorning it entirely with objects from the past. An enormous wall surrounds it, pierced by a single gate. Nothing new can pass through this gate, nothing unused; the wall defends the Kingdom of Dreams from

---

(Paris: Gallimard, 1960). [English translation: *The Morning of the Magicians: The Dawn of Magic* (Rollo Myers trans.) (London: Anthony Gibbs & Phillips, 1963), p. 136.]

every kind of progress which Patera has declared to be inimical. The Kingdom's inhabitants themselves, whether invited or gathered by Patera, wear eighteenth-century clothes, and the artworks bought on Patera's behalf in every land—along with antiques of every kind—must not be any more recent that the 1860s.

This is the exterior face of the Kingdom of Dreams, to which the narrator—who as a child had been a school friend of Paterna—decides to move. And thus he slowly realizes that the Kingdom and its inhabitants are governed by a kind of 'spell' that makes them into slaves at the same time as it gives life to them, and which seems concentrated in Patera himself. A range of events, however, lead him to believe that Patera might be merely the intermediary of some other superior and hidden powers, a demiurge inhabited by terrifying, animating forces that have defined the Kingdom's existence through him. We are told that after an adolescence of vagabondage, Patera acquired his immense riches in some accidental way in China, and that, a little after becoming incredibly rich, he came to know a mysterious indigenous tribe in Tian Shan, comprised of men with light skin and blue eyes, an isolated occurrence among a Mongol population. This tribe conserves unique customs and knowledge, in which Patera participates; wounded in a tiger hunt, he was healed by one of the mysterious wise men, and forged an intimate bond with their tribe: 'when he departed, he left behind rich gifts, making the promise to return soon, very soon. The chiefs accompanied him for a long way, and they say that the parting was most solemn.'

Patera returns to the ancient tribe's land in order to establish the Kingdom of Dreams, and the mysterious community of wise men continues to live in the suburbs of his city, dedicating themselves to meditation and shadowy activities.

In the final section of the novel, the Kingdom of Dreams is gradually destroyed, almost through a phenomenon of organic purification accelerated by the coming of an 'American' who wants to make himself sovereign over the Kingdom and engages in a dramatic conflict with Patera. The final hours of the Kingdom of Dreams are marked by a monstrous proliferation of physical and moral wrongdoings which end with the crumbling of the capital. The suburb of the ancient tribe, nevertheless, remains impervious to every destruction, and, when the palaces of the city are razed by an earthquake, the community of wise men with blue eyes begins a procession towards a temple dug into the mountain which Patera also reaches. In a mysterious chamber in the temple, it seems that the sovereign, far from the anyone's gaze, meets a horrific force which kills him. Having arranged his mysteriously rejuvenated body, the ancient tribe distance themselves for ever. The author concludes: 'The phenomenon of Patera remains unsolved. Perhaps the real rulers were the men with the blue eyes, who activated an inanimate puppet bearing Patera's appearance through magical powers, and who created and destroyed the Kingdom of Dreams for mere pleasure.'*

As a whole and in its many meaningful particulars, the vision—sketched out, we repeat, in 1908—seems to today's eyes to contain the very schema of the events of Nazism and its esoteric structures. As Pauwels and Bergier

---

* Alfred Kubin, *Die andere Seite* (Munich and Leipzig: G. Müller, 1908), p. 335. [Original translation, but also see Michael Mitchell's translation *The Other Side* (Sawtry: Dedalus Books, 2014), here p. 244.]

have noted (in the volume to which we will continue to refer), from 1933 onwards, Nazi Germany truly constituted 'the other side' in the conflict with Western civilization: deliberately isolated from every phenomenon of modern culture, it became subject to rulers who burnt the bridges with almost the whole world, and who wanted to create a 'German science', a 'German philosophy', a 'German art', radically estranged from the creations of the rest of humanity.[18]

Pauwels and Bergier insist on considering this isolation also as a consequence of the desire of certain esoteric groups within the highest ranks of the Nazis, including Hitler himself, who had aimed for the realization of a complete, if not always (nor necessarily) coherent, programme for the renewal of man. The 'new man' who would be born through Hitler's political work and his concurrent efforts in practical magic were meant to include those forces ignored by the rest of 'inferior' humanity. At the basis of this necessary work for the genesis of 'new man' was supposedly a series of dramatic clashes with the laws and institutions of reason, progress and 'materialism', that is, against everything which might represent a state of slumber in the confrontation with the magical awakening of whoever stands in a direct relation with the dark forces. Taken as a whole, all these clashes formed a single, great ritual, a reawakening of the kind described by Dietrich Eckart in the words of a battle hymn later written across Hitler's military standard: 'Germany, awake!'

Our end now is to consider the evidence of Nazi esotericism from a phenomenological standpoint, so as

---

18 Pauwels and Bergier, *Le matin des magiciens*, p. 227. Myers translation p. 219.

to frame Nazism within the context of that phenomenon of the alteration of myth whose traces we have been following. Kubin's novel seems to us particularly significant exactly because it is a document preceding Nazism, manifesting a deformation of myth which in Nazism would become their systematic order, even acquiring a formidable 'secular wing'.

As we have said, at the end of *The Other Side* Kubin asks himself whether Patera were not, in truth, simply a puppet animated by the mysterious Asians with the blue eyes. An analogous question could—with appropriate modification—be put by those considering the statements by Rudolf Hesse on the relation between Hitler and his own secret putative animator, Karl Haushofer, and more generally the rare accounts regarding the so-called Thule Society. This society was probably made up of an esoteric group active in Germany in the first decades of the century and, it seems, connected with analogous Russian circles. The mythical name of Thule, the lost island of the far North, seemed to symbolize a lost civilization whose members held an intimate relation with the dark powers which, as we have said, were to have been the basis for the forces of the 'new man' projected by Nazism. After the disappearance of ancient Thule, the secret of the relations with those powers is supposed to have survived in the hands of a small group of initiates, whose heirs the Thule Society reunited.

The Thule Society included Dietrich Eckart and Alfred Rosenberg—the 'first poet' and 'first ideologue' of the Third Reich, respectively—as well as Rudolf Hess and his teacher Karl Haushofer, professor of geopolitics at Munich University. From 1920, Eckart came into contact with Hitler, in the arena of the small German Workers' Party of which both were a part, and then 'educated' the future Führer for three years, who never reneged on his admiration for him. The Thule Society nonetheless gained particular momentum once Karl Haushofer was a member, who—through Hess—probably met Hitler for the first time while the two were imprisoned at Landsberg. Approaching Haushofer, Hitler came into contact with an esoteric doctrine which, as with Patera, was founded on an Oriental basis. Haushofer had been to India and the Far East many times in order to research the sources of truth, through a path which—Schopenhauer onwards—had been taken by countless Germans of various backgrounds and intellectual tendencies. He epitomized the fascination and influence imposed on the German scene by the esoteric doctrines of the Far East. This was especially true for the Tibetan tradi-tion, of which Sven Hedin—a Tibetanist and friend of Haushofe—had become an important intermediary. Haushofer thus came to know of a Tibetan myth about an ancient race of wise men in communion with great superhuman forces who, after a cataclysm which originated in the Gobi desert, found refuge in a great cavern under the Himalayas, subdivided into two groups: one in Agartha, city of contemplation and non-participation, and the other in Shambhala, city of power and of renewal-determining violence. Shambhala would be the site of the alliance between the heirs to the antique force and the fashioners of the 'new man', guided by Haushofer.

The survival of the Tibetan tradition could, however, also be found in the context of the Thule Society via Alfred Rosenberg, who was in close relation with the emigrants of the Russian White movement; at the end of May 1921, they came together in a congress in Bad Reichenhall in Bavaria, centred round Hetman Skoropadsky (who the Germans had made lord of Ukraine in 1918).

Skoropadsky's partisans, especially his chief press officer
Nemirovic-Dancenko, were to have frequent connection
with the Nazis via Rosenberg, speaking at their meetings
and writing for the *Völkischer Beobachter*. And the
Russian emigrants in esotericist groups had already been
in contact with the interventions of the medium
Badmaiev, trained in Lhasa and friend to the Tsarina
Alessandra Feodorovna. It was she who introduced the
swastika to the Russian court, and thus contributed to the
Nazis' adoption of the symbol, and probably neither
one nor the other was a stranger to the Tibetan inspiration
(it was either Haushofer or Rosenberg who suggested
the swastika to Hitler). The Nazis, on the other hand, did
not cease their interest in Tibetan esotericism at this
point, especially in the context of the research of the
'Ahnenerbe'—the Institute for the study of ancient heritage, officially founded by Himmler in 1935 and incor-
porated into the SS in January 1939. Among the research
missions of the 'Ahnenerbe', a group of scholars were dis-
patched to Tibet, guided by Dr Schäfer, to collect material
on the origins of the 'Aryan' race, and there is even docu-
mentation of the presence of a small Tibetan colony in
Berlin, formed at the wishes of the same men.

If we now consider Rudolf Hess' claims (as gathered
by Jack Fishman) in the light of this discussion[19]—in particular that Haushofer, bearer of the knowledge and
strengths of the Orient, was the Thule Society's 'Master'
and the secret inspiration for Hitler's esoteric activity—
we can note a singular identity between Haushofer and
Hitler on the one hand, and between the Asians with the
blue eyes and Patera on the other. An animated puppet,

---

19 Jack Fishman, *The Seven Men of Spandau* (New York: Praeger,
1954).

moved through magical powers: perhaps this is Patera in Kubin's novel; and whoever probably moves the puppet with secret forces is a mysterious people from central Asia, different from the Mongols, a survival of a remote and ancient past: a community of 'supermen' with a steady blue gaze, whose sacred centre is a temple dug into the mountain, and who remain immune to every upheaval and destruction.

If we did not know that Kubin wrote his novel in 1908, we would recognize the work of one of Haushofer's disciples in *The Other Side*, or the work of Ferdynand Antoni Ossendowski, who spoke of Agartha and Shambhala in in his 1925 essay 'Animals, Peoples and Gods' ['Tiere, Menschen und Götte'] or at least René Guénon. If, however, the novel had a date after the fall of Nazism, we would immediately recognize within it a dramatic—and confusingly precise—allegory for Hitler's life. Kubin narrates, in fact, how a 'kind of secret society' existed in the Kingdom of Dreams, with a specific ritual and unique sacred objects: an egg, a nut, bread, cheese, honey, milk, wine and vinegar. 'This religion, furthermore, could not be exhausted only through food and drink. A little later I learned that hair, horns, pinecones, mushrooms and hay were also sacred. Even horse and cow manure had a higher meaning. Among the internal organs, the liver and the heart had a particular importance, and among animals, fish.'* We have already noted the existence of secret societies and ritual-magical practices in the world of Nazism; to this one could add *Ahnenerbe*. Friedrich Hielscher recounted to Jüngler in 1943 that he had 'established a church' with sacred regulations which recall quite closely those imagined by Kubin; Jüngler wrote in his diary: 'He has moved beyond

---

* Kubin, *Die andere Seite*, p. 93. Mitchell translation, p. 77.

the rules now and is quite advanced in the liturgy. He has shown me a series of songs and a cycle of feasts, "the pagan year", which include an orderly series of divinities, colours, animals, meals, stones and plants.'[20]

And one can also recall the image of Patera himself:

His voice had acquired something fascinating, smooth and stirring. I saw his white teeth gleaming, his movements were heavy and rigid. I understood only a small part of what he said. The sounds were hoarse and choked, his breast puffed up, the veins on his pale neck were ready to explode. Suddenly his face became as grey as stone, and there were only his wide, staring eyes flashing, incandescent with their inexplicable charm.[*]

Is he speaking of the make-believe sovereign of the Kingdom of Dreams, or of Hitler?

* * *

The return of a man towards his infancy, understood as the attempt to valorize the past through myth, without nevertheless transforming into an eternal present, finds an equivalent in the attitude of those who are erected as representatives of a people and engaged in evoking its infancy, attaching the past of their own legacy to a non-genuine myth—for it is a myth which is deliberately 'evoked', personalized and nationalized. This was the attitude of the creators of the 'Germanic renaissance' which proposed, in narrative works and essays from the second half of the nineteenth century onwards, the imagery of a

---

20 Pauwels and Bergier, *Le matin des magiciens*, p. 340; Myers translation p. 208.

* Kubin, *Die andere Seite*, pp. 143–4. Mitchell translation, p. 112.

German past supported not through the scruples and rigour of scientific reconstruction but through the desire to mythologize their own 'national childhood'. It is significant that the most celebrated writers and major success of this work of mythologizing the childhood of the German people pertained to the world or art, and were concerned with supporting their message within an artistic perspective. We think to Julius Langbehn, the author of an anonymously published essay in 1890 and republished many times after that, titled *Rembrandt als Erzieher* [Rembrandt as Educator]; to Ferdinand Avenarius, editor of the journal *Der Kunstwerk* [*The Work of Art*]; to Adolf Bartels, author of a widely read *Geschichte der deustchen Dichtung von Hebbel bis zur Gegenwart* [*The History of Germany Poetry from Hebbel to the Present*]. All of these works focused on the recognition of a German 'quality' in matters of the spirit, the heritage of those who experienced Germanism's childhood, asserting a mythical moment of a non-genuine 'divine childhood'; they all urge on the affirmation and rebirth of a German 'quality' primarily in the sphere of culture, of art, of spiritual activity. This is, in the end, another aspect of the task undertaken by a bourgeois society in order to substitute values of practical activity with those of 'noble contemplation'. Very soon, however, this desire for a contemplation which, even if without admission, implies the realization of the decadence of active functions, transforms into the will for the instrumentalization of contemplative values so as to organize a new activity: it becomes the reform of the active structures of society, based on the values that the mythologization of that society's ethnic, national childhood offers up to contemplation; and it soon became Nazism. Contemporaneously, forms of mysticism or pseudo-mysticism developed out of the values of that mythologized past, the religious equivalent to an aesthetic backwards turn, unable to satisfy the religious needs of a bourgeoisie by now quite distant from the lost paradise of Calvinism. And forms of esotericism were formed that were destined to sustain that phenomenon, almost like a secret theology, explicitly open to death and thus able, in every moment, to carry out that overthrowing of life and death that produces merely a tragic caricature of an otherwise ancient and mysterious paradox.

CHAPTER 6

There is a form of historical space that corresponds to historical time, one that constitutes the locus of epiphany and determines its structure in relation to myth. The relation between time, space and myth is a paradox, for myth is intrinsically atemporal and non-spatial: moreover, every epiphany of myth is paradoxical, within which logic necessarily gives into emotion. And emotion allows myth to 'heal' historical space and time while also providing an innocence, that of the genuinely mythical figure in the presence of the artist. But if the epiphany of myth is no more than mere rubble, the historical space in which it is carried out appears marked by guilt, understood as a ferment of destruction: *guilt* in this case is equivalent to the unreal, or to a death which is not contained within life.

Max Klinger's celebrated *Beethoven*, carved in white marble, sits on a bronze throne decorated with gold and enamel, a robe of yellow agate spread over his knees. The unchanging, crystalline materials bear a singular relation to the appearance of natural reality: a relation both imitative and archetypical, almost as if the marble, bronze, gold and agate, suspended within archetypical space, crystallize the tangible realities immersed within historical space, making their ferment of destruction eternal instead of abstracting these realities from the possibility of decay. In this sense, the *Beethoven* is a profoundly funereal sculpture, for it seems to prolong death, the process of destruction, indefinitely, rather than opposing it as a symbol of incorruptibility. With the *Beethoven*, that is, Klinger had committed the utmost act of devotion to death (a concept he had already encountered frequently in his work): devotion to death as a life-containing interior space, rendered innocent by myth.

A year after the presentation of the *Beethoven* in the Secession exhibition in Vienna (May 1902), Wassily Kandinsky (in his early residency in Munich) took up an old Bavarian folk technique of painting several small pictures on a mirror.[1] In these, the mirror remains clear in the spaces left free between each picture, almost like a gold ground which nevertheless reflects the surrounding reality within the painting itself, and even at times shows the observers. In these young works by Kandinsky, historical space is again directly immersed and rendered perennial in its historicity through the very material of the creation, just as with Klinger's *Beethoven*. Theoretically inalterable, the mirror continues to reflect the semblances of the sensible, historical world, attaching this to the perishable aspects, in an indefinite duration.

And again it is death—death as an interior space—which emerges in this enduring reality, without nevertheless losing its destructive characteristics. The mythological value of Kandinsky's paintings does not consist in the subjects (which are often drawn from fairy tales)—just as the mythological value of the *Beethoven* does not so much consist in the heroic figure—but in the particular manner of conceiving space, in which death is perennially founded within life. Exiting the 'paradise of archetypes,'[2] humankind could no longer ignore historical space, that which is at the same time intrinsically extraneous to myth and

---

1 These paintings are conserved, for the most part, in Munich.

2 According to the expression of Mircea Eliade.

thus has internalized it as the space of death, implicitly conferring onto it a cosmic fullness that gives rise to a kind of vertigo, for within it the earth disappears and one finds oneself suspended in the void of an immense cavern opening up within the most intimate depths of living reality itself.

We have already cited Thomas Mann's novel *The Wardrobe*, and here we can return to it in order to evoke this vertigo in the presence of the space of death, a feeling that characterizes the mysterious experience of Albrecht van der Qualen. But it would be just as appropriate to cite Virgil's last moment in Broch's *The Death of Virgil*, or even the 'night' of the second act of *Tristan und Isolde*. The reduction of historical space to the interior space of death is a phenomenon which deeply marks the mythology of modern German culture, and it does not lie beyond all the efforts of bourgeois culture to rediscover those values of contemplation in the process of opening up history to myth. In *The Elective Affinities*, Goethe had already pointed towards the path of healing through myth, to that of a historical space which comprehends human nature as a complex of alchemical elements inasmuch as it is permeated by death. The mystery which dominates the novel and the cosmic value of the *attractiones electivae* depend exactly on the presence of death within the characters' life, and the healing force of the work derives from the fact that the interior space of death opens up into the flow of myth. The natural, external projection of such an interior space—the park in which the events unfold—assumes the form of a *hortus conclusus*, ordered according to a clearly esoteric widsom. And thus the characters become genuinely mythical figures while also conserving their singular, dynamic emotions, those which Rilke would have called 'the death appropriate to each of them'.

More than a hundred years later, Bertolt Brecht would base his dramatic theory on the dialectical participation of the spectator and the actor in representative theatre; a theory which consists fundamentally in declaring the opening of historical space to mythic epiphany as necessary from the moral point of view. Differing from the aesthetics of traditional theatre, which attempted to involve the spectator in the dramatic activity in a way which offered him a temporary entrance into a sphere apparently alien to historical space, Brecht's theory imposes on the spectator the 'knowledge of being at the theatre' and of discussing that which the actors propose to him, as in a rally.[3] Historical space thus opens up to the drama represented on the stage and permanently makes this its own conflict and imagery. Thus, in other words, one could say that myth becomes history; but it is also significant that history opens itself up to myth and becomes 'healing' in the very moment in which its contingent aspects, those of destruction, become endlessly fixed in the collective consciousness. The transformation of historical space in the interior space of death can take place, indeed, only in terms of the values of collectivity, the only ones capable of integration into genuine epiphanies of myth. The pain of Mother Courage, Johanna Dark and Shen Te is the 'passion' of the great figures of myth and, contemporaneously—or, rather, exactly for this reason—the reality of death which each carries within themselves. But this coincidence can take place only if singular pain and singular destruction are also the pain and destruction *of humankind*, not of *a man*. Otherwise one substitutes the

---

3 The bibliography on Brecht's theory is extensive. We refer in general to the bibliographical essays by Walter Nubel, beginning with 'Bertolt Brecht—Bibliographie', *Sinn und Form* 1–3 (1957): 479–623.

genuine figure of myth with a nocturnal apparition, a false dream.

* * *

At the end of the narration of the death of Charles the Bold, in the second part of *The Notebooks of MLB* [*Aufzeichnungen des Malte Laurids Brigge*], Rilke writes that the court jester was the first to enter the room in which the duke's body had been laid out, examining everything closely, from the jewelled crown perched on his disfigured head, to the huge scarlet boots with their large golden spurs: ' "Very well dressed," he finally said, appreciatively. "Only, a little too theatrical." Death seemed to him like a puppeteer, who quickly needed a duke."*

These words, written in the margins of the manuscript of the *Notebooks*, contain the key to the meaning of the entire episode, leading us to recognize in it the evocation of a history which is not 'healed' by myth, and of a historical space in which death acts as a profane puppeteer, rather than as a force capable of 'healing' the historical reality by attributing it with the most authentic and extra-temporal truth.

The imagery of the marionette also appears in the second of the *Duino Elegies*, juxtaposed to that of the angels in aversion that leaves man with no chance of peace.[4] In a profane history, historical space coincides with the staging of a puppet theatre (a transformed trace,

---

* Rainer Maria Rilke, *Gesammelte Werke* (Cologne: Anaconda Verlag, 2012), p. 336: '"Gut angekleidet", sagte er schliesslich anerkennend, "vielleicht ein Spur zu deutlich". Der Tod kam ihm vor wie ein Puppenspieler, der rasch einen Herzog braucht.' [The Italian version translates 'deutlich' as 'theatrical' rather than 'clear' or 'obvious', which is imprecise—but relevant to Jesi's preceding discussion of Brecht.]

4 See Chapter 1, note 22 (p. 20).

in a negative sense, of Wilhelm Meister's miniature theatre!) in which the angel can intervene; but here the angel is 'terrifying', not the calming angel of myth but the horror of an obscure force which the marionette, distant and menacing, can only foreshadow. Faced with a historical space which has not internalized the site of the personal death, Rilke asks in Elegy III:[5]

> Oh if only we too could find a pure, measured,
>   subtle, human
> strip of fruitful land, our own between stream
>   and rock.

The internalization of historical space as the site of death is rendered arduous through the abandonment of man to the destructive force which is not *his* death, but only the consequence of the limitation of his being within the framework of the cosmos: 'for man feels his destruction there.'[6] Love can be the path which leads to the 'personal' death, that is, to the space of death that each person carries within themselves, for in their embrace, lovers 'attempt a pure life.' ['*einen reinen Vorgang*'—Elegy IV]. And yet:[7]

> To sing the beloved is one thing. Alas,
> that hidden guilty river-god of blood is another.

The destructive flow prevails in the very moment of the experience of love, the impersonal death leading far away from one's *own* death. For Rilke, the figures of 'the abandoned' thus become exemplary: of the women

---

5 See Chapter 2, note 46.

6 Also see Walther Rehm, *Orpheus: Der Dichter und die Toten. Selbstdeutung und Totenkult bei Novalis, Hölderlin, Rilke* (Düsseldorf: Schwann Verlag, 1950).

7 Rilke, *Duineser Elegien,* Elegy III, ll. 1–2.

> Eines ist, die Geliebte zu singen. Ein anderes, wehe,
> jenen verborgenen schuldigen Fluss-Gott des Bluts.

whose love finds no response and, precisely for this reason—because it is not destroyed by a reciprocal destruction—draws on the truth of the personal death.

The figure of the 'abandoned woman' evoked by
Rilke has a mythical precedent in the 'abandoned' and
'rejected' women of Hellenic traditions: Medea, Phaedra,
Arianna. These feminine images are on the other hand
the result of a late metamorphosis of the original *kore*,
the virgin and wife of a god (one thinks of that which we
have already said in Chapter 2 in relation to Rilke's *White
Princess*). In Hellenic mythology, the precarious relation
between the Kore and her infernal spouse was already
frequently resolved through an 'abandonment' suffered
by the Kore herself, *transformed* in a negative sense,
becoming an evil bestower of death rather than a symbol
of the relation between death and rebirth, warden of the
passage to the afterlife. In Rilke's evocation, she fulfils a
further reversion of the mythic pattern, and the abandoned woman returns to being the positive symbol *par
excellence* of femininity: she returns to being, that is, the
original, antique Kore, through whom one reaches the
'personal' healing death, the depository of truth. It will
be another Kore still, the Lament of the *Elegies*, to guide
the young dead man through the path of 'the other kingdom'. In Elegy X, the healing is complete; the seemingly
Egyptian landscape in which the young dead man roams
is not the historical space of Egypt but its 'double', the
result of its internalization as the space of death: Rilke
explicitly states that the Sphinx contemplated by the
young dead man is 'the sister to that of the Nile'.[8]

* * *

---

8 Rilke, *Duineser Elegien,* Elegy X, l. 74:

> Brüderlich jenem am Nil,
> der erhabene Sphinx.

If the mythic epiphany possesses its extra-temporal immobility, the historical time in which it seems to be enacted could be said to be, indeed, 'irredeemable'—as Eliot wrote—'redeemed' once and for all. The activity of the artist who continues to produce a particular historical period throughout their work, and therefore continues to create 'variations' on the same theme which resides in the relation with mythic flow, thus acquires a gratuitous feeling. In reality, however, the necessity—the genuine necessity—of continuing to produce even after one has reached the revelation of epiphany, depends on the dynamic character that death (as an element within life) confers on the course of myth. This dynamic imposed by death could be seen superficially within a struggle for survival, fought by the artist with the weapons that allow him to renew the true experience of myth; but this would lead to viewing death as a perennial enemy rather than a reality of human existence, neither good nor evil, friend nor foe. This is not a struggle, therefore, nor—on the contrary—a sublimation or rising above the utmost communion with death (as Thomas Mann suggests in *Doktor Faustus* in relation to Beethoven's own fate). Rather, it is a constant movement, a dynamic impulse determined by death, which—and this is a secondary fact—from moment to moment seems to come closer to, rather than being more distant from, the persona of the creator. No linear, evolutionary schema can be applied to this phenomenon, for there is no possibility of measuring any supposed greater or lesser proximity of death in the spiritual life of an artist: every instant is permeated by death in terms which escape any attempt to measure the intensity of such a communion.

Analogously, however, one cannot allow the recognition of some new 'discovery' in the perennial movement of creative activity, some 'revelation' which constitutes an extension of experience and knowledge. The uninter-rupted progress of an artist's production is precisely a consequence of the dynamic impulse which derives from death: and, to use a metaphor, a constant stirring of the same cauldron. Continuing with the metaphor, we might add that the activity of every artist is a *single* stirring of the same cauldron: the substance which is moved is always the same and the direction of the move-ment resides in the death that each person carries within themselves.

As such, everyone is bound to renew the movement day after day, even if nothing new can be brought by each rising dawn. God remains the darkness with whom one speaks but of whom one cannot speak, and neither nov-elty nor discovery can exist. The obstacle cannot be over-come through a psychology which identifies within the creative exercise the progressive realization of the Ego, for the Ego is already entirely itself in the first moment of creation: in the first relation with the reality of myth, that is, in the first total subjection to the dynamic impulse that derives from death itself.

* * *

There are versions of the Tristan legend that include the theme of the *Salle aux images*, an underground chamber full of statues where Tristan secretly goes to caress the simulacrum of Isolt.[9] The attitude of the German artists who 'heal' the historical space internalized as the space of 'personal' death could take this *Salle aux images* as its symbol, whose funerary aspect is clear enough. Death as an interior space is precisely an underground cavity dug within the life of each human being, and populated with figures more real than those included within historical

---

9 See Schoepperle, *Tristan and Isolt*, p. 579.

space. If we substitute the statue of Isolt with the imagery of the *kore*—who, in effect, is concealed therein—this solitary devotion is also transformed into a common emotion thanks to the collective value of the genuine epiphany of myth.

The *Salle aux images* is, on the other hand, a kind of subterranean time destined to welcome the manifestation of the mysterious charm of Isolt, and every spontaneous attitude which faces mythic epiphany cannot be deprived of the respect—a truly religious respect—for the mystery which constitutes the most profound foundation of myth. We have spoken at length of the healing power which myth exercises over men and we have observed some manifestations of this within human collectivity. We have not, nevertheless, attempted to advance a hypothesis regarding the profound nature of this healing force, for such a nature can only be glimpsed in the moment of the emotion of those who welcome it with a pure mind. As for the question of the essence of myth, for now we can only reply with Rilke's words: 'Is it not from the pure stars that he has gained the innermost insight into her pure countenance?'[10]

---

10 Rilke, *Duineser Elegien,* Elegy III, ll. 12–13:

Hat er die innige Einsicht
in ihr reines Gesicht nicht aus dem reinen Gestirn?

APPENDIX

PREMISE TO THE APPENDIX

The previously unpublished material we present below is conserved in Jesi's papers. In our opinion, taken together with those already published—such as the epistolary exchange with Karoly Kerényi and the brief exchange with Max Brod and Gershom Scholem cited in the introduction to this volume—these papers represent a nucleus of work that provides an idea of the intellectual task Jesi undertook in preparing his draft of *Secret Germany*.

The first document, to which we have already referred in the introduction, is a synopsis of the book. Written on 18 February 1965, it shows the three main movements, a useful guide for understanding the structure and main themes of the final version (for example, the reasoning behind the woman and the city, the strategy of parody . . .), despite the turn or 'healing' which Jesi's meeting with Kerényi provoked at the end of May that year. The same internal structure of *Secret Germany* can be seen even more clearly, however, if one looks to the edges, or, rather, to the essays, stories, plays and letters that Jesi had already picked out and which he considered publishing in the series he was editing for the Genoan publishing house Silva. These works bear important witness to the 'great mythological work and [. . .] great crisis that has marked German culture'. We have thus published below the first editorial plan for the 'Collection of texts and studies' entitled 'Myth and Symbol in Modern Germany': *Secret Germany* was to be the first of the planned volumes and was, in truth, the only one published (in 1967). Among the variations undergone by the project we recall here that undertaken by Jesi in 1969 when he finished his draft of *Spartakus: Symbology of a Revolt*, defining it as the third volume in the imprint, writing that 'this book follows on from the discussion in *Secret Germany* (n. 1. in the collection).'[1]

These first documents were originally written for Umberto Silva and Sergio Pautasso, Jesi's colleagues at the publishing house. We accompany these first with some writings which one can recognize as first drafts of chapters for *Secret Germany*. In the brief text which we have given the editorial title 'Germanism', Jesi focused on the reasons and meaning behind his own work as Germanist-mythologist by illustrating the exceptional role of German culture within a theoretical context that refers back to (and temporarily preceded) the model of consciousness he had proposed in the important 1965 essay *Myth and the Language of Collectivity*. At the same time, he outlined the limits of the term 'Germanism' in a way that seems to be an early response to Kerényi's advice: 'we do not need to hypostasize matters, as if "myth" or "Germany" were concrete substances.'[2] To aid a certain logical development, we then follow these texts with three closely connected fragments: a draft of the first chapter, entitled 'Culture and Moral Responsibility'; the brief 'Confession and Autobiographical Myth'; and 'Revelation and Morality', the last also conceived of as a possible opening for the book. These fragments focus on the question of the function of the artist inasmuch as he or she is involved in the emergence of the dark forces that— according to Jesi—constitute the most intimate aspect

---

1 See the Editor's Note and the Editorial Schema drawn up by Jesi in *Spartakus*, pp. 167–72.

2 See Kerényi's letter to Jesi, 7 February 1967, in *Demone e mito*, p. 111.

of modern civilization, which in Germany reached a paroxystic intensity of violence in Nazi instrumentalization. Even while there might be various intellectual approaches (Lukács on the one hand, Mann on the other), it is nevertheless the case that in each instance one is dealing with the artist's relation to their own work, their relation to the events or characters through which these dark forces are expressed. The moral problem (of sickness or guilt) thus becomes the problem of mythical autobiography or confession, according to the relation of nonidentification with the novel's characters, obtained 'thanks to art's capacity to understand everything without being understood'. If 'Confession and Autobiographical Myth' was written after Jesi's meeting with Kerényi in Turin (as we are led to believe by the citation of *Fiorenza*), 'Revelation and Morality' can most likely be dated to 17 May 1965, i.e. following the letter in which Kerényi invited Jesi, among other matters, to not ignore Rilke and 'his relation with death'.[3] In a letter from the previous day that was destined to overlap with Kerényi's own, Jesi had written: 'I personally feel [. . .] the need to find some clarity in that part of me closest to and least defended against the dark forces working within German tragedy . . . '.[4] In this draft, Jesi's personal problem—still defined here in Buber's terms as 'speaking with God'—can in truth be overlaid with that of Rilke's own dramatic experience ('speaking of oneself [. . .] speaking of Rilke'). This represent kind of temporary or partial adherence typical to a discussion that aims at truth via a mask or pseudonym, according to 'a concealment that simultaneously reveals'.[5] In the pedagogic strategy of the final lines ('Then [Rilke]

3 See Introduction, p. *xiii* and n7.

4 See Introduction, pp. *xv–xvi* and n21.

5 Martin Heidegger, *Parmenides* (Frankfurt am Main: Klostermann, 1982), p. 53.

would withdraw, leaving each to follow the path in solitude, in the secret of their own being, or to remain and
contemplate distant, unreachable and disturbing dawns'),
Jesi comes upon the first formulation of what would
become a central theme, closely connected to that of
the pseudonym-mask and his monographic work on
Kierkegaard in 1972. This is the question of the
Kierkegaardian 'didactic', led by the 'need to disappear
from the horizon of the reader-disciple after having led
him [. . .] in a particular direction and involved him in
an almost unstoppable motion.'[6] Another piece of writing,
which breaks off all too suddenly, is dedicated to Thomas
Mann's first novel, *Buddenbrooks*, and the entrance of the
suggestive, perturbing figure of Gerda Arnoldsen to the
household. These lines not only contain considerations
on the novel that reappear in *Secret Germany* ('Gerda
introduces a disturbing element into family life, music
[. . .], an activity that coincides with decadence and
death') but also contain an initial formulation of the long
'discussion [. . .] on music and its eventual demonic
transformations' that Jesi would develop above all in the
first chapter of the book, as well as the problem of the
relation between parody and myth that, on the other
hand, cut through the entirety of the book's composition.[7]
As with his rereading of '*Ergriffenheit*' in the Frobenian

6 Furio Jesi, *Kierkegaard* (Turin: Bollati Boringhieri, 2001), pp.
39–40.

7 On parody as 'hatred and love, critique and inevitable
abandonment', see Furio Jesi, 'L'esperienza religiosa di Apuleio nelle
Metamofosi' in *Letteratura e mito*, pp. 215–41. Jesi probably worked
on this essay between 1964 and 1965; he spoke about it with Kerényi
as a work in progress in his letters of 29 October and 7 December
1964, announcing his intention to connect Apuleio's irony with
Mann's own (see *Demone e mito*, pp. 25–6, 31–2). Again on the
problem of parody, see at the very least Furio Jesi, 'Paodia e mito
nella poesia di Ezra Pound' in *Letteratura e mito*, pp. 187–214.

sense of the term', the analogy between music and myth constitutes a fundamental lesson drawn from Kerényi's Introduction to *Science of Mythology*, which Jesi openly reprised and developed, both in this fragment and throughout *Secret Germany*, putting it in conversation with that other typically Kerényian problem, that of the distinction between authentic mythology and technified or non-genuine myth.

'Drums in the Night' is the title we have provided for the first draft of the pages dedicated to Brecht's play of the same name (which Jesi even directed in 1960, in a workshop in Turin), or, rather, to the 'logic' behind the city and its mutations. It seems to us that this text has a particular value not only because it recapitulates the theme developed in the third chapter of the book in short form, but also because it represents, in its own way, a kind of 'original nucleus' for *Spartakus: The Symbology of a Revolt* (and indeed 'Spartakus' was a title initially provided by Brecht for his *Trommeln in der Nacht*), an outcome that was hidden for a long time but we might say matured in these preparatory pages for *Secret Germany*. The text concludes with a meeting between Grosz's watercolour *Twilight*—which Jesi interprets as a figurative equivalent to the drama—and a photograph of the scenery (part of the Expressionist canon) of the first production of *Drums in the Night* (which opened on 22 September 1922, directed by Otto Falckenberg). Jesi received an image of the scene from Helene Weigel, who wrote the peremptory phrase on the reverse: 'Brecht was never an Expressionist!'

The final document which we present below concerns a figurative question. This is a letter written by Jesi to Erwin Panofsky on 15 January 1965, asking his opinion on the paintings of Hieronymus Bosch. As Bosch's name does not appear in *Secret Germany*, and as Jesi turns to Panofsky 'with regards to a study [. . .] on some images of the devil in Egyptian art and in particular of the Egyptian god Bes', the letter might seem to lie outside of the thematic boundaries of the book, even if its is within its temporal ones. However, referring to the apparent absence of the demonic face in the Dutch artist's paintings, Jesi notes that 'Bosch left the presence of the mortal face to be implied, without depicting it: as if the scenes of his paintings lie under the gaze of that face, one which nevertheless remains beyond the frame.' We cannot but think of *Secret Germany* here, and above all the correspondence with Max Brod that Jesi recalls towards the end of Chapter 4. In the letter penned on the same day—15 January 1965—the young mythologist wrote to Brod about his own Jewish heritage and theorized that those origins, from which 'so much uncertainty' derived, had perhaps aided Kafka in 'recognizing the presence of the fascinating and fatal visage that reigns invisibly over the life and efforts of his characters'. Jesi then added a line which, in our view, ideally unified the themes of guilt (and confession), of 'woman', the 'city' (or the *Castle*) and the devil—the schema of the book and the general plan of the series, as well as that of the unpublished pages on Gerda and Rilke and even the letters—in a single constellation: 'I suppose—but only you yourself would be able to confirm this—that this face might be identified with the women that Kafka had loved; before this face he was always immersed in guilt.'[8]

Andrea Cavalletti

---

8 For the letter, see Andrea Cavalletti, 'Alterità divina e femminile in Kafka: una lettera di Furio Jesi a Max Brod' in *il gallo silvestre* 13 (2000): 77–8. For the original version in French, see Andrea Cavalletti, '"Quasi un houyhnhnm". Furio Jesi e l'ebraismo', *Scienza & Politica* 25(48) (2013): 103.

SECRET GERMANY
MYTHS IN TWENTIETH-CENTURY
GERMAN CULTURE

—Morphology of the survival of three fundamental mythic themes:

'woman'   (as symbol of the individual and subjective relation to myth, projected externally): in German literature and figurative arts, the archetypical female image corresponds to a series of figures of Kore, Kore-Aphrodite, Demetra, Demetra-Erynis (=angered-violated), from Wedekind's *Lulu* (to be studied in its various dramatic realizations) to the female characters in Sternheim and Expressionism, up to those of Brecht and even Borchert.

'city'   (as symbol of resolution of collective and social problems in mythic terms): the image of the city (cf. Altheim and Jung's square 'city') corresponds to the various infernal and heavenly cities, which survive both in early Rilke as well as in the literary and figurative arts in revolutions, in particular the Spartacist revolution (Grosz, Brecht, Piscator's productions, Toller, Mehring, etc.). Here one might also add Kraus' clearly apocalyptic 'city'. In a mythical and ethno-logical sense, the 'city' can also include Kafka's *Castle*, and in Wagner the castle was Kundry's rock as much as the underground dominion of Lady Venus.

'shadow'   (i.e. the 'double', the 'other', the 'friend'; as symbol of the individual relation to myth, within oneself. From here, however, through the medium of sexually compen-sating or hermaphroditic 'shadow-doubles', one returns to the external projection of the subjective relation to myth, i.e. the image of 'woman'). The 'shadow' corresponds to vari-ations of 'Serenus Zeitblom' (cf. *Doctor Faustus*) both of Faustian and erotic types. To the medium of this last kind one can add twin couples (*Wälsungenblut, Felix Krull, Der Erwählte*) and thus also grotesque hemaphrodites (*Luischen, Mario und der Zauberer*) and the theme of homosexuality.

—*Relations between literary survivals and scientific inves-tigations into mythic themes*: the various levels of 'scien-tificism', from esotericism to philology 'a là Wilamowitz', and their relations to literature, the figurative arts, music. Stefan George, Klages, Spengler, the theorists of Nazism. The relation to Gnosticism and Hesse's *Demian*. Orient-alist studies: *Siddharta* and the *Transposed Heads*. Frobenius and Kerényi. Kerényi and Heidegger.

—*The two fundamental solutions of the relation with myth*: de-mythification or *mystic union*. Parody (which

does not exclude 'private ecstasy') as Thomas Mann's provisional solution. Parody and 'alienation effect' in Brecht.[9]

---

9 Two pages conserved among Jesi's papers, typed and numbered
with MS date at the foot of the page: '18/02/65', and two
annotations at page 2; the first of these—'around 200 pages / one
year of work'—begins a note, also signed but stylistically later and
with a different pen and stamped date: 'Call from Pautasso: 24
March 1965 / (agreement: the plan is with Silva, will follow
contract)'. Sergio Pautasso was the director of the journal *Sigma*,
edited by Umberto Silva; Jesi had just published the essay 'Cesare
Pavese, il mito e la scienza del mito' (in issue 3–4, December 1964)
which, republished in 1968 in *Letteratura e mito*, would be the
cause of a bitter break with Kerényi (cf. the correspondence from
14 and 16 May 1968, in Jesi, *Demone e mito*, pp. 114–18).

MYTH AND SYMBOL IN MODERN GERMANY
COLLECTION OF TEXTS AND STUDIES

—I would prefer to limit the series title to Germany (rather than Europe) in order to provide it with greater unity and integrity. In order to have any rigour, a 'European' discussion would require a much greater number of volumes than that foreseen (or otherwise the choice would be far too arbitrary). Germany and the German language in general has, on the other hand, been the most important protagonist in relations—genuine and otherwise!—to myths and symbols in modern Europe.

PROJECTED VOLUMES:

Furio Jesi—*Secret Germany* (essay)

Gustav Meyrink—*The Angel of the West Window* (novel)

These have already been discussed.

Alfred Kubin, A. Kolig, C. Moll—*Wrestling with the Angel. Artists' Letters. 1933–1945* (*Ringen mit dem Engel*: Salisbury, 1964)

This is a collection of letters sent by three painters to Anton Steinhart in the Nazi period. It suits the series well because the three writers develop the problem of the artist in a way connected to the irrational, which in the

context of Nazism ran the risk of transforming enlightenment into 'technified myth'. Kubin through his personal, visionary point of view, between Expressionism
and Surrealism; Kolig as an Expressionist and Moll as a
friend of Klimt (with everything that such a friendship
entails) confront the 'struggle with the angel', i.e. with the
forces of irrationality, forces neither to be rejected nor,
however, to be used against humanity. In Kubin's case in
particular, we are in a situation similar to Hesse's own
when he wrote *Demian* or *Journey to the East*: the fascination of the symbol as drive to evocative techniques,
along with a moral rigour that asks for man to be
defended.

Hans Henny Jahnn—Pastor Ephraim Magnus (1919)
(theatrical work)
One of the most relevant works for Expressionist theatre
(which won the Kleist Prize and was staged by Brecht and
Bronnen). It teaches much about the relations between
theatre techniques and the morphology of mythic survivals, in the years in which one spoke of 'cosmic scenery',
'sacred drama', etc. It was all of the drawbacks of the most
violent Expressionism (death, incest, etc.) and thus even
more clearly, without any mystification, shows the structure that binds 'representing' and 'pronouncing symbolic
words'. With the passing of time, Brecht's doctrine of the
'gesture' is disenchanted. Furthermore, the play belongs
to so-called 'apocalyptic Expressionism' and is connected
to the entire symbolism of the cosmic year that ends
with—and death that begins with—the way to myth.

Felix Emmel—*The Ecstatic Theatre* (*Das ekstatische
Theater*, Prien, 1924) (essay)

This essay complements Jahnn's drama, perfectly establishing the relations between Expressionist theatre, symbol and myth through the concept of 'ecstasy'.

Ernst Betram—*Nietzsche. Essay on a Mythology* (*Versuch einer Mythologie*) (essay)

One of the major works on Nietzsche (greatly admired by Thomas Mann, who cited this text alone when suggesting an essay on Nietzsche for Gide). As the title already states, it outlines Nietzsche's experience as a mythological and symbolic presupposition for all of modern German culture. Indeed in a certain sense it was also one of the sources for *Doctor Faustus*.

Gottfried Benn—*Ptolemy's Disciple* (*Der Ptolemäer*: Berlin, 1949) (novel)[10]

One of Benn's mature novels, written 'about a destroyed Berlin'. All of the mythic and symbolic components present in other volumes in the series are reprised here but burned by the devotion to the 'obscure God' that has asked for their evocation and sacrifice, for no other reason than his own being. With a little audacity, one might claim that this is the post-bellum equivalent to Broch's *Death of Virgil*.

These seven works (two novels, a play, a set of letters, three essays) would allow the series to bring together all of the aspects of the great mythological work and, on the other hand, the great crisis that marked German culture. My own book serves as an introduction and sets the scene for the rest. Meyrink represents the fascination with parody of the symbol. Jahnn is the desperate aban-

---

10 Margin note in the MS: NO / EINAUDI HAS IT /

donment in the 'forest of symbols', announcing the end. Emmel's essay represents a guide for whoever finds themselves within that forest. Bertram demonstrates the great humanist jolt that gave rise to all of this, and he views it with the vision of someone who has lived through the consequences with both passion and anxiety. Benn concludes the series by plunging into the deepest straits of that consciousness which has survived and is aware of the crisis.[11]

---

11 The final sentence on Benn is cancelled out with a single line; in the first line, 'two novels' is corrected by hand to 'one novel'.

I [GERMANISM]

'Everywhere Germany extends it ruins culture': Nietzsche wrote these words in *Ecce Homo*, concluding his discussion of Wagner. According to him, the composer 'condescended to the Germans', transforming himself into a 'Reich German'.*

Nietzsche's radical phrase can perhaps be toned down by his own specification a few lines before: 'we who were children in the miasma of the fifties are necessarily pessimistic about the concept "German"; we can be nothing else but revolutionaries.' At the same time, the painful conviction of the presence of a corrupting element within the very nature of Germanism has a moral meaning that transcends historical contingency and political polemic. We are not saying anything particularly new when we affirm that Nietzsche's anti-Germanic attitude is born from a desire for purification and self-punishment, perfectly understandable for a man that 'made mincemeat of himself' and who, beyond his own pronouncements, truly was the tool chosen by the deepest aspect of Germanism in order for it to come into the light.

What lies in the unconscious can be manifested in countless ways; the conscious is not able to oppose itself to that uninterrupted epiphany other than through horror, revealing itself right up to the point in which it too,

***

* Quotations are taken from Duncan Large's translation: Friedrich Nietzsche, *Ecce Homo* (Oxford: Oxford University Press, 2007), pp. 27–8

as in the spasms of an illness, suffers the destructive influence of such 'infernal' spheres. The torment that disturbed all of Nietzsche's life was born precisely from the violence by which those spheres took hold of him as a man, imposing continuous spasms on his conscience, of which the madness of his last years is appropriately emblematic.

Are we thus authorized, however, in defining the revelation of such dark forces 'Germanism', something that, in theory, ought not be susceptible to topographical qualifications but instead ought appear as a constant of human life in any given land? We should thus say from the outset that we do not intend by 'Germanism' any meaning other than that deriving from a comfortable limitation for a subject of study. 'Germanism' for us is simply the name of the manifestation of those dark forces within German land: a name which could be accompanied very well by 'Italianism' or 'Gallicism' if one were to research the study of analogous moments of epiphany in Italy or France. That is, we do not hold that Germany takes pride of place among epiphanies, distinguished from other nations in this regard. It is certainly true that these dark forces represent a typical art of German civilization; but one can equally say that the most typical part of Italian or French civilization is also constituted of the dark forces that they express. Every civilization brings forth similar forces, which no doubt represent that which each civilization possesses on the most intimate level.

If we have thus limited our discussion to German civilization, this is only for a practical reason and not because it seemed impossible to extend our investigation to other civilizations, providing a relatively brief time period and spatial restriction. It nevertheless ought to be explained why Germany is the object of our study and not any other nation. Among the many justifications that might be given, we will choose one that seems of particular importance. Perhaps more than any other nation, modern Germany has possessed men that lived out Nietzsche's tragedy, reflecting its consequences in works of exceptional clarity. These works constitute documents that are more easily utilizable for the purposes of our research.[12]

CHAPTER I. CULTURE AND MORAL RESPONSIBILITY

It would seem dishonest for us not to begin our discussion without clarifying from the outset, in the title of the first chapter, the nature of the most serious problem we desire to confront in this volume. In the opening pages of *Doctor Faustus*, Thomas Mann has the narrator, Serenus Zeitblom, caught by a conflictual scruple:

> Here I break off, chagrined by a sense of my artistic shortcomings and lack of self-control. Adrian himself could hardly—let us say in a symphony—have let such a theme [the pact with the devil] appear so prematurely. At the most he would have allowed it to suggest itself afar off, in some subtly disguised, almost imperceptible way.[*]

There can be no doubt that, under the cover of parody, Mann uses these words to guard against the detached coldness—perhaps even borne out of suffering and fatigue—with which the artist considers and utilizes the subject of his work in the act of composition. Below we will pause on the dangers that stand behind this symptomatic coldness. For now we will accept and adopt the reasoning by which Zeitblom ends by justifying his premature citation of the 'theme' so close to his heart:

---

[*] Mann, *Doctor Faustus*, Woods translation, p. 9.

> For a man like me it is very hard, it affects him
> like wanton folly, to assume the attitude of a cre-
> ative artist to a subject which is dear to him as
> life and burns him to express; I know not how
> to treat it with the artist's easy mastery.*

Culture and moral responsibility: the title of this first chapter refers to the problem provoked by the attitude of the great protagonists of German culture and the even-tual relations between their works and the emergence of Nazism. The problem has posed itself to the conscience of Germanists for a long time now, or rather perhaps to the consciences of all honest, far-sighted persons. In 1938, Edmond Verneil brought together a group of 'the-orists of German nationalism' chosen from among the precursors of Nazism: Spengler, Jünger, Stefan George, Rathenau and Thomas Mann insofar as he was the author of the *Considerations of a Non-political Man*. With the years that have passed since, we can identify two different attitudes in relation to this problem. The first is the atti-tude of the Marxist critic, and above all of György Lukács, who accused both Thomas Mann and Freud, insisting not so much on any personal responsibility but rather on the value of the symptoms of the bourgeois crisis that led to Nazism, a value he attributed to Mann's works: this accu-sation is obviously directed against an entire social class and its culture. Even though Lukács's sharp analysis could not but note Thomas Mann's frequently polemical posi-tion against the bourgeois world, it was inevitable—given the Marxist critic's convictions—that this recognition would not seem to him sufficient in order to redeem his work from a moral point of view; work in which it would be extremely difficult to recognize, aside from a polemic

---

* Mann, *Doctor Faustus*, Woods translation, p. 9–10.

against the bourgeoisie, the preparation for a future world based on Marxist doctrine.

Inasmuch as Thomas Mann may have often shown a lively appreciation for Lukács' analyses of his work, it seems that in a certain sense he returned that basic distrust which the Marxist critic felt for him. Thomas Mann was never Marxist, and his mistrust of ideology as such seems to find concrete expression in the great and tragic emblematic figure of Naphta in *The Magic Mountain*, the human prototype for which was, in fact, Lukács himself.[13]

---

13 Two typewritten and numbered pages, with a small MS addition.

CONFESSION AND
AUTOBIOGRAPHICAL MYTH

In German literature of the first half of the twentieth century, there are oft-recurring moments in which the voices of poets and novelists become those of sick people describing their own illnesses. In the *Notebooks of Malte Laurids Brigge*, Rilke submerges himself in his own neuroses of anxiety; in *Demian*, Hesse gathers together the documents of his own psychic crisis along with the remedies suggested to him by a follower of Jung. Even Thomas Mann's great pedagogic novel, *The Magic Mountain*, is a confession of a sickness, to which the writer opposes a kind of 'dialectical cure': as Maurice Boucher has quite rightly noted, Settembrini, who fights against against sickness and death, is himself incurably ill and 'experiences his own sickness as humiliation'.

Hesse chose a line from Nietzsche as the epigraph to his novella *Zarathustra's Return*: 'Sickness is always the answer, whenever we are inclined to doubt our duty to follow our mission, whenever we begin to make matters easier, one way or another.'* In this formulation sickness is the opposite of election, it is the consequence of uncertainties brought about through effecting one's duty and the doubts arising over morality. There can be no doubt that Hesse's choice of this quotation from Nietzsche was also influenced by the Jungian concept of healing as the realization of the fullness of one's being, the *foundation* of one's self. And as much as this train of thought might

---

* See Chapter 1, note 23 (p. 21).

seem to contradict Thomas Mann's most mature conclusions in *Doctor Faustus*, the suspicion seems justified that at least a part of Mann's soul adhered to Nietzsche's concept and opposed the identification of the state/sickness of demonic 'grace' which only Zeitblom's traditional humanist viewpoint allows. *Doctor Faustus* is not of course a 'thesis novel': Thomas Mann shows himself to be too great an artist to want a work of art to serve the ends of mere demonstration. Thomas Mann is not Adrian Leverkühn, nor is he Zeitblom, just as *Fiorenza* in turn was never neither Lorenzo the Magnificent nor Savonarola. His position lies 'outside' of both characters: he evokes images that represent material within the story of modern civilization, which becomes autobiographical only in the act of inserting his own existence into its narrative flow. His own autobiographical activity can perhaps be read as a confession, from the moment in which he digs down to the foundations of his own twentieth-century German being (and is able to dig so deeply thanks to the capacity of art to understand everything without being understood). Both in *Doctor Faustus* and in *The Magic Mountain*, his confession thus also becomes the discourse of an ill man speaking of his own sickness (or, in a Christian version, of a sinner discussing his guilt). These sicknesses are generated—in Nietzsche's sense of the word—by doubting one's own duty to self-realization, as much as by a 'pact', a relation with an extra-human reality whose help radically solves this doubt and substitutes impure, powerful and guilt-ridden energies for those healthy energies dissipated by doubts.

Both in Rilke's case, and in that of Hesse and Mann, speaking of one's own sickness and one's descent into the depths of the self allows the artist to evoke emblems of extra-human forces that lie 'beyond good and evil'.[14]

---

14 Two typewritten and numbered pages.

CHAPTER I. REVELATION AND MORALITY

Perhaps the most difficult problem that an artist must confront—and in particular the modern artist—lies in the difficulty of unreservedly accepting the epiphanies of forces external to the artist (forces that constitute the very reality of an artwork) while simultaneously non betraying the community of men. It seems to us that such a problem is particularly hard for a modern artist because today, in the Western world at least, they do not experience any organized religion within which such epiphanies might coincide with legitimate revelations of the divine.

One of the most painful events felt by Rainer Maria Rilke, in all likelihood, was precisely the absence of a 'public', collective, organized religion that could set his own spiritual moments within a complex of experiences that heal—or perhaps torment—the devotee's moral consciousness. Rilke's rejection of Catholic religiosity, explicitly so in his later life, challenged him because he felt excluded from the religion of his childhood at the same time as he became aware of his own condition as a poet, a condition that was an essential, unfathomable nucleus of his own being. There was no contemporary religion able to embrace within it those experiences the unique experience of which Rilke felt to be the only possible path open to him. There was no universal, universally true religion for him. And the pain borne from this realization was particularly intense precisely because, certain of the reality of his poetic activities, he wanted above all to transform reality into truth: he felt the resolution of art into moral action as a basic necessity.

How can one distinguish the truth? *Quid est verum?* Pilate's question imposes itself on Rilke's soul as soon as he recognised the real and serious weight of his poetic experience. The forces that spoke through his voice *were*: they were real. But in order to be true, they would need to submit themselves to a consecration to which Rilke devoted his entire life. We will not delude ourselves in trying to understand if he truly reached this goal. The bonds that bind each man's reality with the sacred sphere are genuinely mysterious in the classical sense of *mistero*. As with any mystery, experiencing them relies on an initiation: albeit that which chooses a destiny by directing gestures and thoughts, and consecrating them unbeknownst to the destined one. But one cannot write a book from the results of an initiation. Not so much because they transcend the word—which might not even be true—but due to a shame we believe legitimate and which renders it difficult to bear naked the most intimate truth of our soul: that for which we take responsibility only before the community of men or before God. The only pure way to confess that part of ourselves to the community of our brothers is to act in conformity with it; the only way to confess it to God is to speak with him in solitude.

At this point we will begin with Thomas Mann's *Doctor Faustus.* If we have allowed ourselves to speak personally, to first lay out our own person, we have done so in order to justify—within very restricted limits—our reasons for discussing Rilke. That which we have said about the challenges and qualms of shame that impede out discussion of the truth experienced during initiation can be repeated for Rilke. Rilke was even accused of graphomania due to his tireless desire to speak and write to his vast circle of friends, scholars and devotees who asked him for counsel and insight. And yet no attentive reader of his countless letters could say that these contain the terms or—and this is what counts—the essence of revelation.

Rilke's pedagogic work in relation to his correspondents was always and exclusively propaedeutic. He directed the steps of those who turned to him right up to the threshold of truth. Then he would withdraw, leaving each to follow the path in solitude, in the secret of their own being, or to remain and contemplate distant, unreachable and disturbing dawns.[15]

---

15 Three typewritten and numbered pages.

I [*BUDDENBROOKS*]

'Hera and Aphrodite, Brunhilda and Melusina all in one . . . ': these are the words with which Gosch the broker, in the eighth chapter of Part V of *Buddenbrooks*, greets the appearance of Gerda Arnoldsen, Thomas Buddenbrook's fiancé. Is this merely a stately over-expression? We believe instead that the evoking of these female images in relation to the 'strange' Gerda has a much more genuine mythic quality than the little verse produced in honour of the ancient Buddenbrooks:

> Industry and beauty chaste
> See we linked in marriage band:
> Venus Anadyomene
> And cunning Vulcan's busy hand . . .*

For Thomas Buddenbrook's ancestors, the classical gods contribute to bourgeois luxury, adorning the house on Mengstrasse with white statues. At root, these gossipy interpretations of Thomas's marriage choice ('Well, Consul Buddenbrook himself had a "certain something" about him! . . . ') nevertheless do not lack a grain of truth even while we are led to understand that the last heir of the household has sought out so singular a wife merely in order to enrich his life with a luxury object. The relationship between the old Buddenbrooks and their neo-classical gods was certainly more superficial and simplistic than that between Thomas Mann and his god-

---

* Mann, *Buddenbrooks*, p. 306; Lowe-Porter translation, p. 294.

dess-fiancé. By now we are not dealing with a divine image—holy, restful and reassuring—but, rather, the goddess-woman, fascinating and fugitive, a vehicle of both ecstasy and destruction. It is not without reason that Tony Buddenbrook, bound more passively than his brother to the spirit of the present times, 'reiterated that she had always hated Gerda, but that she for her own part (and her eyes were filled with tears) had always repaid that hatred with love'.* The introduction of Gerda into the family brings a new element with it, both fascinating and terrifying. Thomas Buddenbrook personally assumes the consequences of his choice, showing himself to be incapable of resolving his relation to the woman-goddess within the realm of normal bourgeois life.

On the other hand, what makes the figure of Gerda particularly meaningful—and enigmatic—is that her fatal appearance in the bourgeois world is accompanied by music. Right from her very first appearance in the novel, as Tony's partner in Sesemi Weichbrodt's house, her image is shown connected to a music which is in truth *music itself*, not the superficial habits from the world of sounds that made up part of a young woman's education: 'It appeared that Gerda Arnoldsen did not take piano like the rest of them, but the violin, and that Papa—her Mother was dead—had promised her a real Stradivarius'.†

In that very moment the fundamental extraneity of the Buddenbrooks from music is revealed: 'Tony was not musical—hardly any of the Buddenbrooks and none of the Krogers were. She could not even recognize the chorals they played at St. Mary's . . . '.‡ And when Greda

---

* Mann, *Buddenbrooks*, p. 304. See Chapter 2, note 10 (p. 72).

†Mann, *Buddenbrooks*, p. 60; Lowe-Porter translation, p. 84.

‡ Mann, *Buddenbrooks*, p. 60; Lowe-Porter translation, p. 84.

and Thomas's marriage appears in a very precarious light due to the appearance of lieutenant von Throta, music again functions as a barrier between the woman-goddess and the Buddenbrook: 'Gerda Buddenbrook and the eccentric young officer met each other, naturally, in the world of music.'*

Throughout Thomas Mann's work, music is an art— or rather a reality—with a solemn and fatal presence. From the novella *Tristan* to *Doctor Faustus*, over an arc of forty years, music weighs upon Thomas Mann like the gorgon's face, and with it the thought of Schopenhauer and Nietzsche. In the passage from *Tristan* to *Doctor Faustus*, Mann's attitude towards music became muted, as was also the case with his admiration of Nietzsche. This is the same metamorphosis that led him to go from speaking of the 'Nietzsche's pure and holy name' to writing that the protagonist of *Doctor Faustus* 'shared the same fate as Nietzsche, Hugo Wolf etc., he is a true son of hell'.†

Those who experience within themselves that hard metamorphosis in which, in the end, the confession of one's sins prevails over contemplation, might see themselves portrayed in Hanno Buddenbrook, in the form of a young adolescent marked by music and chosen by death. Von Platen's lines never suited anyone as much as Hanno Buddenbrook:

> Whoever sees beauty with their eyes
> Has already been handed over to death

---

* Mann, *Buddenbrooks*, p. 440; Lowe-Porter translation, p. 249.

† The first quotation is taken from Mann's 1928 essay on Albrecht Dürer: see Thomas Mann, *Altes und Neues. Kleine Prosa aus fünf Jahrzehnten* (Frankfurt am Main: Fischer Verlag, 1953). The second reference is probably to letter to Klaus Mann, 27 April 1943; see Thomas Mann, *Briefe 1937–1947* (Frankfurt: Fischer Verlag, 1963), p. 309.

Will not be good for any work upon this earth
And he will quake before death
Whoever sees beauty with their eyes.*

Like Hanno, von Platen died of a badly diagnosed typhoid infection, 'which was no more than the pretext for death for which he had already been clearly consecrated'. When Thomas Mann wrote these words in his essay on von Platen, he clearly echoed that which he had already written about Hanno's typhoid in *Buddenbrooks*:

> If he shudders when he hears life's voice, if the memory of that vanished scene and the sound of that lusty summons make him shake his head, make hum put out his hand to ward it off as he flies forwards in way of escape that has opened to him—then it is clear that the patient will die.†

Von Platen was gay, and the principle of homosexuality—of sterile love that refuses life—is there in Hanno, in his relationship with his friend Kai. Music, again, is never far off in this relationship, for which it represents an emblem of beauty in opposition to life: it is no accident that, in his novel *Death in Venice*, Thomas Mann took Gustav Mahler as the model for his protagonist's name and profile.

Music: for Hanno Buddenbrook, music means above all Wagner—also the music of seduction in the novella *Tristan*—played almost unwillingly by Pfühl the organist.

---

* 'Wer die Schönheit angeschaut mit Augen,
  Ist dem Tode schon anheimgegeben,
  Wird für keinen Dienst auf Erden taugen,
  Und doch wird er vor dem Tode beben,
  Wer die Schönheit angeschaut mit Augen!'

August von Platen, 'Tristan' in *Sämtliche Werke in vier Bänden. Band 1* (Stuttgart: J. G. Cotta, 1885), p. 131.

† Mann, *Buddenbrooks*, p. 514; Lowe-Porter translation, p. 354.

Lion has insightfully noted that the piece that Thomas Mann chose for the first appearance of music, and of Wagner's music, in *Buddenbrooks* is quite purposefully the *Die Meistersinger.** But the finale of *Die Meistersinger* (again, according to Lion), even while marked by a celebrated, exciting C-major tone, effectively ends the celebration of the serene relation between artists and bourgeoisie in Old Germany with the terrifying prophecy of Hans Sachs: 'Even after the German people and *Reich* has been ruined, "German art" will always survive.' We are here at the other pole from the final scene of *Doctor Faustus*, in which 'German art' and its destiny is emblematic of the guilty destiny of Germany itself. In 1901, Thomas Mann had already made this prophecy within the nucleus of the destruction of the German bourgeois world; and thus the meaning of the presence of *Die Meistersinger* on the threshold o the 'fall of a family' assumed the value of parody—a value which the finale of *Doctor Faustus*, with its Christian touch, emphasized— again in parodical mode. Parody and prophecizing the end: right from the days of his first great novel, Thomas Mann positioned himself against that attitude of esoteric moralism which marked the finale of Mahler's Second Symphony, the composer whose parody appeared as the protagonist in *Death in Venice*: '"Thou shalt arise, surely thou shalt arise." Then appears the glory of God! A wondrous, soft light penetrates us to the heart—all is holy calm! / And behold—it is no judgment—there are no sinners, no just. None is great, none is small. There is no punishment and no reward.'†

---

* Jesi's reference is probably to Ferdinand Lion, *Thomas Mann in seiner Zeit* (Zurich: Niehans, 1935), p. 161.

† Gustav Mahler, *Letters* (Basil Creighton trans.) (New York: Viking, 1946), p. 193.

Writing about his father in his *History of Germany Since 1789*,* Golo Mann says that 'his first novel, *Buddenbrooks*, was later seen as a piece of [critical social history, as the story of the decline of the old, genuine bourgeoisie, and it is true that this was in it, although the author himself was hardly aware of it . . .]'.[16]

---

* Golo Mann, *The History of Germany since 1789* (Marian Jackson trans.) (New York: Frederick A. Praeger, 1968[1958]), p. 370.

16 Four typewritten pages, numbered, with corrections and MSS integrations.

DRUMS IN THE NIGHT

Arnolt Bronnen recounts that in early winter months of 1922, Bertolt Brecht was admitted to the Charité hospital in Berlin for a short time. This was the period in which he began to write *Drums in the Night*:

> Outside, the starving, freezing city played itself out in the sporadic buzz of the tram, betrayed by the bosses who tear each other apart in struggles, upturned by strikes, assemblies, demonstrations, stock market manoeuvres, rhetorical riots. All of this was condensed into the injections which Brecht administered to himself, the sharp, keen actor-spectator with a cynicism like a cut from a jagged blade. 'The play really would be like drums, if all this were in there,' Bronnen observed. 'Very well then,' Brecht agreed, 'I'll put that in there.' 'When?' asked Bronnen. 'It's already there,' Brecht replied.*

As much as Bronnen's observations only refer to one, perhaps superficial aspect of the circumstances in which *Drums in the Night* was written, they serve as a point of departure for understanding at least one fundamental element of the drama, i.e. the image of a city—Berlin—through which the characters pass on a November night, 'from sunset to sunrise'. The city is of noteworthy importance in the play's structure as it seems to reveal its true

---

* See above, Chapter 3, n19 (p. 134).

face only during the disturbed night of the Spartacist revolution, resembling the site of the Apocalypse. The city's nocturnal metamorphosis reveals its depth and the nature of the tragedy into which its inhabitants have fallen. The revolution, its terror and the deformation of human figures lost within it—figures stripped bare by that very deformation—determine the presence of a ferment of destruction within the city, almost the announcement of a coming end. In this looming apocalyptic environment, its arrival beaten out to the rhythm of the drums of the nights, animate and inanimate objects finally show their true nature. The houses and streets show what they truly are in the moment in which they appear as elements in a human tragedy; and the people themselves, when they cover their faces with the stereotypical masks of the play's characters, show their own nature as demonic or painful puppets, an imminent fate looming over them.

Let's read the play's stage directions:

FIRST ACT: Balicke's house. A dark room with muslin curtains. Evening.

SECOND ACT: The Piccadilly bar. Large window in the background. Music. A red moon can be seen through the window. When the door opens: wind.

THIRD ACT: A suburban street. High up on the left and bottom right are the red brick walls of the barracks. Behind, the star-lit city. Night. Wind.

FOURTH ACT: A small gin mill. Glubb, the proprietor, in white, is singing 'The Ballad of the Dead Soldier', accompanying himself on the guitar. Laar and a sinister-looking drunk are staring at Glubb's fingers. A short, thick-set man by the name of Bulltrotter is reading the paper. Manke the writer, brother of Manke at the Piccadilly Bar, is drinking with Augusta, a prostitute. All are smoking.

FIFTH ACT: Wooden bright. Screams. Large red moon.*

If we want an appropriate figurative comparison for these scenes from *Drums in the Night*, we can turn to Georg Grosz's watercolour *Twilight*, in his series *Ecce homo*. Here we see Berlin's tall bourgeois houses immersed in a red, black and green light, between twilight and night-time. A red wall is in the foreground, and upon it are the tragic and demonic faces of the prostitute, the rich, the policeman and the blind beggar. It is under this unravelling light that the woman's face assumes an almost skull-like form and the houses seem to be the depositories of a blood-soaked night, that Brecht's drama takes place. If we look at the photographs of the first production of *Drums in the Night*, put on at the Kammerspiele in Munich, we can see the images of those tall, looming houses in the background, with the red moon hanging between them. Even that moon will reveal itself to be deceptive: in the play's finale, Kragler 'staggers around and throws his drum at the moon which turns out to be a lantern. Drum and moon fall in the river, which has no water in it.'[17]

---

* Bertolt Brecht, *Drums in the Night* (William E. Smith and Ralph Manheim trans.) in *Collected Plays, Volume 1* (New York: Vintage Books, 1971), modified.

17 Two typewritten, numbered pages.

TO ERWIN PANOFSKY

15 January 1965

Dear Professor,

Allow me from the start to apologize for my writing to you in Italian (I read German, but I would not dare write it) and for taking up your time. Perhaps the admiration I hold for your work, and the instruction I have taken from it, can serve as some justification.

I write in order to request your advice regarding a study I have undertaken of demonic images in Egyptian art (I am an Egyptologist), specifically those of the Egyptian god Bes. Please do not think that I mean to ask you questions that lie outside of your own habitual field of studies. In interpreting the image of Bes I have found it necessary to partake in various comparative elements deriving from a variety of cultures, and it is with regards to some of these that your suggestions would be of great assistance.

The question on which permit myself to write to you is the art of Bosch, in particular the magical and mystical components therein. That which has principally drawn my attention in Bosch's paintings is the absence of an undeniable 'face of the demon'. The demons that appear in his paintings provide images of devilish *activity*, but one does not find the depiction of a basic demonic face, as one might find—for example—in Greek art in the face of the Gorgon. To me it seems that Bosch's paintings lack the presence of a 'face of stone', the face of the 'prince' of demons. Perhaps Bosch left the presence of the mortal face to be implied, without depicting it: as if the scenes of his paintings lie under the gaze of that face, one which nevertheless remains beyond the frame.

Reaching some conclusions on this point is particularly important to me, because my current study focuses precisely on the metamorphoses of that demonic face.

Would you mind writing to me with your own opinion on this matter? I would of course be deeply grateful.

I thank you dearly once more, and pray that you will accept my most deferential and devoted greetings.

Furio Jesi.[18]

---

18 Typewritten page with MS title 'To Erwin Panofsky'.

BIBLIOGRAPHY

ADORNO, Theodor, W. *Mahler: A Musical Physiognomy* (Edmund Jephcott trans.). Chicago: University of Chicago Press, 1992.

———. *Mahler. Eine musikalische Physiognomik.* Frankfurt: Suhrkamp, 1960.

———. *Philosophie der neuen Musik.* Frankfurt: Suhrkamp, 1975.

———. *Philosophy of New Music* (R. Hullot-Kentor trans.). Minneapolis: University of Minnesota Press, 2006.

ALLASON, Barbara. *Memorie di un'antifascista.* Milan: Avanti!, 1961.

BECHER, Johannes R. 'Hymne auf Rosa Luxemburg', in K. Pinthus (ed.), *Menschheitsdämmerung. Szmphonie jüngster Dichtung.* Berlin: Rowohlts, 1920.

BENN, Gottfried. *Der Ptolemäer.* Wiesbaden: Limes, 1949.

———. *Doppelleben.* Stuttgart: Klett-Cotta, 1950.

———. *Essays* (E. B. Ashton trans.). London: Bloomsbury, 1987.

———. *Gesammelte Werke. Band II: Prosa und Szenen.* Wiesbaden: Limes, 1958.

———. *Gesammelte Werke. Band III: Gedichte.* Wiesbaden: Limes, 1960.

———. *Sämtliche Werke. Band III: Prosa 1.* Stuttgart: Klett-Cotta, 1987.

———. *Sämtliche Werke. Band IV: Prosa 2.* Stuttgart: Klett-Cotta, 1989.

———. *Sämtliche Werke. Band V: Prosa 3.* Stuttgart: Klett-Cotta, 1991.

———. *Sämtliche Werke. Band VII/1: Szenen / Dialoge / 'Das Unaufhörliche' / Gespräche und Interviews / Nachträge / Medizinische Schriften.* Stuttgart: Klett-Cotta, 2003.

BORCHERT, Wolfgang. *Das Gesamtwerk.* Hamburg: Rowohlt, 1959.

BOUCHER, Maurice. *Le roman allemand (1914–1933) et la crise de l'esprit.* Paris: Presses universitaires, 1961.

BRECHT, Bertolt. *Gedichte, 1918–1929.* Frankfurt: Suhrkamp, 1960.

———. *Hundert Gedichte.* Berlin: Aufbau, 1958.

———. *Trommeln in der Nacht.* Munich: Drei Masken, 1923.

BROCH, Hermann. *Der Schuldlosen.* Frankfurt: Suhrkamp, 1976[1950].

———. *Der Tod des Vergil.* Zurich: Rhein, 1947.

———. *The Death of Virgil* (J. S. Untermeyer trans.). New York: Pantheon Books, 1945.

BRONNEN, Arnolt. *Tage mit Bertolt Brecht. Die Geschichte einer unvollendeten Freundschaft.* Vienna: Henschel, 1960.

BUBER, Martin. 'Dem Gemeinschaftlichen folgen' in *Werkausgabe. Band VI* (Asher Biemann ed.). Gütersloh: Gütersloher Verlaghaus, 2003, pp. 103–23.

———. 'La via della comunità', in *Tempo presente* 5, 1960.

———. 'What Is Common to All' in *The Knowledge of Man: Selected Essays* (Maurice Friedman and Ronald Gregor Smith trans). New York: Harper and Row, 1965, pp. 79–99.

BUTLER, Eliza Marian. *Rainer Maria Rilke.* Cambridge: Cambridge University Press, 1946.

DANTE, Alighieri. *The Inferno* (Robert and Jean Hollander trans.). London: Penguin, 2002.

DÖLGER, Franz Josef. *IXΘΥΣ: Das Fisch-Symbol in frühchristlicher Zeit,* 2nd EDN. Munich: Mohr Siebeck, 1928.

DUSE, Ugo. 'Origini poplari del canto mahleriano'. *L'approdo musicale* 16–17 (1963): 120–55.

ELIADE, Mircea. *Le mythe de l'éternel retour.* Paris: Gallimard, 1949.

———. *Traité d'histoire des religions.* Paris: Payot, 1949.

EURIPIDES. *The Plays of Euripides* (Edward P. Coleridge trans.). London: George Bell, 1891.

FISHMAN, Jack. *The Seven Men of Spandau*. New York: Praeger, 1954.

FOURIER, George. *Thomas Mann: Le message d'un artiste-bourgeois (1896–1924)*. Paris: Les Belles Lettres, 1960.

FROBENIUS, Leo. *Kulturgeschichte Afrikas: Prolegomena zu einer historischen Gestaltlehre*. Zurich: Phaidon, 1933.

GALVANO, Albino. *Per un'armatura*. Turin; Lattes, 1960.

GEORGE, Stefan, and Karl Wolfskehl (eds). *Deutsche Dichtung. Band 3. Das Jahrhundert Goethes*. Berlin: George-Bondl, 1910.

GIUDICE, Gaspar. *Luigi Pirandello*. Turin: Utet, 1963.

GOETHE, Johann Wolfgang von. *Dramatische Dichtungen. Band 2*. Munich: Beck, 2008.

———. *Faust: A Tragedy*. (Bayard Taylor trans.). London and New York: Ward and Lock, 1889.

———. *Goethes Briefe. Band 4*. Hamburg: Wegner, 1967.

GUNDOLF, Friedrich. *Hölderlins Archipelagus*. Heidelberg: Universitäts-Buchhandlung, 1916.

HASENCLEVE, Walter. *Der Sohn*. Stuttgart: Reclam, 1994[1917].

HATTINGBERG, Magda von. *Rilke und Benvenuta. Ein Buch des Dankes*. Vienna: Wilhelm Andermann, 1947.

HEGEL, G. W. F. *Aesthetics: Lectures on Fine Art, Volume 1* (T. M. Knox trans.). Oxford: Clarendon Press, 1975.

———. *Vorlesungen über Aesthetik. Band 2*. Berlin: Duncker and Humblot, 1843,

HESSE, Herman. *Der Steppenwolf*. Frankfurt: Suhrkamp, 1969[1927]

———. *Die Morgenlandfahrt. Eine Erzählung*. Frankfurt: Suhrkamp, 1951.

HEYM, Georg. *Dichtungen und Schriften. Band 1*. Hamburg: Ellerman, 1964.

———. *Umbra vitae. Nachgelassene Gedichte*. Leipzig: Ernst Rowohlt, 1912.

HÖLDERLIN, Friedrich. 'Menons Klagen um Diotima' in *Sämtliche Werke. Band II*. Stuttgart: Kohlhammer, 1953, pp. 78–83. English translation in: *Hyperion and Selected Poems*

(Eric Santner ed., Michael Hamburger trans.). New York: Continuum, 2002.

HOMER. *The Odyssey* (A. T. Murray trans.). Cambridge, MA: Harvard University Press, 1919.

JASPERS, Karl. *Strindberg and Van Gogh* (Oskar Grunow and David Woloshin trans). Tuscon: University of Arizona Press, 1977.'

JENSEN, Adolf Ellegard, and Hermann Niggemeyer (eds). *Hainuvele. Volkserz-ählungen von der Molukken-Insel Ceram.* Frankfurt: V. Klostermann, 1939.

JESI, Furio. 'Il tentato adulterio mitico in Grecia e in Egitto.' *Aegyptus* 42 (1962): 275–96.

———. 'Rilke e l'Egitto. Considerazioni sulla X Elegia Duinese.' *Aegyptus* 44(1–2) (1964): 58–65.

———. 'The Thracian Herakles' (B. Egli trans.). *History of Religions* 3(2) (1964): 261–77.

———, and Philippe Derchain, 'Enqête: Sur les influences osiriaques', *Chronique d'Egypte: Bulletin périodique de la Fondation Egyptologique Reine Elisabeth* 35(69–70) (1960): 184–9.

JUNG, C. G., and Karl Kerényi, *Einführung in das Wesen der Mythologie. Gottkindmythos. Eleusinische Mysterien.* Amsterdam: Pantheon, 1942.

———. *Science of Mythology: Essays on the Myth of the Divine Child and the Mysteries of Eleusis* (R. F. C. Hull trans.). New York and London: Routledge, 2002[1942].

KAFKA, Franz. *The Castle* (Mark Harman trans.). New York: Schocken Books, 1998.

———. *Das Schloss.* Frankfurt: Fischer, 1951.

KERÉNYI, Karl (Károly/Carl). 'Dal mito genuino al mito tecnicizzato', in E. Castelli (ed.), *Atti del colloquio internazionale su 'Tecnica e casistica.* Rome: Istituto di Studi Filologici, 1964, pp. 153–68.

———. *Die Antiken Religion.* Amsterdam: Pantheon, 1941.

———. 'Die goldene Parodie.' *Neue Rundschau* 67 (1956): 549–56.

———. (ed.). *Gespräche in Briefen.* Zurich: Rhein, 1960.

———. 'Hölderlin und die Religionsgeschichte' in *Hölderlin-Jahrbuch*. Tübingen: Siebeck, 1954, pp. 11–24.

———. *La religione antica nelle sue linee fondamentali* (Delio Cantimori trans.), 2nd EDN. Rome: Astrolabio, 1951[1940].

———. 'Nietzsche zwischen Literatur und Religions-geschichte'. *Neue Zürcher Zeitung*, 2 May 1965, pp. 4–5.

———. *The Religion of the Greeks and the Romans* (Christopher Holme trans.). London: Thames and Hudson, 1962.

———. 'Thomas Mann zwischen Norden und Süden'. *Nere Zürcher Zeitung*, 4 July 1955, p. 3.

——, and Furio Jesi. *Demone e mito. Carteggio (1964–1968)* (Andrea Cavalletti ed.). Rome: Quodlibet, 1999.

——, and Thomas Mann, *Felicità difficile: un carteggio* (Ervino Pocar trans.). Milan: Il Saggiatore, 1963.

KLAGES, Ludwig. *Stefan George*. Berlin: Bondi, 1902.

KRAUS, Karl. *Die letzten Tage der Menschheit: Tragödie in fünf Akten mit Vorspiel und Epilog* (Franz Schuh ed.). Salzburg: Jung und Jung, 2014[1919].

KUBIN, Alfred. *Die Andere Seite*. Munich and Leipzig: G. Müller, 1908.

———. *The Other Side* (Denver Lindley trans.). New York: Crown, 1963.

LAWRENCE, D. H. *Lady Chatterley's Lover*. Cambridge: Cambridge University Press, 2002[1928].

———. *The Complete Poems*. London: Penguin, 1993.

LEOPARDI, Giacomo. *Tutte le opere di Giacomo Leopardi: Le poesie e le prose* (Francesco Flora, ed.), *Volume 2/II: Pensieri, discorsi e saggi*. Milan: Mandadori, 1940[1832].

———. *Tutte le opere, Volume 1*. Sansoni: Florence, 1969.

LERBERGHE, Charles van. 'La Faute' in *La chanson d'Eve*. Paris: Mercure de France, 1904.

LEVI, E. *Dogme et rituel de la haute magie*, 2 VOLS. Paris: Germier Baillière, 1861.

MAHLER, Alma. *Gustav Mahler: Erinnerungen und Briefe*. Amsterdam: Allert de Lange, 1940.

———. *Gustav Mahler: Memories and Letters* (Basil Creighton trans.). New York: Viking, 1946.

MANN, Klaus. *Die Wendepunkt*. Frankfurt: Fischer, 1952.

MANN, Thomas. *Adel des Geistes. Sechzehn Versuche zum Problem der Humanität*. Stockholm: Berman-Fischer, 1945.

———. *Buddenbrooks*. Frankfurt: Fischer, 1951.

———. *Der Erwählte*. Frankfurt: Fischer, 1951.

———. *Der kleine Herr Friedemann*. Berlin: Fischer, 1898.

———. *Die vertauschten Köpfe*. Stockholm: Fischer, 1940.

———. *Die Zauberberg*. Frankfurt: Fischer, 1950.

———. *Doktor Faustus*. Stockholm: Bermann-Fischer, 1947.

———. *The Holy Sinner* (H. Lowe-Porter trans.). New York: Alfred A. Knopf, 1951.

———. *Letters of Thomas Mann* (Richard and Clara Winston trans.). London: Penguin, 1975.

———. *Lotte in Weimar*. Frankfurt: Fischer, 1939.

———. *Lübeck als geistige Lebensform: Die Entstehung der Buddenbrooks*. Lubeck: Quitzow, 1926.

———. *Neue Studien*. Frankfurt: Suhrkamp, 1948.

———. 'Tonio Kröger' in *Erzählungen*. Frankfurt: Fischer, 1958.

———. *Tristan*. Berlin: Fischer, 1903.

———. 'Über Goethe's "Faust"' in *Adel des Geistes. Sechzehn Versuche zum Problem der Humanität*. Stockholm: Berman-Fischer, 1945.

———. 'Versuch über Tschechow' [1954] in *Essays VI. Meine Zeit, 1945–1955* (Hermann Kurzke and Stephan Stachorski eds) (Frankfurt: S. Fischer, 1997), pp. 260–79.

——, and Karl Kerényi, *Mythology and Humanism: The Correspondence of Thomas Mann and Karl Kerényi* (Alexander Gelley trans.). Ithaca, NY: Cornell University Press, 1975.

MAYER, Hans. *Thomas Mann: Werk und Entwicklung*. Berlin: Volk und Welt, 1950.

MEIDNER, Ludwig. 'Anleitung zum Malen von Großstadtbildern'. *Kunst und Künstler* 12 (1914): 312–14.

MENC (Ministere de l'Education Nationale et de la Culture). *Le bijou 1900*. Brussels: Hotel Solvay, 1965.

MEYRINK, Gustav. *The Golem* (M. Pemberton and E. F. Bleiler trans.). New York: Dover Publications, 1976.

MITTNER, Ladislao. *La letterature tedesca del Novecento*. Turin: Einaudi, 1960.

MÜLLER, Werner. *Kreis und Kreuz*. Berlin: Widekind, 1938.

MYERS, Bernard Samuel, and Elke Kaspar. *Malerei des Expressionismus. Eine Generation im Aufbruch*. Cologne: Dumont, 1957.

NIETZSCHE, Friedrich. *Sämtliche Gedichte*. Zurich: Manesse, 1999.

——. *The Anti-Christ, Ecce Homo, Twilight of the Idols and Other Writings* (Judith Norman trans.). Cambridge: Cambridge University Press, 2005.

PAUWELS, Louis and Jacques Bergier. *Le matin des magiciens*. Paris: Gallimard, 1960.

——. *The Morning of the Magicians* (Rollo Myers trans.). London: Neville Spearman, 1963.

PELLEGRINI, Alessandro. *Hölderlin, Storia della critica*. Florence: Sansoni, 1956.

——. *Incontri in Europa*. Milan: Garzanti, 1947.

PENSA, Mario. *Stefan George: Saggio critico*. Bologna: Zanichelli, 1961.

PHILLIPSON, Paula. *Untersuchungen über den griecheschen Mythos. Genealogie als Mythische Form. Die Zietart des Mythos*. Zurich: Rhein, 1944.

PISCATOR, Erwin. *Das politische Theater*. Berlin: Adalbert, 1929.

——. *The Political Theatre: A History, 1914–1929* (Hugh Rorrison trans.). London: Methuen, 1980.

PROPP, Vladimir Yakovlevich. *Istoriceskie Korni Volsebnoi Skazki*. Moscow: Labirint, 1998[1946].

RADIN, Paul, C. G. Jung and Karl Kerényi. *Der göttliche Schelm. Ein indianischer Mythen-Zyklus*. Zurich: Rhein, 1954.

——. *The Trickster: A Study in American Indian Mythology* (with translations by R. F. C. Hull). New York: Schocken Books, 1956.

RAUSCHNING, Hermann. *Hitler Speaks: A Series of Political Conversations with Adolf Hitler on His Real Aims* (Ernest Walter Dickes trans.). London: Thomas Butterworth, 1939.

REHM, Walther. *Orpheus: Der Dichter und die Toten. Selbstdeutung und Totenkult bei Novalis, Hölderlin, Rilke.* Düsseldorf: Schwann Verlag, 1950.

RIKLE, Rainer Maria. *Ausgewählte Werke. Band 1: Gedichte.* Leipzig: Insel, 1948.

———. *Briefe. Band 2: 1914–1926* (Ruth Sieber-Rilke and Karl Altheim eds). Wiesbaden: Insel, 1950.

———. *Die Sonette an Orpheus.* Frankfurt: Suhrkamp, 1955.

———. 'Duineser Elegien' in *Werke. Kommentierte Ausgabe. Band 2: Gedichte* (Manfred Engel ed.). Frankfurt and Leipzig: Insel, 1996[1923].

———. *Letters of Rainer Maria Rilke, Volume 2: 1910–1926* (J. B. Greene and M. D. H. Norton trans.). New York: W. W. Norton, 1947.

———. *Sämtliche Werke. Band 1.* Frankfurt: Insel, 1955.

ROMAGNOLI, Ettore. *Minerva e lo scimmione.* Bologna: Zanichelli, 1917.

SCHÖNBERG, Arnold. 'Das Verhältnis zum Text'. *Der blaue Reiter* (1912): 27–33.

———. 'The Relationship to the Text' in *Style and Idea* (D. Newlin trans.). New York: St Martin's Press, 1975.

SCHOEPPERLE, Gertrude. *Tristan and Isolt: A Study of the Sources of the Romance.* Second edition. New York: B. Franklin, 1960.

SCHONAUER, Franz. *Deutsche Literatur im Dritten Reich.* Freiburg: Walter, 1961.

SCHOPENHAUER, Arthur. 'Die Welt als Wille und Vorstellung' in *Sämtliche Werke. Band 1* (Paul Deussen ed.). Munich: R. Piper, 1911.

———. *The World as Will and Idea* (R. B. Haldane and J. Kemp trans.). London: Kegan Paul, Trench and Trübner, 1906.

SCHUMACHER, Ernst. *Die Dramatischen Versuche Bertolt Brechts 1918–1933,* Berlin: Rütten and Loening, 1955.

TREVELYAN, R. C. *Translations from Leopardi*. Cambridge: Cambrdige University Press, 1941.

USENER, Hermann. *Die Sintflutsagen*. Bonn: F. Cohen, 1899.

VAN LERBERGHE, Charles. *La chanson d'Eve*. Paris: Les Editions G. Crès, 1926[1904].

VIGOLO, Giorgio. 'Saggio introduttivo' in Friederich Hölderlin, *Poesie*. Turin: Einaudi, 1958.

WEDEKIND, Frank. *Erdgeist, Earth-Spirit: A Tragedy in Four Acts* (Samuel Atkins Eliot trans.). New York: Albert and Charles Boni, 1941.

———. 'Erdgeist' in *Ausgewählte Werke. Band 2*. Munich: George Müller, 1924.

WERFEL, Franz. *Die vierzig Tage des Musa Dagh*. Berlin: Aufbau, 1955.

WILLET, John. *The Theatre of Bertolt Brecht*. London: Methuen, 1959.